Rethinking the Western Tradition

*The volumes in this series
seek to address the present debate
over the Western tradition
by reprinting key works of
that tradition along with essays
that evaluate each text from
different perspectives.*

Toward Perpetual Peace
and Other Writings
on Politics, Peace,
and History

IMMANUEL KANT

Edited and with an Introduction
by Pauline Kleingeld
Translated by David L. Colclasure
with essays by
Jeremy Waldron
Michael W. Doyle
Allen W. Wood

Yale University Press
New Haven and London

The editor gratefully acknowledges the financial support from the Netherlands Institute for Advanced Study in the Humanities and Social Sciences.

Published with assistance from the Annie Burr Lewis Fund.

Printed in the United States of America by Vail-Ballou Press, Binghamton, New York.

Library of Congress Cataloging-in-Publication Data
Kant, Immanuel, 1724–1804.
[Selections. English. 2006]
Toward perpetual peace and other writings on politics, peace, and history / Immanuel Kant ; edited and with an introduction by Pauline Kleingeld ; translated by David L. Colclasure ; with essays by Jeremy Waldron, Michael W. Doyle, Allen W. Wood.
p. cm. — (Rethinking the Western tradition)
Includes bibliographical references.
ISBN-13: 978-0-300-11794-3 (cloth : alk. paper)
ISBN-10: 0-300-11794-9 (cloth : alk. paper)
ISBN-13: 978-0-300-11070-8 (pbk. : alk. paper)
ISBN-10: 0-300-11070-7 (pbk. : alk. paper)
1. Peace. 2. Political science—Philosophy. I. Kleingeld, Pauline. II. Waldron, Jeremy. III. Doyle, Michael W., 1948– IV. Wood, Allen W. V. Title. VI. Series.
JZ5538.K36 2006
303.6'6—dc22
2006004019

A catalogue record for this book is available from the British Library.
The paper in this book meets the guidelines
for permanence and durability of the Committee on
Production Guidelines for Book Longevity of the
Council on Library Resources.

10   9   8   7   6   5   4   3   2   1

Contributors

David L. Colclasure is assistant professor and head of the German Studies Program at the Monterey Institute of International Studies.

Michael W. Doyle is Harold Brown Professor of International Affairs, Law and Political Science at Columbia University.

Pauline Kleingeld is professor of philosophy at Leiden University, the Netherlands.

Jeremy Waldron is professor of law at the New York University Law School.

Allen W. Wood is Ward W. and Priscilla B. Woods Professor at Stanford University.

Contents

A Brief Sketch of Kant's Life and Works

Immanuel Kant was born in Königsberg, East Prussia, in 1724, as the son of a harness maker. He attended the local university, and from 1747 to 1754 he worked as a private tutor. During this time he submitted two essays as dissertations, which qualified him for a position as an unsalaried instructor at the Königsberg university. He lectured on a broad range of courses in philosophy, mathematics, and the natural sciences, living off his students' course fees and publishing a number of works in philosophy and the natural sciences. His goal was to become a philosophy professor in Königsberg, however, and he rejected several other offers before becoming Professor of Logic and Metaphysics at the University of Königsberg in 1770. This was the start of the so-called silent decade during which Kant published very little and worked out the arguments of the book with which he would establish his lasting reputation: the *Critique of Pure Reason* (1781). In this work, Kant examines the limits and scope of human knowledge, especially metaphysical knowledge. His revolutionary approach was based on the assumption that the specific makeup of the human cognitive faculties determines crucial structural features of how world appears to us and, at the same time, sets radical limits to metaphysical knowledge. Initial misunderstandings among his readers prompted Kant to restate his views in the Prolegomena (1783). Once the revolutionary nature of his theory was understood, Kant became famous.

In the *Critique of Pure Reason* Kant stressed the importance of his new approach for ethics, and a few years later he went on to publish two groundbreaking works in ethical theory: the *Groundwork for the Metaphysics of Morals* (1785) and the *Critique of Practical Reason* (1788). During this time, Kant also wrote the *Metaphysical Foundations of Natural Science* (1786). During the 1780s he published a number of essays in the philosophy of history, touching on matters of politics and international peace: "Idea for a Universal History from a Cosmopolitan Perspective" (1784), "An Answer to the Question: What Is Enlightenment?" (1784), and "Conjectural Beginning of Human History" (1786). In 1790 he published the *Critique of*

Judgment, in which he expounds his theory of aesthetics and theory of biology. His 1793 book, *Religion within the Boundaries of Mere Reason,* involved him in a conflict with the censor. During the 1790s Kant's interest in political theory and practice intensified, as a consequence, no doubt, of the French Revolution and its aftermath. This is evident in "On the Common Saying: This May Be True in Theory, but It Does Not Hold in Practice" (1793), *Toward Perpetual Peace: A Philosophical Sketch* (1795), and the *Metaphysics of Morals* (1797). In 1798 Kant published *The Contest of the Faculties* and *Anthropology from a Pragmatic Point of View,* the latter based on his very popular lectures on the subject.

During the final years of his life Kant suffered from Alzheimer's disease. He died in Königsberg in 1804.

A Note on the Texts

This collection contains Kant's main writings, published during his lifetime, on politics, peace, and history, in a new translation by David L. Colclasure. The translation was based on the text in *Kants gesammelte Schriften,* edited by the Royal Prussian (later German) Academy of Sciences (Berlin: Georg Reimer, subsequently Walter de Gruyter, 1902–), also called the Akademie edition.

Below is a list of the texts included in this volume, with their location in the Akademie edition (volume number: pages), their German title, and bibliographical details of their first publication. The date of the second edition is mentioned where the editors of the Akademie edition used this as their source.

"Idea for a Universal History from a Cosmopolitan Perspective" (Ak 8:15–31)
["Idee zu einer allgemeinen Geschichte in weltbürgerlicher Absicht"]
Berlinische Monatsschrift, November 1784

"An Answer to the Question: What Is Enlightenment?" (Ak 8:33–42)
["Beantwortung der Frage: Was ist Aufklärung?"]
Berlinische Monatsschrift, December 1784

"Conjectural Beginning of Human History" (Ak 8:107–23)
["Mutmaßlicher Anfang der Menschengeschichte"]
Berlinische Monatsschrift, January 1786

Critique of Judgment (entire book: Ak 5:165–485; selected text: § 83–§ 84: 5:429–36)
[*Kritik der Urteilskraft*]
Berlin and Libau: Lagarde and Friederich, 1790
The Akademie edition is based on the second edition, 1793.

"On the Common Saying: This May Be True in Theory, but It Does Not Hold in Practice" (Ak 8:273–313; part 2, 289–306, and 3, 307–13)

["Über den Gemeinspruch: Das mag in der Theorie richtig sein, taugt aber
    nicht für die Praxis"]
Berlinische Monatsschrift, September 1793

Toward Perpetual Peace: A Philosophical Sketch (Ak 8:341–86)
[*Zum ewigen Frieden: Ein philosophischer Entwurf*]
Königsberg: Friedrich Nicolovius, 1795
The Akademie edition is based on the second, augmented edition, 1796.

Metaphysics of Morals (entire book: Ak 6:203–493; selected text: § 43–
    § 62: 6:309–55)
[*Metaphysik der Sitten*]
The selected text was first published in *Metaphysische Anfangsgründe der
    Rechtslehre*. Königsberg: Friedrich Nicolovius, in early 1797. This book
    was later published together with the *Metaphysische Anfangsgründe der
    Tugendlehre* under the title *Metaphysik der Sitten* (Königsberg:
    Friedrich Nicolovius, 1797). The Akademie edition is based on the text
    of the second edition of the *Rechtslehre* (Doctrine of Right), from 1798.

The Contest of the Faculties (entire text: Ak 7:1–116; selected text: part 2,
    7:77–94)
[*Der Streit der Fakultäten*]
Königsberg: Friedrich Nicolovius, 1798

Anthropology from a Pragmatic Point of View (entire book: Ak 7:117–
    333; selected text: 7:321–33)
[*Anthropologie in pragmatischer Hinsicht*]
Königsberg: Friedrich Nicolovius, 1798
The Akademie edition is based on the second edition, 1800.

A Note on the Translation

Translating is not a mechanical endeavor. It is of course important for a translation to be consistent, and thus we have aimed to translate the same German word with the same English word where possible. But when a word has different shades of meaning, and when its meaning is determined by the larger context, assigning it a single English counterpart is neither possible nor desirable.

Also, a translation should not aim to improve the style and contents of the original. If the original is unclear or stylistically ugly, a good translation will be unclear or ugly too — when this is possible. Thus, the English word "also" is used twice within one short sentence because Kant uses the German word *auch* twice, in IUH 8:23. It is not always possible to get this result. A phrase that is ambiguous in German may not have an equally ambiguous English counterpart, for example. We have tried, however, to place the Anglophone reader, as much as possible, in the same position as the reader of the German original when it comes to interpreting and assessing Kant's arguments.

A few terms posed special difficulties. Two issues deserve special mention here:

Mensch. In many other translations, this term is translated as "man," which is then used for both *Mensch* and *Mann.* To preserve the distinction between these two German terms, we prefer to translate *Mensch* as "human being" and reserve "man" for *Mann.*

Recht and its cognates. This term is notoriously difficult to translate because of the structural differences between the juridical systems predominant in the German and English speaking worlds. We have decided to use "right" for *Recht,* which may sound unfamiliar in places, but it may thereby also serve to highlight the different way of thinking about these matters that lies behind Kant's words.

Latin quotes and phrases have been preserved and have been translated separately (between brackets or in a note) only when Kant does not provide a translation himself.

Abbreviations

The marginal numbers in the translations refer to the page numbers of Kant's texts in the standard German edition, the Akademie edition, as indicated in the Note on the Texts.

In the introduction and the essays, Kant's writings are cited by the abbreviated title as indicated below, using the Akademie volume and page numbers. The only exception is the *Critique of Pure Reason,* for which, as is customary, the page numbers of the first (A) and second (B) editions are cited.

A	*Anthropology from a Pragmatic Point of View*
CB	"Conjectural Beginning of Human History"
CF	*The Contest of the Faculties*
CJ	*Critique of Judgment*
CPrR	*Critique of Practical Reason*
CPuR	*Critique of Pure Reason*
G	*Groundwork for the Metaphysics of Morals*
IUH	"Idea for a Universal History from a Cosmopolitan Perspective"
LA	*Lectures on Anthropology*
MM	*Metaphysics of Morals*
PP	*Toward Perpetual Peace: A Philosophical Sketch*
R	*Religion within the Boundaries of Mere Reason*
TP	"On the Common Saying: This May Be True in Theory, but It Does Not Hold in Practice"
WE	"An Answer to the Question: What Is Enlightenment?"

Editor's Introduction

KANT ON POLITICS, PEACE, AND HISTORY

PAULINE KLEINGELD

What is peace? Is it simply the absence of war? Kant thinks not. If peace is no more than a truce used by both parties to regain strength for their next attack, if peace is no more than the continuation of war through political means, if peace is no more than the successful subjugation of one party by another, or if peace is merely local and hence still threatened by the world beyond — then there is no real peace. Real peace, according to Kant, requires the rule of just laws within the state, between states, and between states and foreigners, and it requires that this condition be a global one.

In the texts collected in this volume, Kant and three distinguished commentators from different disciplines discuss the normative and empirical conditions under which genuine peace can be realized. They discuss the question of why individuals should join a state to begin with; what the main characteristics of a just state are; whether and how the state's internal constitution bears on its external behavior toward other states; what form the rule of law should take at the transnational level; and whether and how the goal of perpetual peace can be realized.

Kant's now-classic position on these matters continues to play a vital role in the contemporary discussion of politics and peace and of related issues, such as citizenship, globalization, the United Nations, and the role of the state in the post–cold war world. But, as is so often the case with classic positions, the proper assessment and even the precise meaning of Kant's texts are still much contested. Both the evaluation and the interpretation of the texts are affected by the ever-changing historical context of their readers, and this yields new questions and new critical perspectives regarding the arguments presented in the texts.

For more than two centuries now, Kant has been well known for advocating the establishment of a league of states, and he has often been credited with posthumous influence on the creation of the League of Nations and the United Nations (even if the resulting institutions only partially corresponded to the league proposed by Kant, most notably perhaps because standing armies were not abolished). Since 1989 debates over the role

of the United Nations, its inner workings, and the scope of its powers
have only intensified. Kant's views form an important point of reference in
those discussions. There is much debate, however, about the precise view
that Kant advocated. Did he regard the league of states as the ultimate ideal
or as a transition stage on the path toward a world federation of states?
And in either case, how strong is his argument for this view? "Realists"
strongly reject both versions because they regard the normative principles
expounded by Kant as inapplicable to the international arena. Kant's views
have also found many supporters, however. Many leading political theorists, including, for example, John Rawls, defend a voluntary league via an
explicit appeal to Kant.[1] Others, from Johann Gottlieb Fichte to Jürgen
Habermas, assert that Kant's own theoretical commitments should have led
him to argue for a stronger form of international federation with coercive
military powers.

In the past few decades, attention has also turned increasingly to other
elements of Kant's theory of peace. First, Kant's claim that the *internal*
organization of the state has a crucial influence on a state's external behavior toward other states, more specifically, that "republican" (democratic)[2]
states are more inclined toward peace than despotic ones, has piqued the
interest of political scientists (as well as that of a much broader audience)
ever since Michael Doyle showed that this claim finds at least partial empirical confirmation (see also his contribution in this volume).

Furthermore, Kant's theory of the state is increasingly present in discussions of social and political theory.[3] It presents an alternative to the dominant approaches in debates over the question of what we owe to the state.
Whereas dominant approaches answer this question in terms of consent,
fairness, or utilitarian considerations, according to Kant persons have a
moral duty to join and support a state. Jeremy Waldron carefully lays out
Kant's position on this matter and discusses the seemingly harsh consequences that Kant believes are implied by his position, such as his notorious
views on resistance and revolution.

Third, Kant's notion of "cosmopolitan right" as a category of public
right[4] has turned out to provide a way to capture theoretically the fact that
peace requires the legal regulation not only of the interactions between
states, but also of the interactions between states and foreign individuals or
groups — from refugees to international terrorists. With this insight, Kant
is ahead of his time and remarkably close to developments that took place
in international law in the twentieth century. Moreover, the recent international terrorist attacks by groups who are not acting as representatives of

their own states but who direct their attacks against other states and their citizens painfully underscore the truth of Kant's claim that world peace, that is, the security of the external freedom of all persons, requires more than peace among states. Many questions about the appropriate institutionalization of cosmopolitan right are, however, still open.

Finally, Kant's philosophy of history, long viewed as a very minor matter and an inconsistent one at that, is now increasingly viewed as an integral part of his considered theory of peace. The course of human history is, Kant assumes, an inevitable and proper concern for humans as historical and moral beings. They wonder, first, how much they can *know* about the course of history in general. Second, they wonder what they may *hope* for, which means in the present context whether and how peace, which they ought to promote for moral reasons, may be approximated in reality. Allen Wood discusses some of the questions raised by Kant's answers, for example, what the implications are of the fact that the teleological model presupposed by Kant has lost its currency. But he also argues that the methodological concerns that motivate Kant's philosophy of history have lost none of their relevance.

Kant's Theory of Public Right and the State

Although Kant discussed theories of politics and right at least as early as his lectures of the 1760s, most of his writings on the subject are from the 1780s and 1790s. Events at the time, especially the French Revolution of 1789, had an enormous impact on the evolution of Kant's political theory, particularly on the formulation of Kant's own version of republicanism (TP, PP, and MM).

As mentioned, the details of Kant's theory are subject to debate, but here is one interpretation that can serve as a beginning. Kant starts from the assumption of the freedom and equality of all beings with moral standing.[5] Because agents who live in proximity to one another can influence each other's sphere of activity, and hence can infringe on each other's freedom, the question arises of how to regulate their activity in such a way that the freedom of each is compatible with the freedom and equality of all. This question concerns spheres of action, or what Kant calls "external" freedom (as distinguished from "inner" freedom, the freedom to determine one's will morally, which he discusses in his writings on moral theory).[6] Kant's answer is that securing external freedom requires a system of just public laws and a public authority to enforce these laws, that is, it requires a just state. Therefore, on the basis of the assumption of the freedom and equality of all human beings, he defends the claim that one has a moral duty to join a state and obey its laws (or else withdraw from all interactions with other human beings).[7]

This system of just public laws is called "public right." *Right* is the "restriction of the freedom of each to the condition of its being compatible with the freedom of everyone, to the extent this freedom is possible in accordance with a general law; and *public* right is the sum of *external* laws that make such a universal harmony possible" (TP 8:289–90; cf. MM, 6:230).

In the absence of a system of public right and its enforcement, individuals exist in the so-called state of nature — the condition in which there is no rule of law and no state authority set above the individuals. In that condition, individuals settle their inevitable conflicts on the basis of their respective strength. For even in the best possible scenario, that is, when the individuals are "good-natured and righteous" (MM 6:312) instead of egoistic and violent, they decide their conflicts on the basis of what each *believes* to be right, and since they may not always reach agreement (in time) on this matter, any conflicts in interpretations of what is right (for example, with regard to property claims) cannot be settled in any other way than by might. This situation should be avoided because settling disputes by force is not consistent with the principle of the freedom and equality of all. To avoid this situation one needs a just state. That is to say, the mere possibility of violence requires the just state in order to secure everyone's sphere of freedom.

This raises the question, of course, of under what conditions the state is just. For obviously, the authority of the state itself needs to be compatible with the freedom of all, and the authority assumed by a despotic state clearly is not. Kant's notion of the republic serves to address this issue. In a true republic the people (as citizens) co-legislate via their representatives. That means, Kant writes with an obvious debt to Rousseau, that in a republic the people do not actually relinquish their freedom but rather give it a different form, because they give laws to themselves instead of a foreign authority imposing laws on them. Furthermore, a republic, in contrast to a despotic state, has a separation of powers. The people legislate (via their representatives), but they delegate ruling to the executive (who can be a monarch or a collective, but who should not be the entire people as in a "direct" democracy), and they elect judges and delegate juries.

International and Cosmopolitan Right

If the justification of the state proceeds in terms of securing external freedom for individuals as such, however, right is inherently cosmopolitan in scope. For then the external freedom of *any* individual with moral standing is important (and not just the external freedom of one's compatriots), and so the theory of right is not complete if it limits itself to the internal organization of the state. Moreover, Kant believes that as a practical matter of fact, right cannot be optimally realized within the state unless the relations between this state and others are regulated in accordance with principles of right as well. Thus, the question needs to be addressed of how the interaction between states, and between states and foreign individuals, should be regulated so that it is in accordance with right. In Kant's theory of right, these two questions are answered in his theories of international and cosmopolitan right, respectively.

International right sets out the normative principles for the interaction of states toward each other. During the 1780s, Kant advises the rulers of states to establish a state-like international federation. During the 1790s, however, he advocates the establishment of a voluntary and noncoercive *league* of states, while retaining the federative *state* of states as ideal. This has spawned a lively debate about the coherence of Kant's position. Most authors believe that Kant's considered position is the defense of the league, but many argue that he should instead have defended the establishment of a state-like international federation, and almost all agree that the position as it stands is contradictory.

Perhaps, however, Kant did indeed defend both the league and the stronger form of federation during the 1790s, with the league being regarded as a first step on the way toward the latter. When Kant developed his republicanism more fully during the last decade of the eighteenth century, he started to attribute crucial importance to the republican self-legislation, or autonomy, of the people. As a result, it was no longer possible for him to advocate the international federation as something that rulers should simply decide to bring about (as he had done before). In order not to run counter to the autonomy of the people,[8] a state's joining an international federation should be a voluntary act of the people, not something that states or their rulers can impose on each other as a matter of right. As a result, the *league* of states gets an important historical role for promoting the development toward peace and for helping to prepare populations to *want* peace.[9]

Kant regards the ideal of perpetual peace as feasible. First, he believes that even the forces of simple self-interest will direct humankind to form republics (or, in current terminology, democracies) because every individual has an interest in security and freedom, and these are best guaranteed in a republic. Moreover, despotic states have a tendency to self-destruction in the long run. And Kant believes that republics, in contrast to despotic states, are by nature inclined to form peaceful alliances with other states, since the citizens have a vote in whether to go to war, and they are the ones who will have to bear its burdens (financial and economic burdens, loss of life, and so on). Despots, after all, can pass most of the burdens on to their subjects, and so they have less of an interest in avoiding war. Thus, Kant believes, increased republicanization, or democratization, will lead to more peace.

Second, Kant is aware that the world is the stage not just of states interacting with other states but also of individuals (from refugees to adventurers) and nonstate groups that operate across borders (like businesses or bands of pirates, or, by extension, terrorist groups aiming to attack states). Therefore, Kant introduces a novel, third category of public right, namely, cosmopolitan right. He stresses that this is limited to a "right to hospitality." This term is easily misunderstood as meaning the right to be a guest. What Kant actually means is merely the right to present oneself and initiate contact with a foreign individual or state without being treated with hostility or violence. It remains the right of the visited party, however, to deny visitors entry into its territory, as long as this can be done without causing their death. Kant grounds cosmopolitan right in the original common possession of the surface of the earth and the fact that "originally no one has more of a right to be at a given place on earth than anyone else" (PP 8:358).

In sum, Kant believes that peace in the full sense, and hence perpetual peace, requires that public right be realized at each and all of these three levels (constitutional, international, and cosmopolitan right).

History and the Justification of the Belief in Progress

Kant's theory of constitutional, international, and cosmopolitan right is a purely normative theory. It claims to show what is *correct* on the basis of principles of reason, not on the basis of principles of prudence. The question of what is *right* is fundamentally independent from the question of what is *feasible* or realistic. Yet the normative theory should not contain prescriptions that are absolutely impossible because it is incoherent to prescribe that someone do something that is patently impossible. Thus, Kant needs to be able to show that peace is not empirically impossible — that it is not something that is "true in theory" but "does not hold in practice." Furthermore, even though moral agents, according to Kant, determine what they ought to do on the basis of purely normative principles and not on the basis of considerations of expected results, they do of course wonder what will come of their actions, that is, what they may hope for.

In the first half of the 1780s Kant had already published a teleological account of history, according to which history is to be regarded as progressive. The principle of this process is humankind's gradual development of the use of the rational predispositions of humanity (a development Kant also calls "culture"). Kant views this development as taking place through a distinctive feature of human nature, namely, our "unsocial sociability." This enables him to incorporate much that would otherwise seem counter-purposive, such as conflict, egoism, and jealousy. On Kant's teleological view, the mixed tendency of humans to socialize but also to behave antagonistically toward others leads them to develop their rational potential — they develop skills, prudence, and self-discipline in the process. But, Kant believes, with the general development of their rational capacities even their moral insight will ultimately also develop, and eventually they will gain in moral strength and moral disposition (IUH 8:21, 26).

Kant always attributed a crucial role in this process to political development. And from the outset he regards the improvement of the political organization at the state and the international levels as inherently connected. He believes that it is only in a just state that all "natural predispositions" of humankind can be fully developed; and he believes that this can happen only in a state that has the stability and security that are impossible without international peace. Kant believes, however, that nature is teleologically organized in such a way that it promotes peace: even if their moral disposition is still lacking, humans will be driven in the direction of peace by the forces of self-interest (IUH, TP, PP).

It is important to realize, however, that Kant presents the belief in progress, in the moral and political essays, not as theoretical *knowledge* but as a *belief* on the part of the moral agent. The belief that nature, including of course human nature, will push humans in the direction of what is morally demanded gives the moral agent hope. Thus, in the "Idea for a Universal History," Kant points out the advantages of a teleological view of history for the moral subject and then says that the hope that this perspective provides is no insignificant motivation for choosing this point of view (IUH 8:30; see also CB, TP, PP). We do not have theoretical knowledge of the course of history, Kant writes, but this means it is open to us to *assume for moral purposes* that it is possible to make the world a better place and that our moral agency contributes to a larger historical process toward the better. This form of belief in progress is sufficient for the moral agent, but, importantly, it is not enough to "foretell the future of this peace (theoretically)," as Kant puts it in *Toward Perpetual Peace* (8:368). That is to say: what may at first glance look like a naive claim to knowledge of the actuality of progress is in fact a belief from a moral point of view.

Within the broader Kantian system, the assumption of the teleological model of history is also justified from a theoretical perspective, however, and this is quite important. If the teleological model were not theoretically well grounded, the practical (moral) belief in progress on the part of the moral agent might be incapable of being connected to phenomena in the empirical world.

In the *Critique of Pure Reason* (1781), that is, before his main writings on history, Kant already provides a justification for teleological judgments in general. Here he argues that one cannot *know* whether there are teleological connections in nature, but that the principle to look for such connections is justified as a heuristic principle. Use of this principle encourages new discoveries of connections in nature, and, Kant claims, it allows one to integrate the greatest amount of data into a single systematically organized whole of knowledge. Similarly, in the "Idea for a Universal History," Kant recommends the teleological model of history which he develops in the first seven propositions by pointing out that it can be historiographically "useful" to approach the historical phenomena along the lines he sketches, and that it enables one to present history as a "system," a coherent whole, rather than an aggregate of seemingly chaotic phenomena (IUH 8:29, cf. CPuR A686-8/B714-6).

In short, the theoretical and the moral perspectives converge in the teleological view of history, and the development of just institutions at the level of the state and beyond plays a crucial role in the historical process. Kant's theory of right helps structure his account of the course of history; and conversely, his theory of history addresses the question of the realizability of his theory of right. Therefore, his texts on politics, peace, and history are best read together. This is the reason why they are here, for the first time, brought together in one volume.

Editor's notes have been added where they seemed necessary. Some of these notes occur more than once in this volume, to make it possible for readers to read Kant's texts in a different order or to read some texts but not others.

The three essays in this volume are intended to stimulate further discussion of these and related issues and facilitate active engagement with Kant's texts by providing readers with theses to debate, interpretations to evaluate, and background information to put them in a position to do so. The bibliography provides references to further resources for those who would like to examine other theses, different interpretations, or more extensive background information.

NOTES

1. See John Rawls, *The Law of Peoples* (Cambridge: Harvard University Press, 1999), 10, 19, 21, 22, 36, 54.
2. Kant's claim is nowadays usually discussed as a claim about "democratic" (rather than "republican") states. This change in terminology is appropriate when what is meant is indirect, representative democracy. Kant ranked direct democracy, on the other hand, as a form of despotism because of its lack of a proper separation of powers (cf. PP 8:352).
3. For an extensive discussion of what the state *is,* according to Kant, see the essay by Jeremy Waldron.
4. The term "right" is here used as a translation of the German *Recht.* This term is notoriously difficult to translate because of the structural differences between the juridical systems predominant in the German- and English-speaking worlds. What is meant by the term is explained below.
5. Despite Kant's talk of "all human beings," the textual record shows that Kant did not in fact regard women and men and humans of all "races" as equals for political purposes. In his view, women should never have the right to vote, for example, because of "natural" reasons (not their economic dependence, see TP 8:295; MM 6:314–15). And although his writings from the "critical" period contain fewer comments linking "race" to moral, cognitive, and personal abilities than his earlier writings, such comments can still be found ("On the Use of Teleological Principles in Philosophy," 8:174). Yet it is also clear that Kant regarded humans of all "races" as being in possession of certain elemental rights. See, e.g., his critique of colonialist practices in PP 8:358–59.
6. See, e.g., Kant's *Groundwork for the Metaphysics of Morals,* ed. Allen W. Wood (New Haven: Yale University Press, 2002).
7. Although the duty to join a state is a moral duty, the system of laws

administered by the state itself, however, should not extend to the moral disposition of the subjects but be restricted to what pertains to their "external freedom." That is to say, the laws of the state can and should pertain to behavior only, not to motives.

8. The term "people" should here be taken in the political, not the nationalist sense.

9. I have argued for this position and discussed the current debate in "Approaching Perpetual Peace: Kant's Defense of the League of States and His Ideal of a State of States," *European Journal of Philosophy* 12 (2004): 304–25.

Toward Perpetual Peace *and*
Other Writings on Politics,
Peace, and History

Texts

Idea for a Universal History from a Cosmopolitan Perspective*

Whatever concept of the *freedom of the will* one may develop in the context of metaphysics, the *appearances* of the will,[1] human actions, are determined, like every other natural event, in accordance with universal natural laws. History, which is concerned with giving a narrative account of these appearances, allows us to hope that, however deeply concealed their causes may be, if we consider the free exercise of the human will *broadly,* we can ultimately discern a regular progression in its appearances. History further lets us hope that, in this way, that which seems confused and irregular when considering particular individuals can nonetheless be recognized as a steadily progressing, albeit slow development of the original capacities of the entire species. Thus, given that the free will of humans has such a great influence on marriages, on the births that result from these, and on dying, it would seem that there is no rule to which these events are subject and according to which one could calculate their number in advance. And yet the relevant statistics compiled annually in large countries demonstrate that these events occur just as much in accordance with constant natural laws as do inconstancies in the weather, which cannot be determined individually in advance, but which, taken together, do not fail to maintain a consistent and uninterrupted process in the growth of the plants, the flow of the rivers, and other natural arrangements. Individual human beings and even entire peoples give little thought to the fact that they, by pursuing their own ends, each in his own way and often in opposition to others, unwittingly, as if guided along, work to promote the intent of nature, which is unknown

---

*A statement printed in the short notices in the twelfth issue of this year's *Gothaische Gelehrte Zeitung* (1784), based, no doubt, on a conversation of mine with a scholar who was passing through, compels me to provide the present clarification, without which the statement would make no sense.

1. "Appearance" is the standard English translation of *Erscheinung*. The term is best read in light of Kant's distinction between the world as it is in itself (of which knowledge is impossible) and the world as it appears to us (of which knowledge is possible).

to them, and which, even if it were known to them, they would hardly care about.

Since human beings do not, in the pursuit of their endeavors, follow merely their instincts as do animals, and yet also do not, as would rational citizens of the world, proceed in accordance with a previously arranged plan, it does not seem possible to present a systematic history of them (as could be given for bees or beavers, for instance). One cannot but feel a certain disinclination when one observes their activity as carried out on the great stage of the world and finds it ultimately, despite the occasional semblance of wisdom to be seen in individual actions, all to be made up, by and large, of foolishness, childish vanity, and, often enough, even of childish wickedness and destructiveness. When confronted with this, one does not know, in the end, how one ought to conceive of our species, one so thoroughly conceited about its own superiority. The only option for the philosopher here, since he cannot presuppose that human beings pursue any rational *end of their own* in their endeavors, is that he attempt to discover an *end of nature* behind this absurd course of human activity, an end on the basis of which a history could be given of beings that proceed without a plan of their own, but nevertheless according to a definite plan of nature. — Let us now see whether we can discover a guiding principle for such a history, and then we want to leave it up to nature to produce the man who is able to compile such a history in accordance with this principle. Thus nature produced *Kepler,* for instance, who described, in an unexpected manner, the eccentric orbits of the planets as subject to definite laws, and *Newton,* who explained these laws in terms of a general natural cause.[2]

8:18

FIRST PROPOSITION

All of a creature's natural predispositions are destined eventually to develop fully and in accordance with their purpose. This proposition is supported both by external observation and by internal observation or dissection. An organ that is not meant to be used, or an arrangement that does not achieve its purpose, is a contradiction in the teleological theory of nature. For if we abandon this principle, then we can no longer understand nature as

---

2. Johannes Kepler (1571–1630) joined Tycho Brahe's observatory and later succeeded him. A believer in the Copernican theory, Kepler used Brahe's observations to deduce three fundamental laws of planetary motion. This later enabled Isaac Newton (1643–1727) to formulate his theory of gravitational force and explain the motions of the planets and their moons in detail.

governed by laws, but rather only as playing aimlessly; and the dismal reign of chance thus replaces the guiding principle of reason.

SECOND PROPOSITION

In the human being (as the only rational creature on earth), *those natural predispositions aimed at the use of its reason are to be developed in full only in the species, but not in the individual.* Reason is the ability of a creature to extend the rules and ends of the use of all of its powers far beyond its natural instincts, and reason knows no limits in the scope of its   8:19 projects. Reason itself does not function according to instinct, but rather requires experimentation, practice, and instruction in order to advance gradually from one stage of insight to the next. For this reason any individual person would have to live an inordinately long period of time in order to learn how to make full use of all of his natural predispositions. Or, if nature has limited the span of his life (as has in fact happened), it requires a perhaps incalculable number of generations, of which each passes its enlightenment on to the next, in order to eventually bring the seeds in our species to the stage of development which fully corresponds to nature's purpose. And this point in time must, at least in the idea of what the human being is, be the goal of his endeavors, since otherwise his natural predispositions would have to be regarded as largely futile and pointless. All practical principles would thereby be abolished, and nature, whose wisdom otherwise serves as the basic principle for judging all other arrangements, would thus be suspected of childish play in the case of human beings alone.

THIRD PROPOSITION

Nature has willed that human beings produce everything that extends beyond the mechanical organization of their animal existence completely on their own, and that they shall not partake in any happiness or perfection other than that which they attain free of instinct and by means of their own reason. For nature does nothing superfluous and is not wasteful in the use of its means to attain its ends. The mere fact that it gave human beings the faculty of reason and the freedom of will based on this faculty is a clear indication of its intent with regard to their endowments. They were intended neither to be led by instinct, nor to be supplied and instructed with innate knowledge; they were intended to produce everything themselves. The invention of their means of sustenance, their clothing, their outward security and defense (for which it gave them neither the bull's horns, nor the lion's claws, nor the dog's teeth, but only hands), all the joys that can make life pleasant, their insights and prudence, and even the goodness of their will were intended to be entirely the products of their own efforts. Nature seems to have taken pleasure in its own extreme economy in this regard, and to have provided for their animal features so sparingly, so tailored as to meet only the most vital needs of a primitive existence, as if it had intended that human beings, after working themselves out of a condition of the greatest brutishness to a condition of the greatest skill, of inner perfection in their manner of thought, and hence (to the extent possible on earth) to a state of happiness, should take the full credit for this themselves and have only themselves to thank for it. It thus seems as if nature has been concerned more with their rational *self-esteem* than with their well-being. For in the course of human affairs, humans are confronted with a whole host of hardships. It seems, however, that nature was not at all concerned that human beings live well, but rather that they work themselves far enough ahead to become, through their behavior, worthy of life and of well-being. What is disconcerting here, however, is that previous generations seem to have pursued their arduous endeavors only for the sake of the later ones, in order to prepare for them a level from which they can raise even higher the structure that nature intended; and that nevertheless only the later generations should have the fortune to dwell in the building which was the work of a long series of earlier generations (albeit without this being their intention), without themselves being able to share in the fortune that they themselves had worked toward. But however perplexing this may be, it is nevertheless necessary if one assumes that an animal species should possess reason and, as a class of rational beings, each of which dies, but whose species is immortal, ought nonetheless attain the full development of its predispositions.

FOURTH PROPOSITION

The means that nature employs in order to bring about the development of all of the predispositions of humans is their **antagonism** *in society, insofar as this antagonism ultimately becomes the cause of a law-governed organization of society.* Here I take antagonism to mean the *unsociable sociability* of human beings, that is, their tendency to enter into society, a tendency connected, however, with a constant resistance that continually threatens to break up this society. This unsociable sociability is obviously part of human nature. Human beings have an inclination to *associate* with one another because in such a condition they feel themselves to be more human, that is to say, more in a position to develop their natural predispositions. But they also have a strong tendency to *isolate* themselves, because they encounter in themselves the unsociable trait that predisposes them to want to direct everything only to their own ends and hence to expect to encounter resistance everywhere, just as they know that they themselves tend to resist others. It is this resistance that awakens all human powers and causes human beings to overcome their tendency to idleness and, driven by lust for honor, power, or property, to establish a position for themselves among their fellows, whom they can neither *endure* nor *do without*. Here the first true steps are taken from brutishness to culture, which consists, actually, in the social worth of human beings. And here all of the talents are gradually developed, taste is formed, and, even, through continual enlightenment, the beginning of a foundation is laid for a manner of thinking which is able, over time, to transform the primitive natural predisposition for moral discernment into definite practical principles and, in this way, to ultimately transform an agreement to society that initially had been *pathologically*[3] coerced into a *moral* whole. Without those characteristics of unsociability, which are indeed quite unattractive in themselves, and which give rise to the resistance that each person necessarily encounters in his selfish presumptuousness, human beings would live the arcadian life of shepherds, in full harmony, contentment, and mutual love. But all human talents would thus lie eternally dormant, and human beings, as good-natured as the sheep that they put out to pasture, would thus give their own lives hardly more worth than that of their domesticated animals. They would fail to fill the void with regard to the purpose for which they, as rational nature, were created. For this reason one should thank nature for their quarrelsomeness, for their jealously competitive vanity, and for their insatiable appetite for property and even for power! Without these all of the excellent natural human predispositions would lie in eternal slumber, undeveloped. Humans desire harmony, but nature knows better what is good for their species: it wills discord. Humans wish to live leisurely and enjoy themselves, but nature wills that human beings abandon their sloth and passive contentment and thrust themselves into work and hardship, only to find means, in turn, to cleverly escape the latter. The natural motivating forces for this, the sources of unsociability and continual resistance from which so many ills arise, but

3. The term "pathological" here means "determined by impulses from the senses" (cf. CPuR A802/B830).

8:21

8:22 which also drive one to the renewed exertion of one's energies, and hence to the further development of the natural predispositions, thus reveal the plan of a wise creator, and not, as it may seem, the work of a malicious spirit that has tampered with the creator's marvelous work or ruined it out of envy.

FIFTH PROPOSITION

*The greatest problem for the human species to which nature compels it to seek a solution is the achievement of a **civil society** which administers right universally.* Nature's highest intent for humankind, that is, the development of all of the latter's natural predispositions, can be realized only in society, and more precisely, in a society that possesses the greatest degree of freedom, hence one in which its members continually struggle with each other and yet in which the limits of this freedom are specified and secured in the most exact manner, so that such freedom of each is consistent with that of others. Nature also wills that humankind attain this, like all the ends of its vocation, by its own efforts. Thus a society in which *freedom under external laws* is connected to the highest possible degree with irresistible power, that is, a *perfectly just civil constitution,* must be the highest goal of nature for the human species, since it is only by solving and completing this task that nature can attain its other goals for humankind. It is hardship that compels human beings, who are otherwise so enamored of unrestrained freedom, to enter into this condition of coercion. Indeed, it is the greatest hardship of all, that which human beings inflict on each other, whose natural inclinations make them unable to live together in a state of wild freedom for very long. It is only in a refuge such as a civic union that these same inclinations subsequently produce the best effect, just as trees in a forest, precisely by seeking to take air and light from all the others around them, compel each other to look for air and light above themselves and thus grow up straight and beautiful, while those that live apart from others and sprout their branches freely grow stunted, crooked, and bent. All the culture and art that decorates humankind, as well as its most pleasing social order, are fruits of an unsociability that is forced by its own nature to discipline itself and thereby develop fully the seeds that nature planted within it by means of an imposed art.

8:23

SIXTH PROPOSITION

This problem is both the most difficult and also the last to be solved by the human species. Even the mere idea of this task makes the following difficulty apparent: the human being is an *animal* which, when he lives among others of his own species, *needs a master.* This is so because he will certainly abuse his freedom with regard to others of his own kind. And even though he, as a rational creature, desires a law that sets limits on the freedom of all, his selfish animal inclinations will lead him to treat himself as an exception wherever he can. For this reason he needs a *master* who will break his individual will and compel him to obey a will that is universally valid. But where does he find such a master? In no place other than in the human species. But such a master is just as much an animal in need of a master. He may thus begin in whatever way he likes, yet it is not at all evident how he is to find a supreme authority of public justice that is itself just, whether he seeks such a supreme authority in an individual person or in a group of people chosen for this purpose. For any such person will always abuse his freedom if he has no one above him who can enforce his compliance with the laws. The supreme authority must be just *in itself* but also a *human being.* This task is thus the most difficult of all. Indeed, its perfect solution is impossible: nothing entirely straight can be fashioned from the crooked wood of which humankind is made. Nature has charged us only with approximating this idea.* That this task is also the last to be carried out also follows from the fact that such a constitution requires the right conception of its nature, a great store of experience practiced in many affairs of the world, and, above all of this, a good will that is prepared to accept such a constitution. The combination of all these three elements is very difficult, however, and can occur only late, after many futile attempts.

SEVENTH PROPOSITION

8:24

*The problem of establishing a perfect civil constitution is dependent upon the problem of a law-governed **external relation between states** and cannot be solved without having first solved the latter.* What good does it do to work on establishing a law-governed civil constitution among individuals, that is, to organize a *commonwealth?* The same unsociability that had compelled human beings to pursue this commonwealth also is the reason

---

*Humankind's role is thus very artificial. We do not know how it is with the inhabitants of other planets and their nature, but if we fulfill this task that nature has set us well, then we may well be able to flatter ourselves that we can lay claim to no mean status among our neighbors in the universe. Perhaps in the case of our neighbors an individual is able to fully attain his destiny within his lifetime. In our case it is different: only the species as a whole can hope for this.

that every commonwealth, in its external relations, that is, as a state among states, exists in unrestricted freedom and consequently that states must expect the same ills from other states that threatened individuals and compelled them to enter into a law-governed civil condition. Nature has thus again used the quarrelsomeness of humankind, even that of the large societies and political bodies of this species, in order to invent, through their inevitable *antagonism,* a state of peace and security. That is to say, through wars, through the excessive and ceaseless preparations for war, through the resulting distress that every state, even in times of peace, must ultimately feel internally, nature drives humankind to make initially imperfect attempts, but finally, after the ravages of war, after the downfalls, and after even the complete internal exhaustion of its powers, [nature] impels humankind to take the step that reason could have told it to take without all these lamentable experiences: to abandon the lawless state of savagery and enter into a federation of peoples. In such a federation, every state, even the smallest one, could expect its security and its rights, not by virtue of its own power or as a consequence of its own legal judgment, but rather solely by virtue of this great federation of peoples (*Foedus Amphictyonum*),[4] from a united power and from the decision based on laws of the united will. However wildly enthusiastic this idea may seem to be, and however ridiculed it may have been in the case of the *Abbé St. Pierre* or *Rousseau*[5] (perhaps because they believed its realization was all too near): it is nonetheless the inevitable outcome of the distress to which human beings submit one another which compels states to make precisely the same decision (however difficult this may be for them) that the savage individual, just as reluctantly, was forced to make: to give up his brutish freedom and to seek peace and security in a law-governed constitution. — Accordingly, all wars amount

4. Amphictyonic League: an association of neighboring cities in ancient Greece, established for the protection of a religious center. The most important one was the one related to the Temple of Apollo at Delphi.

5. Charles-Irénée Castel, abbé de Saint Pierre (1658–1743), *Projet pour rendre la paix perpétuelle en Europe* (1713) [Project for Making Peace Perpetual in Europe]. Jean-Jacques Rousseau, "Extrait du projet de paix perpétuelle de Monsieur l'Abbé de Saint Pierre" (1761) (*Oeuvres Complètes,* 4 vols., ed. Bernard Gagnebin and Marcel Raymond [Paris: Gallimard, 1969– 78], 3:561–89). Rousseau's "Jugement sur la paix perpétuelle" [Judgment on Perpetual Peace], written around the same time as the "Extrait," was first published posthumously in 1782 (*Oeuvres Complètes,* 3:591–600). Given that Rousseau distances himself clearly and explicitly from the abbé's proposals in the Jugement, it does not seem that Kant had read this second text.

8:25

to attempts (certainly not in the intentions of humankind, but indeed in the intentions of nature) to establish new relations between states and to create new political bodies by destroying or at least breaking up old ones. Such states are in turn unable, either internally or in their relation to others, to maintain themselves and hence must endure further, similar revolutions, until the point is finally reached where, on the one hand internally, through an optimal organization of the civil constitution, and on the other hand externally, through a common agreement and legislation, a condition is established that, similar to a civil commonwealth, can maintain itself *automatically.*

[There are three questions to consider here:] Whether one ought to expect that, by an *Epicurean*[6] concourse of efficient causes, the states, as do minute particles of matter, through random collisions, will create all sorts of formations which are in turn destroyed upon further impact, until finally a formation is created, *by chance,* which can maintain its form (a fortunate coincidence, which is unlikely ever to occur!); or whether one ought instead to assume that nature pursues a regular course in this regard and gradually leads our species from the low level of animal nature to the highest level of humanity by its own art (an art which nature compels humankind to invent) and develops, in this seemingly disorderly arrangement, those original predispositions in a fully regular manner; or whether one ought rather to assume that nothing, at least nothing sensible, results from all of these actions and reactions of humankind at large, that it shall always be as it always has been, and that one cannot know in advance whether discord, which is such a natural feature of our species, is ultimately setting us up for a hell of ills, however civilized our condition may become, by later perhaps destroying this civilized condition itself and all the advances of culture made thus far by means of barbaric devastation (a fate that one could not resist if one were governed by blind chance, which is indeed one and the same as the state of lawless freedom, unless we assume that such freedom is secretly guided by the wisdom of nature); these three questions all boil down roughly to the question of whether it is reasonable to assume that the order of nature is *purposive* in its parts, and yet *purposeless* as a whole. The purposeless condition of savagery, in which all the natural predispositions in our species lay fallow, subsequently compelled our species, by means of

6. Epicurus (341–270 BCE), ancient Greek philosopher now known primarily for his ethics, but also an important atomist whose physical theory included the claim that the universe is made up of atoms that are in perpetual motion and that form and dissolve compound bodies as they collide and rebound.

the ills to which this condition subjects it, to leave this state and enter into a civil constitution, in which all those seeds would be able to develop. The same holds true for the barbarous freedom of the already established states: through the use of all of the commonwealth's resources to arm for war against others, through the ravages of war, but more still through the need to remain constantly prepared for war, progress toward the full development of our natural predispositions is hindered, but the ills that arise from this, in turn, compel our species to discover a law of equilibrium with regard to the in itself productive resistance between many states which arises from their freedom, and to introduce a united power which lends force to this law. A cosmopolitan condition of public security is thus introduced, which is not completely free of *danger,* so that humankind's powers do not fall into slumber, but also not without a principle of the *equality* of their mutual *actions and reactions,* so that they do not destroy one another. Before this last step (the federation of states) is taken, hence at a point barely halfway through its development, human nature endures the most severe ills deceptively disguised as external prosperity; and Rousseau's preference of the state of savages[7] was not all that far off the mark, that is, if one leaves out this last stage, which our species has yet to surmount. We are *cultivated* to a great extent by the arts and the sciences. And we are *civilized* to a troublesome degree in all forms of social courteousness and decency. But to consider ourselves to be already fully *moralized* is quite premature. For the idea of morality is part of culture. But the use of this idea, which leads only to that which resembles morality in the love of honor and outward decency, comprises only mere civilization. As long as states use all their resources to realize their vain and violent goals of expansion and thereby continue to hinder the slow efforts to cultivate their citizens' minds and even to withhold all support from them in this regard, then nothing of the sort can be expected, because such moral cultivation requires a long internal process in every commonwealth in order to educate its citizens. All that is good yet is not based on morally good convictions is nothing but pure outward show and shimmering misery. The human race will likely remain in such a condi-

7. A reference to Rousseau's "Discourse on the Sciences and Arts" (full title: "A Discourse That won First Prize at the Academy of Dijon. In the Year 1750. On the following question proposed by the Academy: Has the revival of the Sciences and Arts contributed to improving morality?") and his "Discourse on the Origin and Foundations of Inequality Among Mankind" (1755). In Jean-Jacques Rousseau, *The Social Contract and The First and Second Discourses,* ed. Susan Dunn (New Haven: Yale University Press, 2002).

tion until it has worked its way out of the chaotic condition of the relations
between states in the way I have described.

EIGHTH PROPOSITION   8:27

One can regard the history of the human species at large as the realization
of a concealed plan of nature, meant to bring into being an internally and,
to this end, *externally perfect state constitution, as the only condition in*
which nature can fully develop all of its predispositions in humankind. This
proposition follows from the previous one. One sees that philosophy, too,
can have its chiliastic beliefs, but this is a chiliasm the idea of which,
although only from very far away, can itself promote its realization, and
which is, for that reason, anything but fanciful. All that matters is whether
experience can discover any evidence of such a purposeful process in nature. I submit: it can discover *a little.* For this cycle appears to require such a
long time to be completed, that, from within the small part of it that comprises humankind's progress to date along the path toward this purpose, one
can determine the shape of its overall course and the relation between its
parts and the whole only as tentatively as one could establish, on the basis
of all astronomical observations to date, the path that our sun, together with
all of its satellites, takes in the vast system of fixed stars. Yet on the basis of
the general premise that the cosmos is constructed as a system, and on the
basis of the little that has been observed, one can reliably enough conclude
that such a cycle indeed exists. Meanwhile, human nature is such that it
cannot be indifferent even in consideration of the most remote epoch that
shall affect our species, if only it can be expected with certainty. Especially
in our case such indifference is all the less possible, since it appears that we
would be able, by means of our own rational projects, to hasten the arrival
of this point in time, which will be such a happy one for our descendants.
For this reason even the faint signs that we are approaching this point in
time are very important. The states are now in such an artificial relation to
one another that one cannot weaken in its internal culture without losing
power and influence to the others. Thus, even where progress is not guaranteed, at least the preservation of this purpose of nature is secured fairly well
even through the ambitious intentions of these states. Moreover, civil liberties may hardly be encroached upon without negative effects in all indus-
tries, primarily in trade, which would also lead to a decrease in the powers
of the state in its external relations. But these liberties gradually increase. If   8:28
one prevents the private citizen from pursuing his own welfare in any way
that he sees fit, as long as this pursuit is consistent with the freedom of

others, one hinders the vitality of the entire enterprise and thereby diminishes the powers of the whole. For this reason limitations on personal activities are increasingly lifted and the general freedom of religion extended. In this way, although folly and caprice will appear occasionally, *enlightenment* arises as a great good, one which the human race must wrest even from the self-aggrandizement of its masters, as long as they understand their own interests. But this enlightenment, and with it a certain commitment of the heart, which the enlightened person cannot but make to the good that he understands completely, must gradually make its way up to the thrones and even influence their principles of governance. Although, for instance, the rulers of our world have no money to spare for public educational institutions or indeed for anything that has the best interests of the world in mind, since everything is allocated in advance for future wars, they will nonetheless find it to be in their own interest at least not to hinder the efforts, however weak and slow, of their peoples in this regard. Ultimately, war itself will not only become such an artificial undertaking, or one the outcome of which is so uncertain for both parties: the after-pains which the state suffers because of war, through the ever-growing burden of debt (a new invention), the repayment of which becomes immeasurable, will also make war such a dubious activity that the reverberations which upheaval in any one state in our part of the world, so linked in its commercial activities, will have in all other states, will become so clear that these states, compelled by the threat to their own security, albeit without legal standing, will offer themselves up as judges and thus ultimately prepare everything for a future political body the likes of which the earlier world has never known. Although this political body exists presently only in a very rough, rudimentary form, it is just as if a feeling is nevertheless beginning to stir among all the members who have an interest in the preservation of the whole. And this gives us the hope that, after a number of structural revolutions, that which nature has as its highest aim, a universal *cosmopolitan condition,* can come into being, as the womb in which all the original predispositions of the human species are developed.

8:29   NINTH PROPOSITION

A philosophical attempt to describe the universal history of the world according to a plan of nature that aims at the perfect civic union of the human species must be considered to be possible and even to promote this intention of nature. It is indeed an odd and seemingly inconsistent approach to want to narrate a *history* according to an idea of how the course of the world would have to progress if it is to be adequate to certain rational aims; it may seem that such a project could yield only a *novel*. Yet if one may assume that nature itself does not progress without a plan and ultimate intention even in the exercise of human freedom, then such an idea could become useful indeed; and although we are too shortsighted to understand the secret mechanism of nature's organization, this idea may nonetheless serve as a guiding thread with which to describe an otherwise planless *aggregate* of human activities, at least in the large, as a *system*. For if one begins with *Greek* history — through which every other older or contemporaneous history has been passed on to us, or at least must be certified;* if one traces up until our time its influence on the formation and deformation of the *Roman* state which swallowed up the Greek state, and the Romans' influence on the *barbarians* who in turn destroyed them, and if one *episodically* adds to this the history of the states of other peoples, the knowledge of which has gradually been passed down to us from these enlightened nations specifically: then one will discover a regular course of improvement in the constitution of the state in our part of the world (which is likely to provide all others with laws at some future point). By furthermore paying heed in all instances only to the civic constitution and its laws and the relations among states, to the extent that both served for some span of time to elevate and extol peoples (and with them the arts and sciences) through the good that they contained, but which, due to the flaws contained in them in turn collapsed, though in such a way that a seed of enlightenment always remained which developed further through each revolution and prepared a subsequent, even more greatly improved stage: then one will, I believe, thereby 8:30

*Only an *educated audience* that has existed without interruption since its beginning up until the present can certify ancient history. Anything beyond this is terra incognita [unknown territory]. And the history of nations that existed outside of this can only be begun from that point in time at which they entered into it. This happened with the *Jewish people* at the time of the Ptolemies by means of the Greek translation of the Bible, without which one would grant little credibility to its own *isolated* reports. From here on (as long as this point has first been appropriately determined) one can follow its accounts forward. It is the same with all other nations. The first page of *Thucydides* (says *Hume*) is the sole beginning of all real history.[8]

8. David Hume (1711–76), "Of the Populousness of Ancient Nations," in *Essays Moral, Political, and Literary,* ed. Thomas Hill Green and Thomas Hodge Grose, 2nd ed. (London, 1882; repr. Scientia Verlag Aalen, 1992), vol. 1, p. 414: "The first page of Thucydides is, in my opinion, the commencement of real history."

discover a guiding thread that serves not only to explain the convoluted play of human events, nor merely for political fortune-telling regarding future changes in the state (a benefit which one has already been able to derive from human history, if one regards the latter as so many disconnected results of a ruleless exercise of freedom!). Rather, such an examination will reveal a consoling outlook on the future, in which the human species is represented at a remote point in the distant future where it is finally working itself toward the condition in which all the seeds that nature has planted within it can be fully developed and its vocation here on earth can be realized (something that one cannot reasonably hope for without presupposing a plan of nature). Such a *justification* of nature, or rather of *providence,* is no insignificant motivation for choosing a particular point of view when regarding the world. For what good does it do to praise the magnificence and wisdom of creation in the nonrational realm of nature and to recommend the contemplation of it, if there shall remain the constant objection, against that part of the great scene of the most supreme wisdom which contains the purpose of all of this — the history of the human species — the sight of which compels us to reluctantly turn our eyes from it and, as we despair at ever finding in it a completed rational aim, leads us to hope to find it only in another world?

It would be a misinterpretation of my intent to presume that I would wish to suppress accounts of actual history that are merely *empirically* grounded with this idea of a history of the world, which in some sense has a guiding thread *a priori*. It is only a thought about what else a philosophical mind (which incidentally must be extensively familiar with history) could attempt from another perspective. Moreover, the otherwise notable thoroughness with which one currently describes the history of one's time must of course raise the following question to everyone: how will our descendants go about conceiving the burden of history that we would like to leave them with after a number of centuries? Without doubt they will hold in esteem the history of the most ancient time, the documents of which will likely have long since disappeared, only from the point of view of what interests them, namely, what peoples and governments have achieved or harmed, from a cosmopolitan perspective. To take this into account, and at the same time to take into account the desire that heads of state and their servants have for honor, so that they can be directed to the only means that will ensure that they be regarded as praiseworthy into the latest of ages: this too can provide a *small* motivation for attempts at such a philosophical history.

8:31

An Answer to the Question:
What Is Enlightenment?

Enlightenment is the human being's emancipation from its self-incurred immaturity.[1] *Immaturity* is the inability to make use of one's intellect without the direction of another. This immaturity is *self-incurred* when its cause does not lie in a lack of intellect, but rather in a lack of resolve and courage to make use of one's intellect without the direction of another. "*Sapere aude!* Have the courage to make use of your own intellect!" is hence the motto of enlightenment.[2]

Idleness and cowardice are the reasons why such a large segment of humankind, even after nature has long since set it free from foreign direction (*naturaliter maiorennes*),[3] is nonetheless content to remain immature for life; and these are also the reasons why it is so easy for others to set themselves up as their guardians. It is so comfortable to be immature. If I have a book that reasons for me, a pastor who acts as my conscience, a physician who determines my diet for me, etc., then I need not make any effort myself. It is not necessary that I think if I can just pay; others will take such irksome business upon themselves for me. The guardians who have kindly assumed supervisory responsibility have ensured that the largest part of humanity (including the entirety of the fairer sex) understands progress

---

1. "Immaturity" is a translation of *Unmündigkeit,* which can designate both natural and legal immaturity. *Mund* means "mouth," and a primary connotation of the term is not being able to speak (and decide) for oneself. The paradigmatic case of those who are *unmündig* is children. Legal immaturity consists in not being legally allowed to make certain decisions or to represent oneself in legal proceedings, that is, in needing a *Vormund* (translated below as "guardian," but the German word also has connotations of someone who speaks for another). The group of those who are legally immature can comprise more than just children (for example, adults who are not mentally competent or, in the eighteenth century, women).

2. The phrase stems from Horace's *Epistles* 1.2.40 and was a recognized motto in Enlightenment circles.

3. "Those who have come of age naturally."

toward maturity to be not only arduous, but also dangerous. After they have first made their domesticated animals dumb and carefully prevented their tame creatures from daring to take a single step without the walker to which they have been harnessed, they then show the danger that threatens them, should they attempt to walk alone. Yet this danger is not so great, for they would, after falling a few times, eventually learn to walk alone; but one such example makes them timid and generally deters them from all further attempts.

8:36

It is thus difficult for any individual to work himself out of the immaturity that has almost become second nature to him. He has even become fond of it and is, for the time being, truly unable to make use of his own reason, because he has never been allowed to try it. Statutes and formulae, those mechanical tools of a rational use, or rather misuse, of his natural endowments, are the shackles of a perpetual state of immaturity. And whoever would throw them off would nonetheless make only an uncertain leap over even the narrowest ditch, because he is not used to such freedom of movement. Hence there are only very few who have succeeded through their own intellectual toil in emerging from immaturity and who still walk confidently.

It is much more likely that an entire public should enlighten itself; indeed it is nearly unavoidable if one allows it the freedom to do so. For there will always be some independent thinkers even among the appointed guardians of the great masses who, after they themselves have thrown off the yoke of immaturity, will spread the spirit of rational appreciation of one's own worth and the calling of every human being to think for himself. What is particularly noteworthy here is that the public that had previously been placed under this yoke may compel its guardians themselves to remain under this yoke, if it is incited to such action by some of its guardians who are incapable of any enlightenment. So harmful is it to instill prejudices, for they ultimately avenge themselves on their originators or on those whose predecessors invented them. Hence a public can only slowly arrive at enlightenment. A revolution is perhaps capable of breaking away from personal despotism and from avaricious or power-hungry oppression, but it can never bring about a genuine reform in thinking; instead, new prejudices will serve as a guiding rein for the thoughtless masses.

Yet nothing but *freedom* is required for this enlightenment. And indeed it is the most harmless sort of freedom that may be properly called freedom, namely: to make *public use* of one's reason in all matters. But now I hear

8:37

called out on all sides: *do not argue!* The officer says: do not argue, just drill! The tax collector says: do not argue, just pay! The clergyman says: do not argue, just believe! (There is only one master in the world who says: *argue* as much as you like and about whatever you like, *but obey!*) Everywhere here there are limitations to freedom. But what kind of limitation is a hindrance to enlightenment? And what kind of limitation is not, but rather even serves to promote it? I answer: the *public* use of one's reason must be free at all times, and this alone can bring about enlightenment among humans; the *private use* of one's reason may often, however, be highly restricted without thereby especially impeding the progress of enlightenment. By the public use of one's reason I mean the kind of use that one makes thereof as a *scholar* before the *reading world.* I understand the private use of one's reason to be the use that one may make of it in a *civil* post or office with which one is entrusted. For many affairs that serve the interests of the commonwealth a certain mechanism is required, by means of which some members of the commonwealth must play only a passive role, so that they can be led by the government in the pursuit of public ends by means of an artificial unanimity, or at least be kept from undermining these ends. In these cases, of course, one may not argue, but rather must obey. To the extent that this part of the machine is simultaneously a segment of the entire commonwealth and even a part of the society of citizens of the world, and thus acts in his capacity as a scholar who addresses a public through his writings, he can indeed argue, without thereby impairing the affairs for which he is in part responsible through passive service. It would thus be very harmful if an officer who receives orders from his superiors were to publicly question the expediency or usefulness of his orders; he must obey. He cannot, however, justifiably be barred from making comments, as a scholar, on the mistakes in the military service and submitting these remarks to judgment by the public. A citizen cannot refuse to pay the taxes which are required of him; even a presumptuous public rebuke of such levies, if such taxes are to be paid by him, can be punished as causing a public scandal (which could set off a more general resistance). Regardless of this, the same citizen does not contravene his civic duty if he publicly expresses, as a scholar, his thoughts against the impropriety or even injustice of such levies. In precisely such a way a clergyman is bound to render his service to his pupils in catechism and his congregation in accordance with the symbol of the church that he serves, for he has been accepted into his position under precisely this condition. But as a scholar he enjoys full freedom and is even is called upon to communicate to the public all of his own carefully examined and well-intentioned thoughts on what is mistaken in that symbol, as well as his suggestions for a better arrangement of the religious and church-associated institutions. And there

8:38

is nothing here which should be regarded as weighing on his conscience. For what he teaches in accordance with his office as a representative agent of the church, he understands to be something with regard to which he may not merely teach at his own discretion, but rather which he has been employed to present according to instruction and in the name of another. He shall say: our church teaches this or that; this is the evidence that it relies upon. He then derives all practical benefits for his congregation from statutes which he would not himself endorse with full conviction, but the presentation of which he can undertake, for it is after all not completely impossible that truth lies hidden within it, and in any case, however, nothing can be found in it that fundamentally contradicts the inner religion. For if he believed to find such a contradiction therein he would not be able to execute his office in good conscience and would have to resign from it. Hence the use that an employed teacher makes of his reason before his congregation is merely a *private use* thereof: because this is always merely a domestic assembly of persons, however large it may be. And in view of this he is not free as a priest and indeed may not be free, because he is acting on a commission that comes from outside. As a scholar, on the other hand, who, through writings, addresses the true public, namely, the entire world, the clergyman, when making *public use* of his reason, enjoys unrestricted freedom in making use of his reason and in speaking from his own person. For to claim that the guardians of the people (in spiritual matters) should themselves be immature, is an inconsistency that would amount to a perpetuation of inconsistencies.

But should not a society of clergymen, for instance a church assembly, or a venerable *classis* (as it calls itself among the Dutch), be entitled to commit by means of oath among themselves to a certain unchangeable symbol, in order to thereby ensure themselves of constant guardianship over each of their members and thereby over the entire population, and even immortalize their guardianship? I say: that is completely impossible. Such a contract, which is concluded in order to prevent for eternity all further enlightenment for the human race is quite simply null and void, even if it were to be confirmed by the most supreme authority, by means of parliaments or by the most ceremonious of peace treaties. One generation cannot form an alliance and conspire to put a subsequent generation in such a position in which it would be impossible for the latter to expand its knowledge (particularly where such knowledge is so vital), to rid this knowledge of errors, and, more generally, to proceed along the path of enlightenment. That would be a violation of human nature, the original vocation of which consists pre-

8:39

cisely in this progress; and the descendents are thus perfectly entitled to reject those resolutions as having been made in an unjust and criminal way. The touchstone of anything that can serve as a law over a people lies in the question: whether a people could impose such a law on itself. Now this could well be possible for a certain short period of time in order to introduce a certain degree of order, in anticipation of a better law: by allowing every citizen, primarily the clergyman, the freedom to comment publicly, that is, through writings, in his capacity as a scholar, on that which is flawed in the present arrangement while the current order still prevails, until insight into the state of affairs in these matters has publicly progressed to the point where it has shown itself to be generally accepted, such that through a coalition of their voices (even if not a unanimous union) it could present a proposal to the throne to defend those congregations that had agreed upon what they view as a change in their religious organization that constitutes an improvement, without thereby hindering those who would rather leave things as they are. But to agree to a permanent religious constitution that is to be publicly called into question by no one, even within the space of a person's lifetime, and to thereby destroy, as it were, and render vain a span of time in humankind's progress toward improvement and thus make it detrimental to one's descendents, is quite simply impermissible. A human being can postpone enlightenment for his own person, and even then only for a short time, with regard to that which is his responsibility to know. But to renounce it for his own person, and more still for his descendents, amounts to violating the sacred rights of humanity and to trample them under foot. But what a people is not able to legislate over itself, a monarch is even less   8:40 entitled to decree; for his legislative standing is based precisely in the fact that he unifies in his will the collective will of the people. If he only looks to ensuring that all genuine or supposed improvement is consistent with the civic order, then he can for the rest just let his subjects do that which they themselves find necessary to undertake for their own salvation; it does not concern him, but it is his concern to prevent one from hindering another, by forceful means, from working to determine and promote his own salvation with all of his own powers. He would even diminish his own majesty if he were to interfere here and deem writings in which his subjects seek to clarify their insights worthy of supervision by his government. This is true if he did so based on his own supreme insight, in which case he subjects himself to the objection: *Caesar non est supra grammaticos.*[4] And it is just

---

4. "The emperor is not above the grammarians."

as true, and indeed much more so, if he lowers his supreme authority by supporting the spiritual despotism of a few tyrants in his state against his other subjects.

If it is asked, then, whether we live in an *enlightened* age, then the answer is: no, but we do live in an age of *enlightenment.* It is far from the case that humans, in present circumstances, and taken as a whole, are already or could be put in a position to make confident and good use of their own reason in matters of religion without the direction of another. But we have clear indications that they are now being opened up to the possibility of working toward this, and that the obstacles to universal enlightenment, or to the emancipation from one's self-incurred immaturity, are now gradually becoming fewer. In this regard our age is an age of enlightenment, or the century of *Frederick.*[5]

A prince who does not see it as beneath his dignity to say that he regards it as a *duty* to dictate nothing to men in matters of religion, but rather to ensure them perfect freedom in such matters, a prince who thus himself rejects the arrogant name of *tolerance,* is himself enlightened and deserves to be praised both by the grateful world of the present, and by posterity, as the one who first freed the human race, at least from the side of government, from immaturity and let everyone be free to make use of his own reason in all matters of conscience. Under his rule venerable clergymen may, notwithstanding the duties of their office, present, in their capacity as scholars, freely and publicly to the scrutiny of the world, judgments that might here or there deviate from their assumed religious symbol. This is even more the case with any others who are not constrained by duties of office. This spirit of freedom also extends outward, even to where it must struggle with the external obstacles presented by a government that misunderstands itself. For such a government is presented with evidence that granting freedom need not leave one concerned in the least for public order and the unity of the commonwealth. Human beings will gradually work their way out of their condition of brutishness, as long as one does not intentionally meddle in order to keep them in this state.

I have described the main point of enlightenment, that is, the human being's emancipation from its self-incurred immaturity, primarily in terms of *religious matters.* For with regard to the arts and the sciences our rulers have no interest in acting as a guardian of their subjects; moreover, immaturity in matters of religion is the most harmful sort, and hence the most degrading of all. But the way of thinking of a head of state, who encourages

8:41

5. Friedrich II ("the Great") (1712–86), king of Prussia from 1740 to 1786.

freedom in the former, goes even further and recognizes that even with regard to his *legislation*, there is no danger in allowing his subjects to freely make *public* use of their reason and to present publicly their thoughts to the world concerning a better version of his legislation, even by means of a candid critique. We have a brilliant example of this, and the monarch whom we admire has no precedent.

But only he who, himself enlightened, is not afraid of shadows, but at the same time has at his disposal a well-trained and large army for guaranteeing the public peace, can say what a free state may not dare say: *argue as much as you want and about whatever you want, but obey!* Here one finds an odd and unexpected course of human events, just as one does at other times, when one considers the course of human events in the large, in which nearly everything is paradoxical. A greater degree of civic freedom seems to be of benefit to the *intellectual* freedom of the people and yet also sets unsurpassable limitations on such freedom; a lesser degree of civic freedom, by contrast, creates room for the people to extend itself in accordance with all its powers. When nature has fully developed the seed concealed in this hard casing, to which it gives its most tender care, namely, the tendency and the calling to free *thinking,* then this seed will gradually extend its effects to the disposition of the people (through which the people gradually becomes more capable of *freedom of action*) and finally even to the principles of *government,* which find it to be beneficial to itself to treat the human being, who is indeed *more than a machine,* in accordance with his dignity.*   8:42

Königsberg in Prussia, September 30th, 1784.

*I read today, on September 30th, in Büsching's *Wöchentliche Nachrichten* from September 13th, a notice concerning this month's *Berlinische Monatsschrift,* in which Mr. *Mendelssohn's* answer to the same question answered here is cited. I have not yet received the journal, otherwise I would have withheld the present observations, which I offer here only in order to see to what extent chance might yield a unanimity of thoughts.[6]

6. Moses Mendelssohn (1729–86), "Über die Frage: Was heißt aufklären?" [On the Question: What Is Enlightenment?] *Berlinische Monatsschrift* 4 (1784): 193–200.

Conjectural Beginning of
Human History

It is certainly permissible to *interject* speculations in the *course* of an historical account in order to fill gaps in the reports, since what comes before these gaps, the remote cause, and what comes after them, the effect, can provide a reasonably certain means of discovering the intermediate causes, thereby rendering the transitions within the account intelligible. But creating a historical account entirely out of speculations does not seem much better than drafting the plan for a novel. Indeed, such an account could hardly be called a *conjectural history,* but rather only a *fabricated* history. — Yet what cannot rightly be ventured with regard to the progression of the history of human actions can certainly be attempted with regard to its *first beginning,* insofar as *nature* has made this beginning. For this beginning need not be fabricated, but rather can be derived from experience if one assumes this experience was no better or worse in its first beginning than it presently is. Such an assumption is in accordance with the analogy of nature and is altogether safe to make. An account of the earliest development of freedom from its original predisposition in human nature is hence something entirely different than a historical account of the progression of this freedom, an account which can be based only upon historical reports.

Yet speculations cannot make too high a claim on our assent. They cannot lay claim to being serious business, but rather only to being an allowable exercise of the imagination, in the company of reason, for the recreation and health of the mind. They therefore cannot compare to the historical account that is put forward and believed as an actual report of the same event and whose verification is based on grounds entirely different from those of the mere philosophy of nature. It is for precisely this reason, and because I am venturing on a mere pleasure trip here, that I may hope to be favored with permission to use a holy document as my roadmap and also fancy that the route that I take with the help of the imagination, although not without a guiding thread connected to experience by reason, corresponds to precisely the same path laid out historically in that text. The reader can open up this document (Genesis 2–6) and check step by step whether the path that philosophy pursues with concepts coincides with the path set out by history.

If one is not to be overenthusiastic in one's speculations, then one must begin with that which cannot be derived by human reason from preceding causes of nature: the *existence of the human being.* One must begin with the human being, to be precise, as a *fully developed adult,* since he must do without maternal assistance; one must begin with a *couple,* so that the species is propagated; and one must begin with *a single* couple, so that war does not immediately break out when human beings live in close proximity and yet are foreign to one another, and also so that nature is not accused of having neglected, by permitting such diversity in ancestry, to provide in the most appropriate way for sociability in the species, as the greatest end of human destiny. The common descent of all human beings from a single family was without doubt the best arrangement for this. I shall place this couple in a place that is secure against the aggression of predators and that is abundantly supplied by nature with all the means of sustenance, in a *garden,* as it were, in a perpetually mild climate. What is more, I shall consider the human being only after it has made substantial progress in honing it skills in using its naturally given powers, and not begin with the human being in its complete brutishness, for to endeavor to fill the gap between these two points, which would presumably extend across quite a lengthy span of time, could lead for the reader to far too many speculations and far too few probabilities. The first human being was thus able to *stand and walk.* It was able to *speak* (Genesis 2:20),* even *communicate,* that is, to express itself through the use of coherent concepts (v. 23), and consequently to *think.* These are all skills that the human being had to acquire on its own (for if they had been inborn, they would also be passed on, an assumption contradicted by experience). But I shall assume the human being as already in possession of these, simply in order to be able to consider the development of decency and morals in his activities, something which necessarily presupposes the above skills.

8:111

*It must have been the *urge to communicate* that first motivated the human being that was still alone to proclaim his existence to living beings other than himself, primarily to those who make a sound that he can mimic and which can later serve as a name. A similar effect of this urge can be seen in children and thoughtless people who, through their buzzing, screaming, whistling, singing, and other noisy activities (and often also gatherings of this sort), disturb the reflective part of the community. For I see no other motivating reason for their behavior than the wish to make their existence known far and wide.

In the beginning the newcomer must have been lead by instinct alone, this *voice of God* which all animals must obey. Instinct allowed him certain things for nourishment and forbade him others (Genesis 3:2–3). — But it is not necessary to assume that a special instinct, since lost, served this end. It could have been merely the sense of smell and its affinity with the organ of taste, taken together with the well-known sympathy of the latter with the apparatus of digestion, in other words an ability, one which we can still perceive today, to detect in advance the suitability or unsuitability of foods for consumption. Indeed, one may not presume that this sense was any more acute in the first pair of human beings than it is now, for it is well known what difference in perceptive powers can be found between those who are occupied only with their senses and those who are also occupied with their thoughts but who are thereby estranged from their sensations.

As long as the inexperienced human being obeyed this call of nature, all was well with him. Yet *reason* soon began to stir and sought, by comparing foods with what was presented to him as similar to those foods by a different sense than the one to which instinct was bound, say by the sense of sight, to extend his knowledge of foodstuffs beyond the confines of mere instinct (3:6). Even though it was not advised by instinct, this experiment, with luck, could have turned out well, as long as it did not contradict instinct. But it is a peculiarity of reason that, aided by imagination, it can invent desires not only *without* a corresponding natural urge, but even *contrary* to it. In the beginning such desires are called *lasciviousness,* but they eventually engender a whole host of unnecessary and even unnatural inclinations to which the term *luxuriousness* applies. What occasioned the desertion of the natural urges may have been a trifle, but the result of the first experiment, that is, becoming conscious of one's reason as a faculty that can extend itself beyond the boundaries to which all animals are confined, was very important and decisive for the way of life. Perhaps it was only a fruit, the sight of which invited him, through its similarity with other agreeable fruits that he had already tasted, to experiment. Or perhaps an animal whose nature was fit for the consumption of this fruit also provided an example for him, on whom, however, such consumption had an opposite, harmful effect, and was consequently resisted by a natural instinct in him. But this was sufficient to give reason occasion to do injury to the voice of nature (3:1) and, despite its protest, make the first experiment in free choice, an experiment which, as the first one, probably did not turn out as planned. However insignificant the harm done may have been, it sufficed to open the human being's eyes (v. 7). He discovered in himself a capacity to choose a way of life for himself and not, as other animals, to be bound to a single one. The momentary delight caused by his noticing this advantage must have been followed by anxiety and fear as to how he, having not yet known anything according to its hidden traits and remote effects, should proceed with his newly discovered ability. He stood at the edge of an abyss, as it were. For whereas instinct had hitherto directed him to individual objects of his desire, an infinity of such objects now opened itself up to him, from among which he did not yet know how to choose. Yet once he had had a taste of this state of freedom it was impossible for him to return to the state of servitude (under the rule of instinct).

After the instinct of nourishment, by means of which nature preserves each individual, the *instinct of sex* is most prominent, by means of which nature preserves each species. Having now stirred for the first time, reason did not fail to exert its influence on this instinct. The human being soon discovered that the appeal of sex, which in animals is based on stimuli that are merely temporary and mostly periodic, could be extended and even augmented through his imagination, which compelled him, to be sure, with more moderation, but also in a more enduring and consistent manner the more the object is *withdrawn from the senses.* And in this way the human being did not tire of it as he would if a merely animal desire were satisfied,   8:113
Hence the fig leaf (v. 7) was the product of a much greater expression of reason than it had shown during the first stage of its development. For to make an inclination more fervent and lasting by withdrawing its object from the senses already shows the awareness of some degree of mastery of reason over the instincts and not merely, as with the first step, an ability to serve the latter to lesser or greater extent. *Refusal* was the feat by means of which stimuli that were merely sensual were converted to those that were dependent on ideas. Mere animal desire was gradually converted to love and, with this, the feeling of mere pleasure was converted to a taste for beauty, initially only in the human being, but then also in nature. *Decency,* an inclination to inspire the respect of others toward our persons through good manners (the hiding of that which could arouse disdain), as the actual basis of all true sociability, was the first signal to the development of the human being as a moral creature. — A small beginning, but one which is epoch-making insofar as it entirely changes the direction of the way of thinking, is more important than the entire, incalculable series of subsequent expansions of culture.

The third stage of reason, after it had meddled with the immediately felt needs, was the conscious *anticipation of the future.* This ability to enjoy not just the current moment in life but also to represent to oneself the future, often far in advance, is the most distinguishing mark of the human being's capacity to prepare himself for distant ends in accordance with his destiny. But it is also the most inexhaustible source of worry and distress aroused by the uncertainty of the future, something from which all animals are free (vv. 13–19). The man who must provide nourishment for himself, his wife, and his future children foresaw the ever-increasing arduousness of his work. The woman foresaw the tribulations to which nature had subjected her sex and, on top of that, those to which the stronger male subjected her. And beyond that, both of them foresaw with fear, in the background of the picture, that which, to be sure, inevitably comes upon all animals, yet does not cause the latter any worry, namely death, after a life of toil. They seemed to rebuke and make into a crime the use of reason that caused all these ills to befall them. To live through their offspring, who would per-

8:114   haps have it better, or who even as members of a family could ameliorate their woes, was perhaps the only consoling prospect that gave them heart (vv. 16–20).

The fourth and final stage, by means of which reason completely raised the human being above its society with animals, was that he understood (however vaguely), that he was actually the *end of nature,* and that nothing that lived on earth could compete with him in this regard. The first time that he said to the sheep, "*the coat that you wear was given to you by nature not for you, but for me,*" and stripped it of this coat and put it on himself (v. 21), he became aware of a privilege that he, by virtue of his nature, had over all animals. He now no longer viewed them as his fellows in creation, but rather as means at his will's disposal and as tools for attaining any chosen ends. This view of things also implies (however vaguely) the thought of its contrary: that he may not say such a thing to another *human being* but should rather regard the latter as an equal recipient of the gifts of nature. This is a first, remote preparation for the constraints to which reason would later subject him with regard to his fellow human beings, and which is far more necessary than affection or love in establishing society.

And thus human beings became *equals of all rational beings,* whatever their rank may be (3:22), insofar as all rational beings can lay claim to being *ends-in-themselves* and thereby to being regarded as such by every other rational being and not be used by anyone as a mere means to other ends. Herein, and not in reason as it is used merely to satisfy various inclinations, lies the ground for the unlimited equality of the human being even with higher beings who might otherwise far surpass him in their natural gifts, but none of which would thereby have the right to use him however they may see fit. This stage is therefore coupled with his being *released* from the womb of nature, a change which is at once honorable and perilous, insofar as it drives him out from the harmless and secure condition of childcare, from out of a garden, as it were, that took care of him without any effort from him (3:23) and thrust him into the wide world, where so many worries, troubles, and unknown ills awaited him. From this moment on the arduousness of life will bring him the wish for a paradise, a creation of his imagination where he might rest in calm inactivity and perpetual peace and dream and fritter away his existence. But between him and that imagined seat of bliss, his restless reason, which irresistibly drives him to develop the abilities within him, will not allow him to return to the state of brutishness and naiveté from which it had taken him (3:24). It urges him to put himself, despite his hating it, patiently through the toils of life and to pursue all the glitter and baubles that he despises and even to forget death itself, which terrifies him, for all the trifles, the loss of which he fears even more.

8:115

REMARK

From this portrayal of the first history of humankind it follows that the emergence of the human being from the paradise that reason presents to him as the first dwelling of his species had been nothing other than the transition from the brutishness of a merely animal creature to humanity, from the leading reins of instinct to the direction of reason, in a word, from the guardianship of nature into the state of freedom. Whether the human being has won or lost through this change can no longer be the question when one considers the vocation of his species, which consists in nothing other than the *progress* toward perfection, as flawed as the first attempts to reach this goal, even a long series of such attempts, may turn out to be. — Yet this transition, which for the species is *progress* from worse to better, is not the same for the individual. Before reason had awoken, there was neither command nor prohibition and hence no transgression. But as reason began to stir, however weakly, and came into coexistence with animal nature in all its strength, ills arose, and, what is worse, with the cultivation of reason vices arose which were completely foreign to the state of ignorance and hence to the state of innocence.

Thus the first step out of this state was, on the moral side, a *fall*. On the physical side, a series of never-before-known afflictions of life, hence punishment, resulted from this fall. The history of *nature* begins therefore with the good, for it is the *work of God*. The history of *freedom* begins with evil, for it is the *work of the human being*. For the individual that regards only itself in the use of its freedom, such a change was a loss. For nature, which sets its end for the human being in the species, this was a gain. The former

8:116

therefore has cause to attribute all the afflictions that it endures, and all the evils that it perpetrates, to its own fault, but also as a member of a whole (the species) the individual has cause to admire and praise the wisdom and purposiveness of the arrangement. — In this way one can make the so often misinterpreted, seemingly contradictory assertions of the famous *J. J. Rousseau*[1] consistent with one another and with reason. In his paper "On the Influence of the Sciences" and his paper "On the Inequality of Human Beings" he demonstrates quite correctly the inevitable conflict of culture with the nature of the human race as a *physical* species in which every individual is meant to achieve entirely his vocation. But in his *Émile,* his *Social Contract,* and other writings he seeks to solve the more difficult problem of how culture must progress such that the capacities of humankind as a *moral* species properly develop toward its destiny so that the latter no longer conflict with the former as a natural species. It is out of this conflict (since culture, according to true principles *of the education* as both human being and citizen, perhaps has not even really begun, much less been completed) that all true afflictions arise which weigh on human life, and all vices that dishonor it.* Nonetheless the stimuli that precede vice, and which

1. Jean-Jacques Rousseau (1712–78). The full title of the First Discourse is: "A Discourse That won First Prize at the Academy of Dijon. In the Year 1750. On the following questions proposed by the Academy: Has the revival of the Sciences and Arts contributed to improving morality?" The full title of the Second Discourse is: "Discourse on the Origin and Foundations of Inequality Among Mankind" (1755). In Jean-Jacques Rousseau, *The Social Contract and The First and Second Discourses,* ed. Susan Dunn (New Haven: Yale University Press, 2002). Original French titles: "Discours qui a remporté le prix a l'académie de Dijon en l'année 1750. Sur cette question propose par la même Académie: Si le rétablissement des sciences et des arts a contribué à épurer les mœurs" and "Discours sur l'origine et les fondements de l'inégalité parmi les hommes." The books mentioned are *Émile ou de l'éducation* [Émile: Or, On Education] and *Du contrat social ou Principes du droit politique* [Of the Social Contract or Principles of Political Right], both published in 1762.

*To supply but a few examples of this conflict between humanity's striving for its moral destiny, on the one hand, and the unchanging compliance with the laws governing the uncultivated and animal condition in human nature, on the other, I will relate the following.

The age of maturity, i.e., of the urge as well as the ability to propagate one's species, has been determined to be between sixteen and seventeen years. This is an age at which the youth in the uncultivated state of nature literally becomes a man [*Mann*], for he is at this point able to preserve his own life, to propagate his species,

one blames in such a case, are good in themselves and purposive as the predispositions given by nature. But these predispositions, since they were adjusted to the state of nature, are done harm by the progress of culture and do harm in turn to the latter, until complete art again becomes nature. This is the ultimate aim of the moral destiny of the human race.

8:118

---

and to provide for offspring and his wife. The simplicity of his needs makes this an easy task for him. In the condition of culture, however, the latter requires significant means, both in terms of skill, as well as favorable external circumstances, so that this period in the civilized state comes at least some ten years later. Yet nature has not changed its age of maturity to match the progress of social refinement, but rather has stubbornly followed the law that it has laid down for the preservation of the human race as an animal species. From this arises inevitable harm to the end of nature by morals and to the latter by the former. For the natural human being [*Naturmensch*] is at a certain age already a man [*Mann*] when the civilized human being (who does not, however, stop being a natural human being) is still a youth, even perhaps a child. For this is what one would call one who, due to his age (in the state of civilization) cannot provide for himself, much less for a family, even though he has the drive and the ability, thus the call of nature for himself, to propagate his species. For nature has certainly not placed instincts and abilities in living beings so that they should struggle with them and suppress them. Thus this capacity was not adjusted at all to the state of civilization, but rather aimed merely at the preservation of the human species as an animal species. And the state of civilization inevitably comes into conflict with the latter, which can only be resolved by a perfect civil constitution (the ultimate end of culture), since now the space between them is commonly filled with vices and their consequence, manifold human misery.

Another example of the truth of the proposition that nature has placed in us two predispositions to two different ends, namely, of humanity as an animal species and of the same as a moral species, is the following: *Ars longa, vita brevis* [the art (of medicine) is long, life is short] from Hippocrates.[2] The arts and sciences can be brought much further by a mind that is made for them, if it has come to the proper state of maturity through practice and learned knowledge, than they could by entire, consecutive generations of scholars, if only that mind lived with the same youthful strength through the span of time that is given to all these generations. Yet nature has taken its decision with regard to the lifespan of the human being from a different perspective than that which would promote the sciences. For when the most fortunate mind is on the verge of the greatest discoveries that he can hope to attain given his skill and experience, age sets in: his mind becomes dull and he must leave it to a second generation (which must start again with its ABCs and tread the same path

END OF THE CONJECTURAL HISTORY

The beginning of the subsequent period was when the human being emerged from the epoch of leisureliness and peace and entered into the epoch of *toil and discord* as a prelude to unification in society. Here we must again make a great leap and put him already in possession of tamed animals and the plants that he farmed himself for his nourishment by sowing or planting (4:2), even though his advancement from the wild life of hunting to the possession of tamed animals and from the sporadic digging of roots or collecting of fruits to agriculture may have come about quite slowly. This is where the strife between human beings who had to date coexisted peacefully had to begin, and the consequence of this was their separation on the basis of their different ways of life and their becoming scattered across the earth. The *pastoral life* is not just leisurely, it also provides the most secure livelihood, since, when for miles around there are no other inhabitants, it cannot lack in food. *Agriculture* or planting are quite toilsome by comparison, since they are dependent on the variations in weather and hence are uncertain. They also require permanent dwellings, ownership of the land and sufficient power to defend the latter. The shepherd hates this ownership,

---

that has already been followed) to add a step to the progress of culture. The human species' advance in attaining its full destiny thus seems to be continually interrupted and in constant danger of regressing into the old brutishness again. And it was not without reason that the Greek philosopher lamented *that it is a shame that one must die when one has just begun to recognize how one should have lived.*

A third example could be the *inequality* among human beings, and yet not an inequality in their natural gifts or in the means placed at their disposal by chance, but rather the inequality in universal *human right*. This is an inequality about which *Rousseau* complains with a great deal of truth, but one which is not to be separated from culture, as long as it proceeds without a plan (which is also inevitable for quite a length of time), and one for which nature has certainly not destined the human being, since it gave the human being freedom and reason, with which the human being is to restrict this freedom by means of nothing other than its own universal lawfulness, an external lawfulness to be precise, which is called *civil right*. The human being ought to work its way out of the brutishness of its natural predispositions and, in raising himself above them, nevertheless take care that he does not do violence to them. This is a skill that he can attain only late in life and after many unsuccessful attempts. In the meantime, humanity will heave deep sighs under the weight of the afflictions that it brings upon itself out of inexperience.

2. Hippocrates' *Aphorisms* I.I.

however, as it limits his freedom of pasture. Considering the shepherd's life, it could seem that the farmer would envy the shepherd as more favored by heaven (v. 4). Yet the shepherd instead became an annoyance to him as long as he stayed in his vicinity, for the grazing livestock pay no heed to his crops. It is no trouble for the shepherd who causes such damage to move his herd far away and escape responsibility, since he does not thereby leave anything behind that he cannot find just as easily any other place. For this reason it was probably the farmer who first used force to prevent such harms, harms which the other did not consider unallowed, and ultimately (since the occasion for that would never fully cease to exist), to *move* as far *away* as possible from those who lead the pastoral life if he was not to lose the hard earned fruits of his labor (4:16). This separation initiates the third epoch. 8:119

A tract of land that, if it is to provide a livelihood, must be worked and planted (primarily in the case of trees), requires permanent dwellings. The defense of these dwellings against harm requires a group of people who will lend one another assistance. Those living the agricultural way of life could thus not spread themselves out in single families, but rather had to stay together and found villages (improperly called towns), in order to protect their property against wild hunters or hordes of roving herdsmen. The primary needs of life, the provision of which requires a *different way of life* (v. 20), could now be *exchanged.* This inevitably gave rise to *culture* and the beginning of *art,* of leisure and of industriousness (vv. 21–22). But above all a civil constitution and public justice began to be instituted. Initially such justice was concerned only with the most violent acts, and the revenge for these was no longer, as in the savage condition, left to the individual, but rather to a lawful power that held the whole together. That is to say, it was left to a kind of government which itself was subject to no other use of force (vv. 23–24). — From this first and brutish arrangement all human art, of which the art of *sociability and civil security* is the foremost fruit, could eventually develop step by step, as the human race multiplied and spread from a center like beehives, sending out cultured colonists in all directions. With this epoch *inequality* among human beings also began, this rich source of so much evil, but also of all good, and became ever greater.

As long as the nomadic herdsmen, who recognize only God as their master, flocked around the town dwellers and farmers, who have a human being (the authorities) as their master (6:4),* and, as sworn enemies of land 8:120

---

*The Arab *Bedouins* still call themselves children of a former *sheikh,* the founder of their tribe (such as *Beni Haled* and others). The latter is in no way their *master* and cannot exercise power over them as he sees fit. For among a pastoral

ownership, treated the latter with hostility and were hated by them for it, there was continual war between them, or at least the continual threat of war, and both peoples were at least able to enjoy the priceless good of internal freedom. — (For the threat of war is also today the only thing that moderates despotism: since wealth is required for a state to be a power, yet without *freedom* there is no industriousness that can produce wealth. Instead of such wealth a poor people must have extensive concern for the preservation of the commonwealth, which is only possible when people feel free in it.) — But in time the increasing luxury of the town dwellers, above all, however, the art of pleasing, a matter in which women from the towns far surpassed the unkempt girls of the desert, must have been a tremendous attraction for the herdsmen (v. 2) to enter into relations with the former and let themselves be taken in to the glittering misery of the towns. And here, in this joining of two otherwise hostile peoples, comes the end of all threat of war and with it the end of freedom. For on the one hand, the despotism of powerful tyrants arose, and on the other hand, however, with a culture that has barely begun to develop, a soulless lavishness, in the most depraved kind of slavery, together with all the vices of the state of barbarism, brought the human race inevitably off the course charted for it by nature in the development of its capacities for the good, and it thereby made itself unworthy even of its existence as a species meant to rule over the earth and not to indulge itself as a brute and serve as a slave (v. 17).

CLOSING REMARK

The reflective human being feels a sorrow, one that can even become a moral corruption, of which the thoughtless person knows nothing. He feels dissatisfaction with providence, which governs the course of the world as a whole, when he considers the ills that so afflict the human race without, as it seems, there being hope for something better. But the following is of the greatest importance: *to be content with providence* (even though it has laid such a toilsome path for us in our earthly world), in part so that one can still take heart in the face of such labors, and in part in order to not, by placing the blame on fate, lose sight of our own fault, which may perhaps be the only cause of all these ills, and fail to seek help against them in self-improvement.

One must concede that the greatest ills that afflict civilized peoples are

---

people any family can easily separate itself from the tribe and join another if it dislikes where it is, since no one has fixed property that it thereby leaves behind.

brought upon us by *war,* albeit not so much by the actual past or present war, but rather by the never subsiding and even ever increasing *arming* for a future war. All the powers of the state, all the fruits of its culture, which could be used toward an even greater culture, are used to this end. Freedom is harmed in so many places and the maternal care of the state for individual members turned into an unrelenting toughness of demands, however these demands may well be justified by the fear of external threats. Yet would this culture, would the close association of social estates within the common-wealth that promotes their mutual prosperity, would such a large popula-tion, would even the degree of freedom that remains, albeit under very restrictive laws, still be seen if that much-feared future war did not demand even of the heads of states this *respect for humanity?* One need only con-sider China, which, due to its location could perhaps suffer an occasional unforeseen attack but has no powerful enemy to fear, yet in which for that very reason every trace of freedom has been erased.— At the level of culture at which the human race still stands, therefore, war is an indispens-able means of bringing about progress in culture. And only after culture has been perfected (only God knows when this would be) would a lasting peace be salutary for us and only through such culture would it become possible. We are thus, as concerns this point, most likely ourselves to blame for the ills about which we so loudly complain. And the holy scripture is com-pletely right to portray an amalgamation of peoples into a single society and their complete liberation from external threats as a hindrance, since their culture had but hardly begun, to all further culture, and as a descent into incurable corruption.   8:122

The human being's *second dissatisfaction* concerns the order of nature with regard to the *brevity of life.* One must have little appreciation of the value of life if one wishes it to last longer than it actually does, for this would merely extend a game of constant struggles with hardships. But one cannot blame those with a childish judgment for fearing death without loving life and who, although it becomes difficult to carry on their existence with some degree of satisfaction, nevertheless can never have enough days in which to repeat this torment. But if one only considers how much worry consumes us about the means to pass such a short life, and how much injustice is brought about in the hope of a future enjoyment that lasts such a short time, then it is reasonable to believe that if human beings could look forward to a lifespan of 800 or more years, that a father's life would hardly be secure in his son's hands, nor that of one brother in those of another, nor that of one friend in those of another, and that the vices of a human race which lived so long would become so great that it would become deserving of no better fate than to be exterminated from the face of the earth in a great flood (vv. 12–13).

The *third* wish, or rather the empty longing (for one is conscious of the fact that what is wished for can never be had) is the shadow image of that time praised by the poets as the *Golden Age*. This is an age where one is freed from all the imagined needs that luxuriousness loads upon us, where a modest life with only the needs of nature is supposed to exist, a universal equality of human beings, an everlasting peace among them, in a word, the pure enjoyment of a carefree life of lazy daydreaming or a life frittered away with childish games. — This is a longing that makes the tales of Robinson Crusoe and the travels to the South Sea Islands so attractive, yet which demonstrates how the reflective human being wearies of civilized life when he seeks its value merely in *enjoyment* and, when reason, for instance, reminds him that life is given value by his *actions,* counteracts such a thought with laziness. The emptiness of this wish to return to the age of simplicity and innocence is sufficiently demonstrated when one takes heed of the above representation of the original state: the human being 8:123   cannot remain in this state because he is not satisfied with it. He is even less inclined to ever return to it, hence he always has to attribute his present state of arduousness to himself and his own choice.

Such a portrayal of his history is fruitful for the human being and serves to teach and improve him when it shows him the following: that he may attribute no blame to providence for the ills that afflict him; that he is not justified in attributing his own trespass to an original sin of his ancestors, by means of which a tendency to commit similar trespasses had purportedly been inherited by subsequent generations (for voluntary acts do not lead to hereditary features); it shows him rather that he ought to acknowledge fully that which they made happen as if he had done it himself, and that he ought to attribute completely the blame for all the ills that arise from the misuse of his reason to himself. This he does by realizing that under the same circumstances he would have behaved in just the same way and first used reason by misusing it (even against the warning of nature). Once the blame for moral ills has been correctly attributed, actual physical ills can hardly tip the balance of merit and blame in our favor.

And thus is the outcome of an attempt to write, through philosophy, the most ancient part of human history: satisfaction with providence and the course of human events as a whole, a course which does not progress, beginning with good, toward evil, but rather develops gradually from worse to better. Everyone is called upon by nature itself to contribute, to the best of his ability, his part to this progress.

Critique of Judgment, § 83–§ 84

Ak 5:429

§ 83. ON THE ULTIMATE END OF NATURE AS A TELEOLOGICAL SYSTEM

We have shown above that we have sufficient reason to regard the human being not merely as an end of nature like all other organized beings, but rather also as the *ultimate* end of nature here on earth, in relation to which all other things of nature compose a system of ends, according to principles of reason, though for the reflective, and not for the determining, faculty of judgment.[1] If one must find in the human being himself that which is to be promoted as an end through his association with nature, then the end must be such that either the end itself can be satisfied by nature 5:430 through its beneficence, or the end is the suitability and skill to attain all kinds of ends for which the human being can use nature (external and internal). The first end of nature would be human *happiness,* and the second would be human *culture*.

The concept of happiness is not one that the human being abstracts from his instincts and thereby derives from the animal nature within him; rather it is a mere *idea* of a state, an idea to which he wishes to make his condition adequate, under merely empirical conditions (which is impossible). The human being invents this idea himself and indeed does so in such a varied manner by means of his intellect, which is so entangled with his senses and his imagination; he even changes this concept so often that nature, even if it were subjected fully to his volition, could simply not adopt a determinate, universal, and fixed law by means of which it could be brought into harmony with this vacillating concept and hence with the end that each would arbitrarily set for himself. But even if we were to either reduce this concept

1. By "reflective faculty of judgment" Kant means the faculty that finds the rule or concept under which a given particular falls. By "determining faculty of judgment" is meant the faculty of applying a given rule or concept to particulars. Kant has argued in the preceding that humans are to be regarded not merely as one species of organisms among others, but as organisms which provide the principle of the teleological organization of nature.

to the genuine needs of nature, with regard to which our species is in universal agreement, or, on the other hand, to augment the skill at achieving ends that one has imagined for oneself as much as we want to: even then what the human being understands happiness to be, and what is in fact his own ultimate natural end (not the end of freedom), would never be attained by him. For his nature is not the kind that can finish and be satisfied through possession and pleasure. At the same time it is far from the case that nature has chosen the human being as her special favorite and charitably favored him above all other animals. Indeed, nature has spared him as little as any other animal, in its harmful effects, from pestilence, hunger, the threat of flooding, frost, attack by other animals large and small, and other such threats. But more still, the contradictions in his *natural predispositions* that cause him and others of his species self-inflicted troubles through the oppression of domination, the barbarism of wars, etc., place him in a state of such distress, and he himself, to the extent he is able, works toward the destruction of his own species, such that even with the most charitable nature external to us, the end of the latter, if it were oriented toward the happiness of our species, could not, in a system of such ends, be attained on earth, since the nature within us is not receptive to it. He is thus always merely a link in the chain of the ends of nature: indeed, a principle with regard to many an end for which nature seems to have determined him according to its design, insofar as he makes himself into that; but he is also nonetheless a means to maintaining purposiveness in the mechanism of the other links. As the only being on earth that possesses reason and which therefore has the capacity to freely set ends for itself, he is indeed properly regarded as a master of nature, and when one understands nature as a teleological system, he is, according to his vocation, the ultimate end of nature. But he is this only conditionally, to the extent that he understands this and possesses the will to establish a relationship of means and ends between himself and nature that, independent of nature, can be sufficient unto itself and hence a final end, and which must not at all be sought in nature.

But in order to discover in what aspect of the human being we must at least set that *ultimate end* of nature, we must seek out that which nature is able to accomplish, in order to prepare him for that which he must do himself in order to become a final end, and separate this from all other ends the possibility of which relies on conditions that one can expect from nature alone. Happiness on earth is of the latter sort of end, and by happiness we mean the sum of all human ends that are possible through nature inside or outside of humankind; that is, the matter of all of his ends on earth, which, if he were to make it into his whole end, would make him unable to set a final end for his own existence and to bring his existence into harmony with it. Of all of his ends in nature there thus remains only the formal, subjective condition, namely, of the aptitude for setting oneself ends at all and (independent of the role of nature in his determination of ends), in general, of using nature as a means in a manner appropriate to the maxims of his freely chosen ends, as that which nature can accomplish with regard to the final end that lies outside of it and which hence can be regarded as its own ultimate end. Making a rational being fit to pursue any ends whatsoever (and consequently also to pursue ends that are chosen freely) is *culture*.[2] Thus only culture can be the ultimate end which one can reasonably attribute to nature with regard to the human species (and not his happiness on earth, or even that he is merely the primary tool for creating order and harmony in the nonrational nature external to him).

But not every culture is sufficient to attaining this ultimate end of nature. The cultivation of *skillfulness* is the foremost subjective condition for one's being fit to promote ends in general. But it alone is not sufficient to promote   5:432 the *will* in the determination and selection of one's ends, which is an essential part of the entire scope of fitness for ends. The latter condition of such fitness, which one might call the culture of discipline, is negative and consists in freeing the will from the despotism of desires that make us, bound to certain elements of nature, unable to choose for ourselves, by allowing our drives to become shackles, drives which nature has given to us as guiding threads in order that we not neglect, or even violate, the characteristic of animality in us, while we are in fact free enough to tighten or relax these guiding threads, to extend or shorten them, all in accordance with the demands of rational ends.

Skillfulness cannot very well be developed in the human species except by means of inequality among human beings: the greatest number of people look after the necessities of life more or less mechanically, in a way that does not require any particular art, and do so for the comfort and leisure of others who work on the less necessary elements of culture, science and the arts, while the former are subjected by the latter to oppression, unpleasant work, and little enjoyment, whereby some of the culture of the higher class nonetheless also gradually spreads among this other class. But with the advance of this culture troubles grow equally extensively on both sides (the pinnacle of which is known as luxury, if that which is indispensable begins

2. The etymological roots of the term "culture" are still clearly visible in Kant's usage. It is to be understood as synonymous with "cultivation," "development."

to be abandoned in favor of what is dispensable), on the side of the lower class by means of violence imposed from without, and on the side of the higher class through internal insatiability; but the glaring misery is connected with the development of the natural capacities of the human species, and the end of nature itself, although it is not our end, is nonetheless attained. The formal condition that must be satisfied in order that nature can attain this end, its final aim, is a constitution that governs the relations of human beings among one another, and in which the damage to freedom that results from the mutually conflicting exercise of freedom is opposed by a lawful force embodied in a whole, which is called *civil society;* for only in such a society can the greatest development of the natural predispositions occur. Even if human beings were clever enough to invent such a system and were wise enough to willingly subject themselves to its authority, such a society would, however, also require a *cosmopolitan* whole, that is, a system of all those states which would otherwise be in the position to act to the detriment of each other. In the absence of such a system, and given the obstacle presented by the lust for honor, by the thirst for power, and by greed, primarily among those who have it in their power to oppose even the possibility of this project, *war* is inevitable (partly war in which states are split up and break into smaller states, partly war in which a state merges other, smaller states with itself and strives to form a greater whole). War, just as much as it is an unintentional attempt on the part of human beings (prompted by unbridled passions), is also a deeply concealed, perhaps intentional attempt of the most supreme wisdom, if not to establish, then at least to prepare lawfulness along with the freedom of states and thereby the unity of a morally grounded system of states. And despite the most horrible sufferings that it imposes on the human race and the perhaps even greater sufferings brought on by the condition of being constantly prepared for it during peacetime, war nonetheless constitutes another motivating force (while the hope for a people's happiness in a state of peace becomes more remote) for developing, to the highest degree possible, all the talents that serve culture.

5:433

As concerns the discipline of the inclinations, for which the natural capacity is entirely purposive with regard to our vocation as an animal species, yet which impede the development of humanity very greatly: in view of this second requirement to promote culture, too, it is evident that nature strives by design for a development that makes us receptive to ends higher than those that nature itself can give us. The predominance of ills that we are inundated with by the refinement of taste to the point of its idealization, and even by luxury in the sciences, as nourishment for vanity, through the insatiable quantity of further inclinations produced by these, is not to be denied. On the other hand, the end of nature is also not to be misconstrued, viz., that we should gain increasingly more against the brutishness and impetuosity of those inclinations which belong more to our animal nature and which are most opposed to the development toward our higher vocation (the inclinations of pleasure) and make more room for the development of humanity. Fine art and sciences, which, by means of a pleasure that can be communicated universally, and through the way in which they enhance and refine society, make humankind, if not moral, then at least better behaved, gain very much against the tyranny of our sensible tendency, and thereby prepare the human being for mastery by no other power than reason; while the afflictions with which, in part nature, and in part the intolerant selfishness of human beings, torment us, also call on, intensify, and toughen the resources of the soul, in order that we will not fall prey to such afflictions and in order to thereby make us feel an aptitude to higher ends that lies concealed within us.* 5:434

§ 84. ON THE FINAL END OF THE EXISTENCE OF A WORLD, THAT IS, CREATION ITSELF

A *final end* is that end which requires no other end as a condition of its possibility. If one accepts the mere mechanism of nature as sufficiently explaining the purposiveness of nature, then one cannot ask why the things in the world exist. For one thus speaks, according to such an idealistic system, only of the physical possibility of things (which for us to regard as

---

*The value that life has for us, if it is assessed merely on the basis *of that which one enjoys* (the natural end of the sum of all inclinations, i.e., happiness) is easy to determine. It is less than zero; for who would wish to begin life anew under the same conditions, or even according to a new, self-designed plan, albeit one consistent with the course of nature, if such a plan were oriented simply toward enjoyment? The value that life would have, what it would contain if conducted according to the end that nature has for us, and which would consist in *that which one does* (and not merely enjoys), where we would be, however, always only a means to an indeterminate final end, has been shown above. There is thus likely nothing that remains other than the value which we ourselves give our lives by means of not merely what we do, but also do so purposively and independently of nature, that even the existence of nature can be an end only under this condition.

ends would constitute mere sophistry without an object): now one might interpret this form of things as due to chance or blind necessity, but in both cases the question would be baseless. But if we assume the relation of ends in the world to be real and further suppose a particular kind of causality that governs this relation, namely, a cause that *acts intentionally,* then we may not simply stop at the question of why things in the world (organized beings) take this or that form, or are placed by nature in this or that relation with others. Rather, since we already conceive of an intellect which must be regarded as the cause for the possibility of such forms as they really mani-

5:435   fest themselves in things in the world, then one must also ask about the objective ground that could have determined this productive intellect to have such an effect, which is hence the final end to which such things exist.

I have said above that the final end is not an end which nature alone is able to bring about and realize in accordance with the idea of that same end, because it is unconditioned. For there is nothing in nature (as a sensible being), of which the determining ground that is found in nature itself is not in turn conditioned; and this is true not only of nature external to us (material nature), but rather also of that within us (thinking nature): it must be understood, of course, that I regard only that in myself which is nature. But a thing that necessarily, due to its objective make-up, is to exist as the final end of an intelligent cause, must be of the sort that it depends on no other condition in the organization of ends other than the idea of it.

We have only one kind of being in the world of which the causality is teleological, that is, oriented toward ends, and yet simultaneously is made up in such a way that the law, according to which it is to set ends for itself, is conceived by such beings themselves as unconditioned and independent from natural conditions, yet as necessary in itself. The human being is this kind of being, but only when considered as a noumenon. It is the only natural being in which we can cognize, on the basis of its own make-up, a supersensible ability (*freedom*) and even the law of causality, together with the object of the latter that it can set as its highest end (the highest good in the world).

One cannot then ask, regarding the human being as a moral being (and likewise in the case of any rational being in the world): for what (*quem in finem*) he exists. His existence has its highest end in itself, an end to which, to the extent he is able, he can subject all of nature, at least against which he may not regard himself as subject to any influence of nature. Now if the things in the world, as, according to their existence, dependent beings, require a supreme cause that acts purposively, then the human being is the final end of creation. For without the human being the chain of ends orga-

nized in super- and subordinate relations to one another would ultimately be baseless; and only in the human being, and even in the human solely as a subject of morality, can the unconditioned legislation with regard to ends be found, which therefore makes him alone able to be a final end, to which all   5:436
of nature is teleologically subordinated.*

*It would be possible that the happiness of rational beings in the world were an end of nature, and in that case it would also be its *ultimate* end. At least it cannot be understood a priori why nature should not be organized in such a way, since this effect would well be possible by means of its mechanism, at least as far as we understand. But morality and a causality according to ends that is subordinate to this morality simply due to causes of nature are absolutely impossible. For the principle of its determination to act is supersensible and is thus the only possible thing in the order of ends, which in view of nature is quite simply unconditioned, and only its subject thereby qualifies as the *final end* of creation, to which all of nature is subordinate. — *Happiness,* on the other hand, is, as shown in the previous § according to the evidence of experience, not even an *end of nature* in view of the human being as possessing an advantage over other creatures: let alone that happiness should be the *final end of creation.* Human beings may always make happiness into their ultimate subjective end. But if I ask about the final end of creation: why did human beings have to come into existence? then I thereby ask about his own internal objective, supreme end, such as the highest reason would require for its creation. If one then answers: so that beings exist for whom that supreme cause can do good, then one contradicts the condition to which the human being's reason subjects even his most fervent desire for happiness (namely, harmony with his own internal moral legislation). This proves: that happiness can be only a conditional end, that the human being can thus be the final end of creation only as a moral being; as far as his condition is concerned, however, happiness is connected with that final end, as the end of his existence, only as a consequence in proportion to the harmony with that end.

On the Common Saying:
This May Be True in Theory, but
It Does Not Hold in Practice,
Parts 2 and 3

Ak 8:289

II. On the Relation of Theory to Practice in
Constitutional Right

(Against *Hobbes*)[1]

Of all the contracts by means of which a number of human beings unites itself into a society (*pactum sociale*), the contract to establish a *civil constitution* among them (*pactum unionis civilis*) is of such a peculiar kind that, even though it may have, with respect to its *execution,* much in common with all others (which are equally directed at some chosen end to be promoted jointly), it is nonetheless essentially distinct from all others with regard to the principle of its institution (*constitutionis civilis*). The union of many for some common end (which all *have*) is found in all social contracts; but a union of the same that is in itself an end (which each of them *ought to have*), hence a union which is an unconditional and primary duty in any external relation among human beings in general who cannot avoid mutually influencing one another, is to be found only in a society which is in a civil condition, that is, which constitutes a commonwealth. The end, then, which in such an external relation is in itself duty and the supreme formal condition (*conditio sine qua non*) of all other external duty, is the *right* of human beings *under public coercive laws* by means of which it can be determined for each what is his own and the latter can be secured against the infringement of others.

The concept of external right in general originates solely from the concept of *freedom* in the external relations among human beings and has nothing at all to do with the end that all human beings naturally have (the

---

1. Thomas Hobbes (1588–1679). Hobbes's *De Cive* [On the Citizen] was published in 1642. His more famous work, *Leviathan, or the Matter, Form, and Power of a Commonwealth, Ecclesiastical and Civil* was published in 1651.

objective of happiness) and the prescription of the means to arrive at it. The end of happiness therefore must never be commingled with the laws of external right as a determining ground thereof. *Right* is the restriction of the freedom of each to the condition of its being compatible with the freedom of all, to the extent this is possible in accordance with a general law. And *public law* is the sum of *external laws* that make such a universal harmony possible. Since every limitation of freedom through the will of another is known as *coercion,* it then follows that the civil constitution is a relation among *free* human beings who (notwithstanding their freedom in the whole of their union with others) are nonetheless subject to coercive laws, since reason wills it to be this way, specifically pure, a priori legislating reason, which pays no regard to any empirical end (all of which are conceived under the general name of happiness). For with respect to their empirical end and what it consists in human beings think very differently, such that their will cannot be brought under a common principle and hence also under no external law that is in harmony with the freedom of all.

8:290

The civil condition, considered purely as a legal condition, is grounded on the following a priori principles:

1. The *freedom* of every member of society, as a *human being.*
2. The *equality* of every member with every other, as a *subject.*
3. The *independence* of every member of the commonwealth, as a *citizen.*

These principles are not so much laws that the already established state promulgates, rather, only on the basis of these principles is it possible at all to establish a state in accordance with pure rational principles of external human right. Thus:

1. As for the *freedom* [of every member of society] as a human being, I express this principle for the constitution of a commonwealth with the following formulation: No one can force me to be happy in his way (according to how he conceives the welfare of other human beings), rather each may pursue happiness in the way that he sees fit, as long as he does not infringe on the freedom of others to pursue a similar end, which can coexist with the freedom of everyone in accordance with a possible general law (that is, with the same right of another). — A government that would be established on the basis of the principle of benevolence toward the people, as a *father* vis-à-vis his children, that is, a *paternalistic government* (*imperium paternale*) would be the greatest imaginable *despotism* (a constitution that nullifies all freedom of the subjects, who thus have no rights). Such a government is one where the subjects, as dependent children, cannot decide what is useful or damaging to them and are required to behave

8:291

merely passively. How such passive citizens should be happy depends only on the judgment of the head of state, and his willing them to be so would be merely due to his kindness. Not a *paternalistic,* but rather only a *patriotic* government (*imperium non paternale, sed patrioticum*) is the one which can be conceived for human beings who are capable of rights, and also the only one that can be conceived for a benevolent ruler. *Patriotic* is namely that way of thinking whereby every one in the state (the head of state not excluded) regards the commonwealth as the maternal womb or the country as the paternal land from which and on which one has come into being, and which one must leave behind as a treasured pledge. Each thus considers himself authorized only to protect the rights of the same through laws of the common will, but not authorized to subject it to his own absolute discretionary use. — He, the member of the commonwealth, is entitled to this right of freedom as a human being to the extent that the latter is a being capable of rights in general.

2. As for the *equality* as a subject, for this the formulation can read: Every member of the commonwealth has coercive rights vis-à-vis every other member, from which only the head of state is excepted (for the reason that he is not a member of the commonwealth, but rather its creator or preserver). The head of state alone is authorized to coerce without himself being subject to coercive laws. But everyone who is *subject* to laws is a subject in a state, and thus is subject to coercive law just as are all other members of the commonwealth, the only exception (physical or moral person) being the head of state, through which alone all legal coercion can be exercised. For if the head of state could also be coerced, he would not be the head of state and the series of subordination would continue upward into infinity. And if there were two of them (persons not subject to coercion), then neither of them would be subject to coercive laws and neither could do the other wrong, which is impossible.

This universal equality among human beings in the state as subjects of the same is perfectly consistent with the greatest inequality in the quantity and degree of their possessions, be it with regard to physical or intellectual superiority over others or with regard to riches external to them and rights in general (of which there can be many) with respect to others. There may be such inequality between them that the welfare of the one depends greatly on the will of the other (that of the poor person on that of the rich person), such that the one must obey (as a child obeys its parents or a woman her husband) while the other commands, or such that the one serves (as a wage-earner) while the other pays, etc. But according to *right* (which as the pronouncement of the general will can only be singular, and which concerns the form of what is right, not the matter or the object with regard to which I have a right), both as subjects are nonetheless equal, since no one can coerce another other than through public law (and through its executor, the head of state). Yet through public law every other person resists him in the same degree, while no one loses this authority to coerce (that is, to have a right vis-à-vis others) except through his own crime and cannot surrender it, say, through a contract. That is, there is no legal action that he can perform, such that he has no rights but only duties, since he would thereby rob himself of the right to make a contract and would thus nullify the contract itself.

From this idea of the equality of human beings as subjects in the commonwealth the following formula also follows: Every member of the commonwealth must be permitted to attain any degree of rank in it (that a subject can attain) that he can earn through his talent, diligence, and luck. And his fellow subjects may not, by virtue of a *hereditary* prerogative (as wielding the privilege of a certain rank), stand in his way in order to hold him and his descendants eternally down under it.

For all right consists merely in the limitation of the freedom of others to the condition [*Bedingung*] that it is consistent with mine in accordance with a general law, and public right (in a commonwealth) is merely the condition [*Zustand*] of a real legislation in accordance with this principle and coupled with power, by virtue of which all those who belong to a people are subjects in a juridical condition (*status iuridicus*) in general, that is to say, are in a condition of equality of action and reaction of a mutually limiting choice in accordance with the general law of freedom (which is called the civil condition). For this reason the *innate* right of everyone in this condition (that is, before any legal acts of the same), with respect to the authority to coerce all others so that the use of their freedom always remains within limits of consistency with my freedom, are universally the *same*. Since birth is not a *deed* of the one who is born, and since he can thereby incur no inequality in his legal status and no subjugation to coercive laws other than to the sole, supreme legislating power that is common to all, there can be no innate privilege of one member of the commonwealth as a fellow subject before others. And no one can bequeath the privilege of a *rank* which he possesses in the commonwealth to his descendants and therefore can also not, as if they were qualified by birth to the ruling class, forcibly prevent others from rising, through their own merits, to higher positions in the social hierarchy (of superior and inferior, but not a relation of *imperans* [ruler] and *subiectus* [subject]). Everything else that is a thing (not concerning his personality) and can be acquired as property and disposed of he may bequeath, which,

8:293

after a series of descendents, may bring about a considerable inequality in wealth among the members of a commonwealth (between employee and employer, between landowner and farm laborer, etc.). Only he may not prevent that these, if their talent, diligence, and fortune enable them to, might rise to similar circumstances. For he would thereby be permitted to compel without being compelled in turn by others and thereby rise above the position of fellow subject. — No human being who lives in the legal condition of a commonwealth can depart from such equality except through his own crime. But he can never depart from it through contract or military occupation, for he cannot cease by means of a legal act (neither his own, nor that of another) being owner of himself and join the class of domestic animals that one uses for all ends as one wishes, and for as long as one wants without obtaining its consent, even if under the condition (which is sanctioned from time to time by religion, as in India) that one does not cripple or kill it. One can consider him happy in any condition as long as he is conscious that it is due solely to himself (his capacities, or genuine will) or to circumstances, which he can blame on no one else, but not due to the irresistible will of others, that he does not rise to a level with others, for they, as his fellow subjects, have no advantage over him as concerns their rights.*

8:294

*If one wishes to associate a determinate concept with the word *gracious* (as distinct from *kind, charitable, protective,* etc.), then it can be applied only to those against whom there is *no coercive right.* Thus only the head of the *government* (for the *sovereign* that gives the laws is as it were invisible; it is the personified law itself, not its agent), who causes and grants all benefits that are possible according to public laws, can be given the title *gracious lord,* as the only one against whom there is no coercive right. Thus in an aristocracy, such as, for example, in Venice, the *senate* is the only gracious lord. The nobility of which the senate is constituted are all subjects, from which even the *Doge* is not excluded (for only the *grand council* is the sovereign). As concerns the execution of the law, they are equal to all other subjects, namely, insofar as the subject has a coercive right against each of them. Princes (i.e., persons who are by hereditary right entitled to governments) are called (i.e., by courtly etiquette, par courtoisie) gracious lords with regard to their prospect of becoming so and due to their claim to it. As owners of property they are, however, fellow subjects, against which even the lowliest of their servants must have through the head of state a coercive right. There can thus be no more than one single gracious lord in the state. As concerns the gracious (actually distinguished) women, they can be regarded as entitled to this designation by their *rank* and *sex* (consequently only vis-à-vis the *male* sex), and this by virtue of a

3. As for the *independence* (*sibisufficientia*) of a member of the commonwealth as *citizen*, that is, as co-legislator: Regarding legislation itself, all are free and equal under already present public laws, yet not all are to be regarded as equal as concerns the right to make these laws. Those who are not capable of this right are nonetheless, as members of the commonwealth, subject to the obedience of these laws and thereby share in the protection that these offer, but as *protected compatriots,* not as *citizens.* All right depends namely on laws. Yet a public law which determines for all what they are legally allowed and not allowed to do is an act of a public will from which all right issues and which therefore must not be able to do anyone wrong. But this is possible only with the will of the entire people (since all decide over all, and hence each decides over himself). For no one can do wrong to himself. But if it is another, then the mere will of one different from him cannot decide anything over him that would not be wrong. His law would therefore require another law that limits his legislation, hence no particular will can legislate for a commonwealth. (Actually the concepts of external freedom, equality, and *unity* of the will *of all* come together in order to constitute this concept. The prerequisite for this unity, since it requires a vote [if freedom and equality are present] is independence.) This basic law, which can arise only from the general (united) will of the people, is called the *original contract.* 8:295

The one who has the right to vote in this legislation is known as the *citizen* (*citoyen,* that is, *citizen of the state,* not citizen of the city, *bourgeois*). The only quality required for this, beside the *natural* one (that it is neither woman nor child) is: that one is *one's own master* (*sui iuris*), and thus that one has some *property* (which also includes any skill, trade, fine art, or science) that provides for one. That is to say that in those cases where he must earn his livelihood from others, he earns it only by *selling* what is *his,** not by means of granting others the right to make use of his powers,

---

refinement of manners (known as gallantry) according to which the male sex believes to honor itself more, the more it concedes privileges over itself to the fairer sex.

*He who completes a piece of work (*opus*) can through *sale* render it to another, just as if it were his property. Guaranteeing one's labor (*praestatio operae*), however, is no sale. The house servant, the shop helper, the day laborer, even the hairdresser are mere laborers (*operarii*), not artists or artisans (*artifices* in the broader meaning of the word) and not members of the state, thus also are not qualified to be citizens. Although the one to whom I give my firewood to have it cut

thus that he not *serve* anyone, in the true sense of the word, but the commonwealth. In this, artisans and large (or small) estate owners are all equal to one another, namely, all are entitled to one vote. For as the latter are concerned, we shall not even consider the question how it could rightly have come about that one has received more land as his own than he could use with his own hands (for acquisition by means of military seizure is no first acquisition), and how it happened that many people who together would otherwise have been able to acquire a permanent property are thereby instead brought to merely serving him in order to live. It would already come into conflict with the earlier principle of equality if a law granted them the privilege of their descendents either always remaining large (feudal) landowners without their land being sold or divided through inheritance and thus becoming useful to multiple people, or even in the case of division, only those belonging to an arbitrarily determined class of human beings being able to acquire it. The large landowner does away with so many smaller landowners and their votes as could otherwise take his place; he thus does not vote in their name and has only one vote. — It ought to be left solely to the abilities, diligence, and luck of every member of the commonwealth that each can acquire a part of it and that all can acquire the entirety of it, while differences in this regard cannot come into consideration within the general legislation. Therefore, the number of those entitled to vote on legislation must be calculated according to a head count of those in possession of property and not according to the size of their possessions.

However, *all* who have this voting right must agree to this law of public justice. For otherwise a legal conflict would arise between those who do not agree to it and those who do, which would require even a higher principle of right in order to be resolved. Unanimity among an entire people cannot be expected, rather one can expect only to attain a majority of votes, that is, not a majority of direct votes among a large people, but rather only a majority of votes of delegates as representatives of the people. One must assume, therefore, that the principle of allowing the majority to suffice has universal

---

and the tailor to whom I give cloth to have it turned into a garment seem to stand in very similar relation to me, each of them is nonetheless distinct, as the hairdresser is distinct from the wig maker (whom I may have even given the hair to for it), or the day laborer is distinct from the artist or artisan, who makes a work that belongs to him as long as he is not paid for it. The latter sells his property as one engaged in a trade to another (*opus*), while the former grants the use of his powers to another (*operam*). — It is, I confess, somewhat difficult to determine the requirement for laying claim to the class in which one is one's own master.

agreement and that it is accepted by means of a contract, and this must serve as the ultimate grounds for the establishment of a civil constitution.

Conclusion   8:297

Here, then, is an *original contract* on which alone a civil, thus universally juridical constitution among human beings can be founded and a commonwealth established. — Only it need not be supposed that this contract (called either *contractus originarius* [original contract] or *pactum sociale* [social pact]), as a coalition of every particular and private will in a people into a common and public will (for the end of a merely rightful legislation), exists as a *fact* (indeed as such it is completely impossible). Such an assumption would proceed as if one must first prove from history that a people into whose rights and obligations we enter as descendants had once actually performed such an act and must have left us a certain report or instrument of it either orally or in writing so that we would know ourselves as bound to an already existing civil constitution. It is rather a *mere idea* of reason, yet one which has unquestionable (practical) reality. Namely, this idea obligates every legislator to pass laws in such a way that they *would have been able* to arise from the united will of an entire people and to regard every subject, insofar as it wishes to be a citizen, as though it has given its assent to this will. For that is the touchstone for the lawfulness of any public law. If a public law is so composed that an entire people *could not possibly* give its assent to it (as, for example, in the case of a certain class of *subjects* having the hereditary privilege of a *ruling rank*), then it is unjust. If it is *only possible,* however, that a people could agree to it, then it is a duty to regard the law as just, even if the people were now in such a state or attitude of mind that, if it were asked, it would probably withhold its agreement.*

*If, for instance, a proportional war tax were collected from all subjects, the latter could not, because the tax is oppressive, say that it is unjust because, for instance, the war in their opinion was unnecessary. For they are not entitled to make such judgments, since it always remains *possible* that the war was inevitable and the tax indispensable. Such a tax thus must be considered lawful in the judgment of the subject. If, however, certain property owners were subjected to levies while others of the same class were spared, then one can easily see that an entire people could not agree to such a law and the people is thus authorized at least to make representations against the law, since it cannot regard this unequal distribution of burdens as just.

But this restriction clearly applies only to the judgment of the legislator, not to the subject. Thus if a people should judge that it would in all probability forfeit its happiness under a law that currently is in force, what should it do? Should it not resist? The answer can only be that the people has no option other than to obey. For we are concerned here not with the happiness that the subject can expect from the institution or administration of the commonwealth. We are concerned foremost merely with the right that is thereby to be secured for each. This is the supreme principle from which all maxims that concern a commonwealth must issue, and it is limited by no other principle. With regard to the former (happiness), no generally valid principle for laws can be given at all. For the temporal conditions as well as the very conflicting and always changing illusions in which each person expects to find happiness (and where he finds happiness cannot be prescribed for him by anyone) makes all fixed principles impossible and happiness unfit as a principle for legislation. The proposition *salus publica suprema civitatis lex est*[2] remains undiminished in its value and high regard, but the public good that is to be considered *first* is precisely that legal constitution that secures for each his freedom through laws, whereby he remains free to seek his happiness in any way that seems best to him, insofar as he does not violate that general lawful freedom and thereby the rights of other fellow subjects.

When the supreme authority passes laws that are aimed primarily at happiness (the prosperity of the citizens, increased population, etc.), this happens not because this is the purpose of establishing a civil constitution, but rather only as a means of *securing* the *juridical condition* primarily against external enemies of the people. The head of state must be authorized to himself be the sole judge of whether such laws are necessary for the prosperity of the commonwealth, which is required to protect its strength and steadfastness internally, as well as against external enemies. Such laws are not enacted in order to make the people happy against its will, but rather only such that it exist as a commonwealth.* In his judgment whether those measures are *prudent* or not the legislator may err, but he cannot err in

*This includes certain import restrictions, so that the livelihood of the subject and not the advantage of foreigners and encouragement of the industriousness of others are promoted, because without the prosperity of the people the state would not possess enough powers to resist foreign enemies or to preserve itself as a commonwealth.

2. The public well-being is the supreme law of the state. Cf. Cicero, *De legibus* 3.3: "*Salus populi suprema lex esto.*" (The well-being of the people is the supreme law.)

asking himself whether the law is consistent with the principle of right. For here he has the idea of the original contract as an infallible standard and has it indeed a priori at hand (and need not wait for experiences that instruct him with regard to the suitability of his means, as he would if he adopted the principle of happiness). For as long as there would be no contradiction if an entire people were to agree to such a law, however unpleasant it may find it to be, then it is in accordance with right. Yet if a public law meets with such agreement, and consequently is *irreprehensible* with respect to right, then this is bound up with the authority to coerce on the one hand and the prohibition of actively resisting the will of the legislators on the other. That is to say that the power of the state which makes the law effective is also *irresistible,* and there is no lawfully constituted commonwealth without such power to put down all internal resistance, since such resistance would occur according to a maxim which, if made general, would obliterate all civil constitution and destroy the condition in which human beings can be in possession of rights in general.

From this it follows that all resistance against the supreme legislating authority, all incitement in order to express through action the dissatisfaction of subjects, all revolt that leads into rebellion, is the highest and most punishable offense in the commonwealth because it destroys the latter's very foundations. And this prohibition is *unconditional,* such that even if the legislative authority or its agent, the head of state, violates the original contract and thereby surrenders, in the perception of the subjects, the right to be legislator by authorizing the government to act thoroughly violently (tyrannically), the subject is still not allowed to resist in any way. The reason for this is that under an already existing civil constitution the people 8:300 has no right to judge how the constitution is to be administered. For if one supposes that the people has such a right to judge and that its judgment is in conflict with that of the actual head of state, then who shall decide who is right? Neither of the two can decide as a judge in their own case. There would therefore have to be a head above the head of state, who would decide between him and the people, which is a contradiction. — Neither can for instance a right of necessity (*ius in casu necessitatis*), which, as a purported *right* [*Recht*] to do *wrong* [*Unrecht*] in the greatest circumstances of (physical) need, is preposterous anyway,* enter the picture here

*There is no *casus necessitatis* except in the case where duties, particularly an *unconditional* duty and a (albeit perhaps great, nonetheless) *conditional duty,* conflict with one another. For example, when it is important to avert a misfortune befalling the state by the betrayal of someone who stands in a relationship such as

and help raise the obstacle that restricts the people. For the head of state can just as well think it can justify its heavy hand against its subjects due to their rebelliousness as the subjects can think to justify their rebellion against him with their complaint of unreasonable suffering, and who is to decide the matter? Whoever is the supreme administrator of justice, and that is precisely the head of state, alone can decide. And no one in the commonwealth can thus have a right to dispute his authority in this.

8:301   Nevertheless I find respectable men who assert this authority of the subject to use violence against his superiors under certain circumstances. Of these I wish to cite only *Achenwall*,[3] who is very cautious, precise, and modest in his theories of natural law.* He writes: "If the danger which threatens the commonwealth as a result of continued tolerance of the injustice of the head of state is greater than that which results from taking up arms against him, then the people can resist the head of state and, in pursuing this right, abandon its contract of subjugation and dethrone him as a tyrant." He then concludes: "In this way the people returns (with respect to its previous ruler) to the state of nature."

I would like to think that neither *Achenwall,* nor any of the worthy men who have speculated in agreement with him on this matter would ever have advised or condoned such risky undertakings in a concrete case. There is hardly a doubt that if the revolts by which Switzerland, the United Nether-

---

that of father to son to another. Here the aversion of the ill of the former is an unconditional duty, while that of the misfortune of the latter is only a conditional duty (that is, it applies only if the latter is not guilty of a crime against the state). The latter may report the plans of the former to the authorities only with the greatest reluctance, but he is bound to do so by (moral) necessity. — If, however, someone who pushes another shipwrecked person from his board in order to save his own life claims that he has a right to it due to his (physical) necessity, his claim is entirely false. For saving my own life is only a conditional duty (applies only if I can do it without committing a crime), whereas not taking the life of someone who has not injured me and not even *put* me in jeopardy of losing mine is an unconditional duty. The teachers of general civil right are entirely consistent, however, when they concede a legal authority to such measures in emergencies. For the authorities can attach no *punishment* to the prohibition since the punishment would have to be death. Yet it would be an illogical law to threaten someone with death if he did not voluntarily submit to death in dangerous circumstances.

Ius Naturae. Editio Vta. Pars posterior §§ 203–6.

3. Gottfried Achenwall (1719–72), whose *Ius Naturae* [Natural Law] was first published in 1755–56 (2 vols.).

lands, or Great Britain attained their much-acclaimed constitutions had failed, the reader of the history of these uprisings would see in the execution of their now so celebrated initiators nothing other than the deserved punishment of persons guilty of high treason. For the outcome commonly colors our judgment of rightness, even though the former is uncertain, while the latter is certain. Yet it is clear, as concerns rightness, that the people has committed a wrong of the highest degree in seeking their rights in this way, even if one concedes that no wrong has been done to the sovereign prince through such revolt (perhaps since he had violated a real basic contract with the people, such as the *joyeuse entrée*).[4] For this way of seeking one's right (taken as one's maxim) makes all lawful constitutions uncertain and leads into a state of complete lawlessness (*status naturalis*), where all right ceases, or at least ceases to be effective. — I wish, in light of this tendency of so many well-thinking writers to side with the people (to its own detriment), to remark that it is partly caused by the common delusion of substituting the principle of happiness for the principle of right in one's judgments. It is also partly caused by the fact that, where no instrument of a contract that was presented to the commonwealth and subsequently accepted by its ruler and sanctioned by both can be found, they assume that the idea of an original contract, which always lies in reason as the basis, is something that must have *actually* occurred. They thus always reserved for the people the authority to abandon the contract at its own discretion whenever, though in its own judgment, there is a gross violation of it.*

8:302

One obviously sees here what havoc the principle of happiness (which is

*Even if the actual contract of the people with its ruler is violated, the people cannot immediately respond *as a commonwealth,* rather only as mobs. For the previously existing constitution was torn to pieces by the people, and the organization into a new commonwealth has yet to happen. Here the state of anarchy ensues, with all of the horrors it brings with it. And the wrong that is done here is the wrong that each party in the people does to the other, as can be seen in the cited example, where the rebellious subjects of that state ultimately wanted to violently impose a constitution on the others that would have been far more oppressive than the one they had abandoned, namely, one in which they were devoured by clergy and aristocrats, rather than being able to expect more equality in the distribution of political burdens under a single ruler who ruled all.

4. Translated: "joyous entry." The ceremonial first visit of a prince to his country, during which the subjects would officially grant or confirm the royal privileges. In 1789–90, Joseph II had tried to repeal the Joyeuse Entrée charter of Brabant, provoking Brabant's revolt.

actually not capable of a determinate principle at all) wreaks in constitutional right, just as it does in morality, even if the teacher thereof has the best of intentions. The sovereign wants to make the people happy according to his own concepts and becomes a despot; the people does not wish to give up on the general human claim to happiness and becomes a rebel. If one had first asked what is right (where the principles stand fixed a priori, where no empiricist can meddle), then the idea of the social contract would remain with its unquestionable authority. But it would not exist as a fact (as *Danton*[5] would have it, who declares that without it all existing rights and property under actually existing constitutions are null and void), but rather only as a rational principle in judging all public lawful constitutions in general. And one would thereby see that, before the general will exists, the people possesses no coercive right against its ruler, since it can legally coerce only through him. But once the general will exists, there can be no coercion of the ruler, since then the people would be the supreme ruler. The people thus never has a coercive right against the head of state (insubordination in words or in deeds).

8:303   We also see this theory sufficiently confirmed in practice. In the case of Great Britain, where the people boasts about its constitution as if it were a model for all the world, we nevertheless find that it is completely silent about the authority belonging to the people, should the monarch transgress against the contract of 1688. Thus the people secretly reserves the right to rebellion against him if he wanted to violate it, since there exists no law about this. For it would be a clear contradiction if the constitution were to contain a law concerning this case, one which enabled the overthrow of the existing constitution, from which all particular laws are derived (even presuming the contract had been violated). It would be a contradiction because the constitution would have to contain a *publicly constituted** counter-authority, and there would therefore have to be a second head of state which would protect the rights of the people against the first, but then also a third head of state which would decide which of the two sides was right. — Those leaders (or, if one wishes, guardians) of the people, fearing such an accusation if their undertaking were to fail, preferred to *impute* to the mon-

---

*No right in the state can be concealed maliciously, as it were, by means of a secret reservation, least of all the right that a people presumes for itself as part of the constitution, because all laws of this constitution must be thought of as flowing from a public will. If it allowed revolt, the constitution would have to publicly declare the manner in which the right to revolt is to be made use of.

5. Georges-Jacques Danton (1759–94), French revolutionary leader.

arch who had been frightened off by them to a voluntary relinquishment of the government, rather than presuming a right to dethrone, by which they would have brought the constitution into contradiction with itself.

Since certainly no one will counter my assertions with the objection that I flatter the monarch too much with this inviolability, so too, hopefully, will I be spared the objection that I assert too much in favor of the people when I declare that the people similarly has inalienable rights vis-à-vis the head of state, although these cannot be coercive rights.

Hobbes is of the opposite view. According to him (*De Cive*, ch. 7, § 14) the head of state is obligated by the contract to nothing vis-à-vis the people and can do no wrong to the citizen (whatever he may want to do to him). — This proposition would be entirely correct, if by "wrong" one means such an injury by which the one injured obtains *coercive right* against the one who does him wrong. But stated in such a general fashion the proposition is frightening. 8:304

The nonrebellious subject must be able to assume that his ruler does not *want* to do him harm. Thus, since every human being indeed has his inalienable rights, ones that he cannot surrender even if he wanted to and with regard to which he has the authority to pass his own judgment, the wrong that befalls him in his own view occurs, as long as the above condition is met, only due to error or ignorance of certain consequences of laws on the part of the highest power. The citizen must therefore be authorized, with the approval of the ruler, to publicly make known his opinion about what in the ruler's decrees seems to be a wrong against the commonwealth. For to assume that the ruler cannot err or cannot be unknowledgeable of a certain matter would be to presume him blessed with divine inspiration and elevate him above humanity. Thus the *freedom of the pen* is the only protector of the people's rights — as long as it is held within the bounds of a great respect and love for the constitution within which one lives by a liberal way of thinking among subjects, which the constitution itself instills in them. (And the pens limit one another themselves, so that they do not lose their freedom.) To want to deny this freedom to the people is not so much to deprive it of any claim to a right with respect to the supreme commander (according to Hobbes) as it is rather to divest the latter, whose will commands subjects as citizens merely through the fact that he represents the general will of the people, of all knowledge of that which, if he knew about it, he would change himself, and thereby places him in contradiction with himself. To instill fear into the ruler that thinking to oneself or thinking out loud could cause unrest in the state is the same as awakening mistrust against his own power or hatred toward his own people.

The general principle, however, according to which a people can judge *negatively,* that is, judge whatever it may regard as *not decreed* in good will by the supreme legislator is contained in the following proposition: *Whatever a people cannot decide over itself cannot be decided over it by the legislator.*

8:305   If the question is, for example, whether a law that pronounces that a certain, previously established ecclesiastical constitution be considered permanently valid can be regarded as issuing from the actual will of the legislator (according to its intention), then one must first ask whether a people would be *allowed* to make into a law for itself that certain doctrinal content and forms of external religion that were assumed at one point in time are supposed to remain for ever. One must thus ask whether it would be permitted to hinder itself in its descendants from progressing in its religious insights or changing earlier errors. Then it becomes clear that an original contract of the people that made this into a law would be in itself null and void because it conflicts with the vocation and end of humanity. Therefore a law given in this way could not be regarded as the actual will of the monarch, and one could present him with counterarguments against it. — In all cases, however, if such a law were passed by the supreme legislator, one can pass general and public judgments on it but could never resist it in either word or deed.

In every commonwealth there must be *obedience* under the mechanism of the state constitution in accordance with coercive laws (which apply to the whole). But there must also be a *spirit of freedom* since, as concerns general human duties, everyone requires, to avoid self-contradiction, to be convinced by reason that this coercion is consistent with one's rights. Obedience without freedom is the cause that occasions all *secret societies.* For it is the natural calling of humanity to communicate with one another, above all about what concerns the human being in general. Those secret societies would fall away if this freedom were encouraged. And in what other way could the government itself obtain the knowledge that promotes its own essential intention, than by letting the spirit of freedom, in its origin and effects so worthy of respect, freely express itself?

* * *

Nowhere does practice that foregoes all principles of pure reason more presumptuously deny theory than in the question concerning the requirements for a good state constitution. The cause of this is that a constitution that has existed for a long time has gradually accustomed a people to a rule to judge their happiness as well as their rights according to the state of affairs under which everything has peacefully progressed to date. But they are not accustomed to conversely evaluating the current state of affairs according to concepts of happiness and right that are given to them by reason. They are rather prepared to prefer the passive condition to the perilous state of seeking a better condition (this is a case where what Hippocrates told doctors to take to heart holds true: *iudicium anceps, experimentum periculosum*).[6] All constitutions that have existed for some time, whatever flaws they may have, have, despite all their difference, one result which is the same, namely, being satisfied with the state in which one is. Thus, when one considers the *well-being of the people,* nothing at all depends on any theory but rather everything depends on a practice derived from experience.

8:306

If there is, however, something in reason that is expressed by the word *constitutional right,* and if the concept of it has a binding force and thus objective (practical) reality for human beings who stand in an antagonistic relation to one another due to their freedom, without regard for the good or ill that this may produce for them (for knowledge of this rests on experience), then it is grounded in a priori principles (for experience cannot teach us what is right), and there is a *theory* of constitutional right, to which any practice that is to be held valid must conform.

No objection can be made to this but that, although human beings have the idea of rights to which they are entitled in their head, they are, due to the intractability of their hearts, incapable and unworthy of being treated in accordance with them. Therefore a supreme authority that operates according to mere rules of prudence may and must keep them in order. This leap of desperation (*salto mortale*) is, however, such that when the concern is not of right, but rather only of might, the people may attempt its own power and thus make all legal constitutions uncertain. If there is nothing that through reason compels immediate respect (such as human rights), then all influences on the choice of human beings are incapable of containing their freedom. But if right speaks out next to benevolence, then human nature will show itself not so despoiled that its voice will not be heard deferentially by the latter. (*Tum pietate gravem meritisque si forte virum quem Conspexere, silent arrectisque auribus adstant.* Virgil.)[7]

6. Hippocrates, *Aphorisms* 1.1. "Judgment is uncertain, experiment is dangerous."

7. Virgil, *Aeneid* 1. 151–52: "then, if haply they set eyes on a man honoured for noble character and service, they are silent and stand by with attentive ears" (trans. H. Rushton Fairclough).

III. On the Relation of Theory to Practice in *International Right*. Considered from a Universal Philanthropic, That Is, Cosmopolitan Point of View*

Against *Moses Mendelssohn*[8]

Is the human race as a whole to be loved? Or is it an object that one must regard with reluctance, an object that (in order not to become misanthropic) one wishes all the best to even though one does not, however, actually expect it for him, and therefore must prefer to turn one's eye from? The response to this question depends on the answer that one gives to another question: Are there predispositions in human nature from which one can conclude that the species will always progress toward the better and the evil of present and past times will be lost in the good of future times? For in this way we can love the species at least for its constant approach to the good, otherwise we would have to hate or despise it, whatever posturings of universal love of humanity we might be presented with as proof of the opposite (it would be at most love in the form of benevolence,[9] not love on the basis of pleasing). For what is and remains evil, especially the intentional and mutual violation of the most sacrosanct of human rights — even with the greatest attempt to force oneself to love — we cannot avoid hating. Although we do so not in order to bring harm to human beings, we thereby want to have as little to do with them as possible.

Moses Mendelssohn was of the latter opinion (*Jerusalem,* second section, pp. 44–47), which is opposed to his friend *Lessing's* hypothesis of a divine education of the human race.[10] This is a mere fantasy to him: "that

---

*It is not immediately clear how a universal-*philanthropic* presupposition points to a *cosmopolitan* constitution or how the latter points to the grounding of *international right* as a state in which alone the predispositions of humankind can appropriately be developed which make our species worthy of love. — The conclusion of this section will make this connection clear.

8. Moses Mendelssohn (1729–86), *Jerusalem, oder über Religiöse Macht und Judentum* [Jerusalem, or on Religious Power and Judaism], 1783.

9. Cf. MM 6:449, where Kant contrasts love understood as feeling, that is, "pleasure in the perfection of others" with "practical love," which consists in the adoption of "the maxim of *benevolence* . . . , which results in beneficence."

10. Gottfried Ephraim Lessing (1729–81), whose final work, *Die Erziehung des*

the whole of humanity here on earth should, in the progression of time, continually move forward and perfect itself. — We see," he writes, "that the human race as a whole makes small oscillations; and it has never made steps forward without soon thereafter slipping back into its previous states with twice the speed." (This is precisely the boulder of Sisyphus,[11] and one thereby takes, as do the Hindus, the earth to be the site of atonement for old sins that are no longer in memory.) — "The individual human being goes on, but humankind vacillates up and down between fixed boundaries, maintaining in all time periods, considered as a whole, more or less the same level of morality, the same measure of religion and irreligiosity, of virtue and vice, of happiness (?) and misery." — These assertions he introduces (p. 46) by writing: "You wish to guess what intentions providence has with humankind? Do not construct hypotheses" (he had earlier called these theory); "merely look around at what is really happening and, if you can get an overall view of the history of all times, at what has always happened. This is fact, this must have been part of the intention, and must have been approved in the plan of wisdom, or at least have been taken up with it."

8:308

I am of a different opinion. — If it is a sight worthy of a deity to behold a virtuous man struggling with unpleasant circumstances and temptations to evil and nonetheless to withstand it, then it is a sight not only unworthy of a deity, but also highly unworthy of the most common but well-thinking person to see the human race make steps upward toward virtue from time to time, only to fall back just as far down into vice and misery soon thereafter. Watching such a tragedy for a while may perhaps be moving and instructive, but ultimately the curtain must fall. For in the long run it becomes a mockery. And even if the actors do not tire of it, because they are fools, the spectator will nonetheless tire of it after one or two acts of it, when he can conclude with good reason that the never-ending piece will be an eternal monotony. If it is a mere play, the punishment that comes at the end can put right the unpleasant sensations of the spectator throughout. But having vice pile upon countless vice (even if interspersed with virtue) in reality so that there may come a day of great punishment is, at least according to our concepts, even contrary to the morality of a wise creator and ruler of the world.

Menschengeschlechts [The Education of Humankind], 1780, voices belief in the perfectibility of humankind.

11. Sisyphus, the cunning king of Corinth, was, according to Greek mythology, punished in Hades by perpetually having to roll up a hill an enormous stone that would roll down again as soon as it reached the top.

I will thus be allowed to assume that since the human race is constantly progressing with respect to culture as the natural end for the same, it is also progressing toward the better with respect to the moral end of its existence, and that this progress will occasionally be *interrupted* but never *broken off*. It is not necessary for me to prove this supposition, rather my opponent has the burden of proof. I rely here on my innate duty to affect posterity such that it will become better (something the possibility of which must thus be assumed) and such that this duty will rightfully be passed down from one generation to another — I am a member of a series of generations, and within this series (as a human being in general) I do not have the required moral constitution to be as good as I ought, and therefore to be as good as I could be. However many doubts about my hopes may be given by history that, if they were sufficient proof, could move me to give up on a seemingly futile task, I can nonetheless, as long as this cannot be made entirely certain, not exchange my duty (as the *liquidum*)[12] for the prudential rule not to work toward the unattainable (as the *illiquidum,* since it is mere hypothesis). And however uncertain I am and may remain about whether improvement is to be hoped for the human race, this uncertainty cannot detract from my maxim and thus from the necessary supposition for practical purposes, that it is practicable.

This hope for better times, without which a serious desire to do something that promotes the general good would never have warmed the human heart, has always had an influence on the work of the well-thinking. And the good *Mendelssohn* must also have had it in mind when he made such eager endeavors for the enlightenment and welfare of the nation to which he belonged. For he could not reasonably have hoped to bring this about himself, if others did not continue on the same path after him. Faced with the tragic sight not so much of the ills that oppress the human race from natural causes, but rather those that human beings cause one another, the heart is enlivened by the prospect that it could get better in the future. And this arises from unselfish benevolence, [since it comes] at a time when we have long been in the grave, and we will not harvest the fruits that we ourselves, in part, have sown. Empirical evidence against the success of these resolutions made in hope has no bearing here. For the argument that what has not yet succeeded will therefore never succeed does not even justify giving up on a pragmatic or technical aim (as, for example, flights with aerostatic balls). It is even less a justification to give up on a moral aim, which, as long as it is not demonstratively impossible to effect it, is a duty.

12. "What is evident." *Illiquidum*: "what is not evident."

Moreover, there is ample evidence that the human race as a whole has actually made considerable progress morally in our age when compared to all others (brief pauses in such progress do not prove anything to the contrary). There is also evidence that all the fuss about the unending and increasing debasement of the human race comes precisely from the fact that when one stands at a higher stage of morality one sees even further ahead and one's judgment about what one is, compared to what one ought to be, hence our self-censure, becomes all the more critical the more steps of morality we have climbed in the entirety of the course of the world that is known to us.

If we now ask by what means this continual progress toward the better might be maintained and even accelerated, one soon sees that the success of this, which reaches immeasurably far out, depends not so much on what we do (for example, on the education that we give the younger world) or the method by which we ought to proceed in order to bring it about, as it does on that which human *nature* will do in us and with us in order to *compel* us into a track into which we will not ourselves easily follow. For from nature, or, rather (since the highest wisdom is required for the completion of this end), from *providence* alone can we expect a success that affects the whole and from there the parts. Human beings, by contrast, proceed with their *plans* only from the parts and are likely only to stick with them, since the whole as such, which is too large for them, is something to which their ideas can extend, but not their influence. This is especially true since they conflict with one another in their plans and would be unlikely to unite themselves out of their own free volition.

Just as omnipresent violence and the duress that arises from it must ultimately bring a people to the decision to subject itself to the constraint that reason itself prescribes as a means, namely, public laws, and enter into a state constitution, so too must the duress of the constant wars in which states seek to diminish or subjugate one another ultimately bring them, even against their will, to enter into a *cosmopolitan* constitution. Or, if such a state of universal peace (as has likely happened several times with overly large states) is itself even more dangerous in that it brings about the most horrible despotism, this duress must force states into a condition which is admittedly not a cosmopolitan commonwealth under one head, but nonetheless a legal condition of a *federation* according to a commonly agreed-upon *international right*.   8:311

The progressing culture of states, together with the growing tendency to expand at the expense of others, either through violence or deceit, must multiply the number of wars. It also causes the costs of the standing armies to rise, which are always increased (with the same amount of pay) in number and must be continually trained and supplied with ever greater amounts of equipment. The prices of all the needs thus continually rise without the hope of a proportionately increasing growth in metal currencies. No peace can last long enough that the savings accrued in that time would be sufficient to meet the expense of the next war. The invention of state debts was an ingenious measure against this, but it is ultimately a self-destructive one. Thus fatigue must ultimately do what good will should have done but did not: each state must be organized internally such that not the head of state, whom the war does not actually cost anything (since he wages it at the expense of another, namely, of the people), but rather the people, whom it ultimately costs, ought to have the deciding voice in whether to wage war (which of course necessarily presupposes the realization of that idea of an original contract). This is so since the people is likely to refrain from placing itself at risk of personal poverty, which does not affect the head of state, out of the mere desire to expand or due merely to purported verbal injuries. And thus posterity (on which no burdens are undeservedly conveyed) will be able always to progress toward the better in a moral sense, without love of posterity, but rather only the self-love of every age being the cause of this, by every commonwealth, incapable of harming another through violence, having to abide by what is right on its own, but having reason to hope that other commonwealths so constituted will lend assistance to it in this endeavor.

But this is mere opinion and hypothesis: it is uncertain, as are all judgments which claim to describe the only appropriate natural cause of an intended effect that is not entirely under our control. And even as such it does not contain a principle for the subject in an already existing state to attain the intended effect by force, rather it applies only to heads of state, who are free from coercion. Although it does not lie in the nature of the human being according to the normal order to voluntarily relinquish power, even though it is not impossible under urgent circumstances, one can take it to be a not inappropriate expression of the moral wishes and hopes of human beings (being conscious of their own inability) to expect from *providence* the circumstances required for it. The end of *humanity* as an entire species, that is, the attainment of its ultimate destiny through the free use of its powers, as far as they extend, will be brought by providence to an outcome which the ends of *human beings,* considered separately, work against. For precisely the opposition of the inclinations among one another from which evil arises, provides reason with free play to subjugate them

8:312

altogether and, rather than evil, which destroys itself, to make the good, which, once it exists, preserves itself, dominant.

* * *

Human nature seems nowhere less worthy of love than in relations among entire peoples. No state is secure for a moment against another with regard to its independence or its property. The will to subjugate one another or diminish what belongs to the other is always there, and arming for defense, which often makes peace more oppressive and destructive for internal welfare than the war itself, may never abate. Against this there is no other expedient possible than an international right that is founded on public laws that are backed with power and to which every state must subject itself (in accordance with the analogy with civil or constitutional right among individual persons). — For an enduring general peace by means of the so called *balance of powers in Europe* is, like *Swift's* house, which was built so perfectly by a master builder according to all the laws of equilibrium that it immediately collapsed when a sparrow landed on it, is a mere fantasy. — But states, one will say, will never subject themselves to such coercive laws, and the proposal of a general state of peoples, under whose authority all individual states ought to voluntarily adapt themselves to in order to obey its laws, might sound nice in the theories of the abbé of *St. Pierre* or *Rousseau*,[13] but it is not valid in practice. Such an idea has always been ridiculed by great statesmen, even more so by heads of state, as a pedantically childish notion from the schools.

8:313

— For my part, I place my trust in what the theory that is based on the principle of right says about how relations *ought to be* among human beings and states and which extols the maxim to the earthly gods to always act in their conflicts with one another such that such a general state of peoples could thereby be introduced and therefore to assume that it is possible (*in praxi*) and that it *can exist*. — But I also trust (*in subsidium*) in the nature of

13. Abbé Charles-Irénée Castel de Saint Pierre, *Projet pour rendre la paix perpétuelle en Europe* (1713). Jean-Jacques Rousseau, *Extrait du projet de paix perpétuelle de Monsieur l'Abbé de Saint Pierre* (1761) (*Oeuvres Complètes,* vols. 1–4, ed. Bernard Gagnebin and Marcel Raymond [Paris: Gallimard, 1969–78], 3:561–89). Rousseau's *Jugement sur la paix perpétuelle,* written around the same time as the *Extrait,* was first published posthumously in 1782 (*Oeuvres Complètes,* 3:591–600). Given that Rousseau distances himself clearly and explicitly from the abbé's proposals in the *Jugement,* it does not seem that Kant had read this second text.

things, which compels one in a direction one does not wish to go (*fata volentem ducunt, nolentem trahunt*).[14] In this human nature is also brought into consideration, which, since respect for right and duty are still animate in it, I cannot or do not want to regard as so sunken in evil that moral practical reason cannot, after many unsuccessful attempts, ultimately triumph over evil and show it to be worthy of love. Thus, from the cosmopolitan point of view, too, the assertion still stands: Whatever reason shows is valid in theory, also holds true for practice.

14. "The Fates lead the willing but drag the unwilling," Seneca, *Epistles* 107.11. Also quoted in PP 8:365.

Toward Perpetual Peace:
A Philosophical Sketch

"To Perpetual Peace"[1]

We can leave open the question whether this satirical caption to the picture of a graveyard, which was painted on the sign of a Dutch innkeeper, applies to *human beings* in general, or specifically to the heads of state, who can never get enough of war, or even just to philosophers who dream the sweet dream of perpetual peace. The author of this essay shall, however, stipulate one condition: since the practical politician tends to look disdainfully upon the political theorist as a mere academic, whose impractical ideas present no danger to the state (since, in the eyes of the politician, the state must be based on principles derived from experience), and who may show his hand without the *worldly* statesman needing to pay it any heed; then, in case of a conflict with the theorist, the statesman should deal with him consistently and refrain from any allegations of perceived threat to the state in whatever views that the theorist might dare set forth and publicly express. With this *clausula salvatoria* the author of this essay is hereby invoking the proper form to protect himself from any malicious interpretation.

First Section,
Which Contains the Preliminary Articles for
Perpetual Peace among States

1. "No peace settlement which secretly reserves issues for a future war shall be considered valid."

1. *Translator's note:* The German preposition *zu* can mean both "to" and "toward." In its citation in Kant's text it has been translated as "to" in order to maintain the character of a dedication in the name of the inn. In the title of Kant's essay it has been translated as "toward" since Kant sees perpetual peace as a state that should be approached, but not as one that can be attained.

For such a treaty would represent a mere cease-fire, a postponement of hostilities, and not peace. For *peace* signifies the end to all hostilities, and even merely adding the adjective *perpetual* to the term renders it a suspicious-looking pleonasm. The existing causes of a future war, even if perhaps not yet known to the parties themselves, are nullified without exception by a peace settlement, however acutely and shrewdly they might be ferreted out of archival documents. Each party might make a tacit reservation (*reservatio mentalis*) of old pretensions to be elaborated only at a later point in time, and not make any mention of them at present, since both parties are too exhausted to continue waging war but sustain the ill will to make use of the first good opportunity to this end. If, however, one considers the character of such an action in itself, such a tacit reservation belongs to Jesuitical casuistry and is beneath the dignity of a ruler, just as the compliance with such reasoning is beneath the dignity of this ruler's minister.

8:344

But if, on the basis of "enlightened" concepts of political prudence, the true honor of the state is thought to lie in the continual expansion of its power by any means whatsoever, then such a judgment will surely seem academic and pedantic.

2. "No independently existing state (irrespective of whether it is large or small) shall be able to be acquired by another state through inheritance, exchange, purchase, or gift."

For a state is not a possession (*patrimonium*), as is, for instance, the territory on which it exists. It is, rather, a society of human beings, whom no one but the state itself may command or dispose of. To annex a state, which, like a tree trunk, has its own roots, and thus to treat it as a graft onto another state, is to annul its existence as a moral person and to treat this moral person as a mere thing. Doing so hence contradicts the idea of the original contract, an idea without which no right over a people is conceivable.*

Everyone knows the danger that the presumptive right to this manner of acquisition has brought to Europe — for the custom is unknown in other parts of the world —, even in the most recent times. It is thought that even states can marry one another, in part as a new kind of industry by which one can effortlessly increase one's power through familial alliances, and in part as a means to expand one's land possessions. — The hiring out of the troops

---

*A hereditary kingdom is not a state that can be inherited by another state. Only the right to rule it can be inherited by another physical person. The state thus acquires a ruler, whereas the ruler as such (i.e., who already possesses another kingdom) does not acquire the state.

of one state to another for the purpose of fighting an enemy not common to both parties is a further instance of this. For the subjects are thus treated as objects to be used and used up at will.   8:345

3. "Standing armies (*miles perpetuus*) shall gradually be abolished entirely."

For they continually threaten other states with war by their willingness to appear equipped for it at all times. They prompt other states to outclass each other in the number of those armed for battle, a number that knows no limits. And since the costs associated with maintaining peace will in this way become more oppressive than a brief war, these armies themselves become the cause of offensive wars, carried out in order to diminish this burden. Moreover, being hired out to kill or be killed seems to constitute a use of human beings as mere machines and tools in the hand of another (the state), a use which is incompatible with the rights of humanity in our own person. The situation is quite different, however, when citizens of the state voluntarily and periodically undertake training in the use of weapons in order to protect themselves and their country from attacks from the outside. — It would be precisely the same in the case of hoarding riches, since this would be viewed by other states as a threat of war and would force other states to carry out preemptive attacks (since of the three types of power — *military power,* the *power of alliances,* and the *power of money* — the third may well be the most reliable tool of war), if it were not for the difficulty of assessing the extent of the wealth of a state.

4. "The state shall not contract debts in connection with its foreign affairs."

There is nothing questionable about seeking financial assistance from sources either outside or within the state for the sake of the domestic economy (for the improvement of roadways, for new settlements, for the provision of food reserves for bad harvest years, etc.). But, as an instrument in the struggle of state powers with one another, the credit system, the ingenious invention of a commercially active people in this century, represents a dangerous monetary power. For while the holders of the debts thereby incurred are secured from present claims (since not all creditors demand payment at the same time), these debts can grow without limit. This credit system can be used as a war chest that surpasses in size the wealth of all other states combined and which can be fully exhausted only by the eventual loss of tax revenues (a loss which can nonetheless be staved off for a long period of time by the stimulation of the economy through the effects that the credit system has on industry and commerce). This ease with which one can wage war, combined with the inclination of those in power to do so, an inclination which seems to be an essential aspect of human nature, is thus a great hindrance to perpetual peace. This hindrance ought therefore to be prohibited, and this prohibition ought all the more to serve as the basis of a preliminary article of perpetual peace, since the ultimately unavoidable bankruptcy of one state would necessarily involve other states in the loss, though at no fault of their own, which would thus cause them a public injury. Other states are therefore at least justified in allying themselves against such a state and its presumptuous behavior.

8:346

5. "No state shall forcibly interfere in the constitution and government of another state."

For what can justify its doing so? The offense, perhaps, that it causes the subjects of another state? It can rather serve as a warning, by means of the example of the great ills that a people has brought upon itself through its lawlessness. And, in general, a bad example which one free person sets for another (as *scandalum acceptum*) does not constitute an injury of the latter. — It would be an altogether different matter if a state, through internal conflict, were divided into two parts, each of which regarded itself a separate state that laid claim to the whole. In this case, an external state could not be charged with interference in the constitution of the other by lending assistance to one of these parts, for in this case there is anarchy. But as long as this internal conflict is still undecided, the intervention of external powers would constitute a violation of the rights of a people, a people which is dependent on no other and is merely struggling with its own internal infirmity, and such an intervention would itself therefore be an offense and render the autonomy of all states insecure.

6. "No state shall allow itself such hostilities in wartime as would make mutual trust in a future period of peace impossible. Such acts would include the employment of *assassins (percussores), poisoners (venefici), breach of surrender, incitement of treason (perduellio)* within the enemy state, etc."

These are dishonorable stratagems. For there must remain, even in the middle of war, some degree of trust in the enemy's manner of thinking, since otherwise no peace could possibly be reached, and hostilities would degenerate into a war of extermination (*bellum internecinum*). For war is only the regrettable expedient in the state of nature (where there exists no court that could adjudicate the matter with legal authority) to assert one's rights by means of violence. In war neither of the two parties can be declared an unjust enemy (since such an assessment presupposes a judicial decision). It is rather the *outcome* of the war (or "divine judgment," as it were) which decides whose side is in the right. A punitive war (*bellum punitivum*) between states is inconceivable (since there exists between them no relation of superior to subordinate). From this it follows that a war of extermination, in which both parties and, moreover, all right can be eradicated simultaneously, could bring about perpetual peace only over the great graveyard of humanity. Such a war, therefore, and hence the use of the means which would lead to it, must be utterly forbidden. — But it is clear that the means named above would inevitably lead to such a war of extermination, since once they were used, such diabolical arts, malicious in themselves, would not long hold themselves within the boundaries of war, as for instance with the use of spies (*uti exploratoribus*), where only the dishonorableness of *others* (which can never be fully eliminated) is used; instead, these malicious practices would be carried over into peacetime and thus destroy its purpose altogether.

* * *

Although all the laws cited above are objectively — that is, in the intention of those in power — , purely *prohibitive laws* (*leges prohibitivae*), some of them are nonetheless of a *strictly* valid kind, which are applicable irrespective of circumstances (*leges strictae*), and which require that violations thereof be abolished *immediately* (such as nos. 1, 5, and 6). But others (such as nos. 2, 3, and 4), although not exceptions to the legal rule, nonetheless allow for some subjective latitude with regard to their application, depending on circumstances (*leges latae*) and permit a *postponement* of their execution, as long as one does not lose sight of the end that allows this postponement. The restoration of freedom that has been taken from certain states in accordance with no. 2, for instance, may not be postponed to a nonexistent date (*ad calendas graecas,* as Augustus was in the habit of promising), which would amount to the nonrestoration of those states' freedom. Rather, postponement is permitted only so that such restoration not be implemented too hastily, thus counteracting the very purpose of the legal rule. For the prohibition here concerns only the *manner of acquisition* that is henceforth to be prohibited, but not the *status of possession.* Although it does not have the required legal basis, this status was nonetheless, in public opinion at the time, considered lawful by all states (at the time of the putative acquisition).*

*One has previously doubted, and not without basis, whether there exist, beyond laws of commandment (*leges praeceptivae*) and laws of prohibition (*leges*

Second Section,
Which Contains the Definitive Articles of
8:348   Perpetual Peace Among States

The state of nature (*status naturalis*) is not a state of peace among human
8:349   beings who live next to one another but a state of war, that is, if not always
an outbreak of hostilities, then at least the constant threat of such hostilities.

---

prohibitivae), *laws of permissibility* (*leges permissivae*) based on pure reason.
For all laws imply a ground of objective practical necessity, whereas permission
implies a ground of the practical contingency of certain actions. A *law of permissibility* would therefore imply an obligation to carry out an action to which one cannot
be obligated. And this, if the object of the law has the same meaning in both respects,
would be a contradiction. — But here the prohibition that is presupposed in the law
of permission concerns only the future manner of acquiring a right (e.g., through
inheritance), whereas the exemption from this prohibition, i.e., the permission,
concerns the current status of possession. In accordance with the law of permissibility of natural right, the current state of possession can, in the transition from
the state of nature into the state of civil society, continue to be preserved as an,
although not lawful, nonetheless *honest possession* (*possessio putativa*). This obtains for such a putative possession as soon as it has been recognized as such in the
state of nature, even though a similar manner of acquisition in the subsequent state
of civil society (after the transition) is prohibited. This authorization of continued
possession would not exist if such a putative acquisition had occurred in the state of
civil society. For in the state of civil society such possession would constitute an
injury and have to end immediately after the discovery of its unlawfulness.

I wanted only to draw the attention of teachers of natural law to the concept of a
lex permissiva here, which inevitably offers itself to systematically classifying
reason, primarily since it is frequently used in civil law (statutory law), but with the
difference that the law of prohibition stands on its own, whereas the feature of
permissibility is not introduced into the law as a restrictive condition (as it should
be), but rather is counted among the exceptions. — Here it is said: this or that is
forbidden, *unless* no. 1, no. 2, no. 3, and so on indefinitely, since permissions
become part of law not in accordance with a principle, but rather by probing
among actual cases. For otherwise the conditions would have to have been introduced *into the formulation of the law of prohibition,* which would have rendered it
a law of permissibility. — Therefore it is regrettable that the profound but still
unsolved problem of the prize competition of the wise and astute *Count von
Windischgrätz,*[2] which insisted on precisely the latter, was abandoned so quickly.

Hence the state of peace must be *established*. For refraining from hostilities does not guarantee a state of peace, and when one neighbor does not guarantee the peace of the other (which can occur only in a *juridical* condition), the other neighbor who called upon the first to do so can treat him as an enemy.*

For the possibility of such a formulation (one similar to a mathematical formula) is the only genuine touchstone of a kind of legislation that remains consistent, without which the so-called *ius certum* will always remain a mere pious wish— Otherwise one will have nothing but *general* laws (which are valid *for the most part* [*im Allgemeinen*]), and no universal laws (which are valid *in all cases* [*allgemein*]), as the concept of law seems to require.

2. Joseph Nikolas von Windischgrätz (1744–1802) had proposed a question for a prize essay, namely, how property contracts can be drawn which will be entirely unambiguous and rule out any lawsuits.

*One generally assumes that I may treat no one with hostility except if the other has actively harmed me, and this is completely right, if both parties exist in the *civil juridical* condition. For by entering into this condition, one party guarantees another party the necessary security (by means of the authorities, which have power over both). — But a person (or a people) in a mere state of nature deprives me of this security and harms me through this very state by existing next to me, although not actively (*facto*), nonetheless through the lawlessness of his state (*statu iniusto*), by means of which he represents a constant threat to me. I can thus require of him that he either enter into a state of common civil law or remove himself from my vicinity. — Hence the postulate on which all of the following articles are based is that all people who can mutually exert influence on one another must be party to some civil constitution.

Yet any juridical constitution, with regard to the persons that are subject to it, takes one of the following forms:

1. one based on the right of *citizens of a state* governing the individuals of a people (*ius civitatis*),

2. one based on *international right* governing the relations of states among one another (*ius gentium*),

3. one based on *cosmopolitan right,* to the extent that individuals and states, who are related externally by the mutual exertion of influence on each other, are to be regarded as citizens of a universal state of humankind (*ius cosmopoliticum*). This classification is not arbitrary but necessary with respect to the idea of perpetual peace. For if only one party were able to exercise physical influence on the other and yet were in the state of nature, then this would amount to the state of war, and it is emancipation from precisely this state of war that is the aim here.

FIRST DEFINITIVE ARTICLE OF PERPETUAL PEACE:
THE CIVIL CONSTITUTION OF EVERY STATE
SHALL BE REPUBLICAN

The republican constitution is a constitution that is established, first, according to principles of the *freedom* of the members of a society (as human beings), second, according to principles of the *dependence* of all on a single, common legislation (as subjects), and third, according to the law of the *equality* of the latter (as *citizens of the state*).* The *republican* constitution

8:350

---

*Juridical (and hence external) *freedom* cannot, as one conventionally does, be defined as the authority to do anything that one wants, as long as one does no one any wrong. For what is meant by *authority?* The possibility of an action, insofar as one does no one any wrong in so acting. The definition of *freedom* would thus be as follows: freedom is the ability to act in ways in which one does no one any wrong in so acting. One does no one any wrong (one may do whatever one wants), only to the extent that one does no one any wrong: this is thus an empty tautology. — My external (juridical) *freedom* must rather be described in this way: it is the authority to obey no external laws than those to which I have been able to give consent. — In the same way external (juridical) *equality* in a state is that relationship among citizens of a state according to which no one can place another under a legal obligation without similarly submitting himself to a law according to which he *can* be placed under a similar obligation by the other. (There is no need to describe the principle of *juridical* dependence, since this principle lies in the concept of a state constitution as such). The validity of these innate rights, which necessarily belong to humankind and are inalienable, is confirmed and elevated by the principle of the juridical relations that a human being can have to higher beings (when he conceives of such beings), by imagining himself, in accordance with precisely the same principles, as a citizen of a supersensible world. For, as concerns my freedom, I have no obligation even with regard to the divine laws, which are known to me by means of mere reason, other than the laws I have myself been able to agree to (for I conceive of the divine will only by means of the law of freedom of my own reason in the first place). As far as the principle of equality is concerned, with regard to the most sublime being in the world that I can conceive of outside of God (a great Aeon, for instance), there is no reason why, if I do my duty in my position, as it does in its position, I should only have to the duty to obey, while the former is entitled to the right to command. — The reason that this principle of *equality* does not apply (as with the principle of freedom) to the relationship to God is that this being is the only one where the concept of duty ends.

But as concerns the right of equality of all citizens as subjects, answering the question of the coincidental nature of *hereditary nobility* is solely a matter of

is the only kind of constitution that follows from the idea of an original contract, upon which all laws legislated by a people must be based, and is therefore, as concerns right, itself the one on which all the civil constitutions are originally based. Now it is just a question of whether the republican constitution is also the only kind that can lead toward perpetual peace.   8:351

Besides the purity of its origin, that is, its having sprung from the pure source of the concept of right, the republican constitution also offers the prospect for the desired consequence, namely, perpetual peace. The reason for this is as follows: if (as must be the case in such a constitution) the agreement of the citizens is required to decide whether or not one ought to wage war, then nothing is more natural than that they would consider very carefully whether to enter into such a terrible game, since they would have to resolve to bring the hardships of war upon themselves (which would include: themselves fighting, paying the costs of the war from their own possessions, meagerly repairing the ravages that war leaves behind, and, finally, on top of all such malady, assuming a burden of debt that embitters the peace and will never be repaid [due to imminent, constantly impending wars]). By contrast, in the case of a constitution where the subject is not a citizen of the state, that is, in one which is not republican, declaring war is the easiest thing in the world, because the head of state is not a fellow citizen, but rather the owner of the state, and hence forfeits nothing of his feasts, hunts, summer residences, court festivals, and such things due to the war. The head of state can decide to wage war for insignificant reasons as a kind of game for amusement and can, for the sake of decency, indifferently leave its justification up to his diplomatic corps, which always stands ready for such tasks.

* * *

whether the *rank* granted by the state (of one subject above another) must precede *merit* or merit must precede rank. — So much is clear: that if rank is associated with birth, then it is not at all certain whether merit (skill in and loyalty to one's office) will also follow. This therefore amounts to the favored one being granted his position (to be commander) without any prior merit. This is something which the general will of the people would never agree upon in an original contract (which is, however, the principle of all rights). For a nobleman is not consequentially a *noble* man. — As concerns *nobility of office* (which one could call the rank of a high magistrate, and which one must acquire by means of one's merits), the associated rank does not adhere to the person like property, but rather to the position, and the law of equality is not thereby violated. This is so because when they resign from their office, they also resign from the rank assigned to it and return to the people.

The following clarifications must be offered, so that one does not (as often happens) confuse the republican constitution with the democratic constitution. The forms that a state (*civitas*) takes can be classified either according to the persons who hold the position of highest authority in the state or according to the *manner* in which the head of state *governs* the people (whoever the head of state may be). The former is properly called the *form of sovereignty* (*forma imperii*), and only three such forms are possible, since either only *one* person, a *group* of associated persons, or *everyone* who makes up the civil society can possess sovereign power (autocracy, aristocracy, and democracy; the authority of the monarch, of the nobility, or of the people). The second is the *form of government* (*forma regiminis*) and concerns the manner, based on the constitution (the act of general will by which a crowd becomes a people), in which the state makes use of its power. The state is, in this regard, either *republican* or *despotic. Republicanism* is the principle by which the executive power (the government) of a state is separated from the legislative power. Despotism is the principle by which the state executes, on its own authority, laws that it has itself made. Under despotism the public will is therefore treated by the monarch as his individual will. Among the three forms of state, *democracy* is, according to the proper sense of the term, necessarily a form of *despotism,* because it establishes an executive power whereby "all" make decisions over, and if necessary, against one (who therefore does not agree). Thus "all" who are not actually all make decisions, which means that the general will stands in contradiction with itself and with freedom.

Any form of government that is not *representative* is, properly speaking, without form. This is so because one and the same person can be legislator and executor of his will at the same time just as little as the universal of the major premise in a syllogism can at the same time be the subsumption of the particular under it in the minor premise. And although the two other forms of sovereignty [that is, autocracy and aristocracy] are always imperfect to the extent that they allow for a despotic form of government, it is at least possible that these two forms assume a form of government that is in accordance with the *spirit* of a representative system. Thus Frederick II[3] at least *said* that he was merely the highest servant of the state.* The democratic

___

3. Friedrich II ("the Great") (1712–86), king of Prussia from 1740 to 1786.

*The lofty designations often given to a ruler (that of one who is divinely anointed, of embodiment and representative of the divine will on earth) are often criticized as coarse, dizzying blandishments, but, I think, wrongly so. — It is far from the case that these should make the ruler of the land arrogant, rather they

form of sovereignty, by contrast, makes this impossible, because under it
everyone wishes to be the ruler. — One can therefore say: the smaller the
personnel exercising state power (the number of rulers), and the greater
its representativeness, the more the constitution of the state tends toward
republicanism, and the more it can hope to raise itself to republicanism
through gradual reforms. For this reason it is more difficult under aristocracy than under monarchy, yet impossible under democracy, to achieve this,
the only perfectly juridical constitution, by any means other than violent
revolution. But the form of government* is of incomparably greater concern to the people than the form of state (although very much does indeed
depend on the degree to which the latter is fit for the purpose of attaining the
end of such a constitution). If it is to be in accordance with the concept of
right, the form of government must include a representative system, the

necessarily humble him in his soul if he has intellect (which one must certainly
assume) and considers that he has taken on an office that is too great for a human
being, namely, to administer the holiest thing that God has on earth, the *rights of
human beings,* and that he must be concerned at all times that he not offend God's
most treasured possession.

*In his seemingly brilliant, yet ultimately hollow and meaningless words, Mal-
let du Pan boasts that many years of experience have finally led him to be convinced
of the truth of the following well-known saying by *Pope:* "For forms of government
let fools contest; whate'er is best administered is best."[4] If this is meant to express
that the best administered government is administered best, then he has, as Swift
would say, bitten open a nut only to find a maggot therein. But if this is meant to say
that the best administered government is also the best manner of governing, i.e., the
best state constitution, then the saying is fundamentally false, since examples of
good governments do not demonstrate anything about the manner of governing. —
Who ruled better than a *Titus* and a *Marcus Aurelius?* Yet the former left *Domitian*
as his successor, and the latter *Commodus.*[5] This could not have happened had there
been a good state constitution in place, since their unsuitability for the post was
known from early on, and the ruler's power was also sufficient to exclude them.

4. Jacques Mallet du Pan (1749–1800), *Über die französische Revolution und die
Ursachen ihrer Dauer,* trans. from the French by Friedrich Gentz (Berlin, 1794) [*Con-
sidérations sur la revolution de France et sur les causes qui en prolongent la durée*
(Brussels, 1793)].

Alexander Pope, *Essay on Man* (London, 1734), Epistle 3, 303–4.

5. Titus (39–81; ruled 79–81) and Marcus Aurelius (121–180, ruled 161–180),
Roman emperors with a reputation of beneficence; Domitianus (51–96; ruled 81–96) and
Commodus (161–192; ruled 180–192), Roman emperors with a reputation of cruelty.

only kind of system in which a republican form of government is possible, and without which the government will be despotic and violent (whatever form the constitution may be). This system was not known to any of the old, so-called republics, and it is for this reason that they simply had to dissolve into despotism, which, under the rule of a single individual, is still the most tolerable kind of all.

8:354   SECOND DEFINITIVE ARTICLE OF PERPETUAL PEACE: INTERNATIONAL RIGHT SHALL BE BASED ON THE *FEDERALISM* OF FREE STATES

Peoples, as states, can be judged as individual human beings who, when in the state of nature (that is, when they are independent from external laws), bring harm to each other already through their proximity to one another, and each of whom, for the sake of his own security, can and ought to demand of others that they enter with him into a constitution, similar to that of a civil one, under which each is guaranteed his rights. This would constitute a *federation of peoples,* which would not, however, necessarily be a state of peoples. Herein would lie a contradiction, because every state involves the relation between a *superior* (who legislates) and a *subject* (who obeys, namely, the people), whereas many peoples within one state would make only one people, which contradicts the presupposition (since we are to consider the right of *peoples* in relation to one another here insofar as they make up so many different states and are not to be fused together into one state).

We view with great disdain the way in which savages cling to their lawless freedom, preferring to fight continually amongst one another rather than submit to a lawful coercion that they themselves establish, and thereby favoring mad freedom over rational freedom. We consider this a barbaric, unrefined, and a brutish denigration of humanity. One would thus think, then, that civilized peoples (each united into a state) would be in a hurry to emerge from such a depraved condition as soon as possible. Instead, however, each *state* sees its majesty (for it would be nonsensical to speak of the majesty of the people) in its being subject to no external legal coercion, and the splendor of its head as consisting in his having many thousands at his disposal to have sacrificed for a cause that does not concern them at all, without him being required to place himself in jeopardy.* The main differ-

---

*In this spirit a Bulgarian prince gave the following answer to the Greek emperor, who had good-naturedly offered to settle their quarrel by means of a duel:

ence between the European and the American savages is that while many of the tribes of the latter have been entirely eaten by their enemies, the former know how to put their conquered to better use than to consume them, and prefer to increase the numbers of their subjects and hence also the number   8:355 of tools at their disposal for even more extensive wars.

The maliciousness of human nature, although quite concealed by the coercion of government in the state of civil law, can be observed openly in the free relations between the peoples. It is therefore astonishing that the word *right* has not yet been able to be fully banished from war politics as pedantic, and that no state has yet dared to publicly endorse doing so. For while *Hugo Grotius, Pufendorf, Vattel*[6] and many others (all tiresome comforters) are still faithfully cited to *justify* an offensive war, even though their codex, whether formulated philosophically or diplomatically, does not have the least amount of *legal* force and cannot have such force (since states as such are not subject to common external coercion), there is no example of a state having ever been moved by arguments armed with the testimony of such important men to desist from its intentions. — This homage paid by every state to the concept of right (at least through their words), demonstrates, however, that there is an even greater, although presently latent, moral predisposition to be found in the human being, to eventually overcome the evil principle within himself (the existence which he cannot deny) and also to hope that others do the same. For otherwise of states who wish to feud with one another would never utter the word *right,* except to use it in jest, as a Gallic prince once declared: "It is the prerogative that nature has given the stronger that the weaker ought to obey him."

Although states can pursue their rights only through war, and never by means of a trial before an external tribunal, war and its favorable conclusion — *victory* — never determines right. And while a *peace treaty* achieves an end to the present war, it does not achieve an end to the state of war (always allowing a pretext to be found for a new war). The state of war cannot

---

"A blacksmith who has tongs will not use his own hands to grab the red-hot iron from the embers."

6. Hugo Grotius (1583–1645), *De jure belli ac pacis libri tres* [Of the Law of War and Peace] (1625); Samuel von Pufendorf (1632–94), *De iure naturae et gentium* [Of Natural Law and the Law of Nations] (1672); Emerich de Vattel (1714–67), *Le droit des gens ou Principes de la loi naturelle appliqués à la conduite et aux affaires des nations et des souverains* [The Law of Nations, or Principles of the Law of Nature, Applied to the Conduct and the Affairs of Nations and Sovereigns] (1758).

exactly be declared unjust, however, since in this situation each state acts as judge in its own case. Yet what applies under natural law to human beings in the lawless condition, namely, that they "ought to emerge from this condition," cannot also apply to states under international right (since, as states, they already have an internal legal constitution and have thus outgrown the coercion by which others subject them to a broader legal constitution according to others' conception of right). Nonetheless, from the throne of the highest moral legislative authority, reason looks down on and condemns war as a means of pursuing one's rights, and makes peace an immediate duty. But peace can be neither brought about nor secured without a treaty among peoples, and for this reason a special sort of federation must be created, which one might call a *pacific federation* (*foedus pacificum*). This federation would be distinct from a *peace treaty* (*pactum pacis*) in that it seeks to end not merely *one* war, as does the latter, but rather to end *all* wars forever. This federation aims not at the state's acquisition of some sort of power, but rather at its securing and maintaining the *freedom* of a state for itself and also the freedom of other confederated states without these states thereby being required, as are human beings in the state of nature, to subject themselves to public laws and coercion under such laws. It can be shown that the idea of *federalism,* which should gradually encompass all states and thereby lead to perpetual peace, is practicable (that is, has objective reality). For if fortune so determines that a powerful and enlightened people can constitute itself as a republic (which according to its nature necessarily tends toward perpetual peace), then this republic provides a focus point for other states, so that they might join this federative union and thereby secure the condition of peace among states in accordance with the idea of international right and gradually extend this union further and further through several such associations.

It is understandable that a people would say: "There shall be no war among us, for we desire to form ourselves into a state, that is, to establish a supreme legislative, executive, and judicial authority over ourselves that will settle our disputes in a peaceful manner." But when this state says: "There shall be no war between myself and other states, even though I acknowledge no superior legislative authority that guarantees me my rights and to which I guarantee them theirs," then it is not at all clear what the confidence in my own rights is based on, if not on a surrogate for the compact of civil society, namely, a free federalism, which reason must necessarily connect with the concept of international right, if the latter is to mean anything at all.

8:356

One cannot conceive of international right as a right *to* war (since this would be a presumptive right to determine what is right, not according to universally valid external laws that restrict the freedom of every individual, but rather by means of violence, according to one-sided maxims); one would have to mean by it that it is perfectly just that people who are so disposed annihilate each other and thereby find perpetual peace in the vast grave that covers all the horrors of violence together with their perpetrators. As concerns the relations among states, according to reason there can be no other way for them to emerge from the lawless condition, which contains only war, than for them to relinquish, just as do individual human beings, their wild (lawless) freedom, to accustom themselves to public binding laws, and to thereby form a *state of peoples* (*civitas gentium*), which, continually expanding, would ultimately comprise all of the peoples of the world. But since they do not, according to their conception of international right, want the positive idea of a *world republic* at all (thus rejecting *in hypothesi* what is right *in thesi*),[7] only the *negative* surrogate of a lasting and continually expanding *federation* that prevents war can curb the inclination to hostility and defiance of the law, though there is the constant threat of its breaking loose again (*Furor impius intus — fremit horridus ore cruento.* Virgil).[8]*

8:357

*It may not be at all improper for a nation to announce, when concluding peace, a day of repentance to follow the festival of thanksgiving for the victory in war, during which it would appeal to the heavens in the name of the state for mercy for the great sin that the human race commits again and again by not desiring to submit to a legal constitution governing the relations among states, and instead, proud of its independence, making use of the barbaric means of war (which does not even achieve what is sought after, namely, the rights of each individual state). — The festivals of thanksgiving for a *victory* during a war, the hymns sung (in the style of the Israelites) to the *Lord of Hosts,* stand in no less sharp a contrast to the moral idea of the Father of mankind, because they, beyond their indifference toward the manner in which peoples seek to attain their mutual rights (which itself is lamentable enough), also take pleasure in having annihilated a great number of human beings or their fortune.

7. In "On the Common Saying" Kant explains this terminology: *in thesi* means "in theory," *in hypothesi* is equivalent to "in practice," TP 8:276.

8. "Within, impious rage . . . roars savagely with bloody lips," Virgil, *Aeneid* 1.294–96.

THIRD DEFINITIVE ARTICLE OF PERPETUAL PEACE: *COSMOPOLITAN RIGHT* SHALL BE LIMITED TO THE CONDITIONS OF UNIVERSAL *HOSPITALITY*

As in the previous articles, we are concerned here with *right,* not with philanthropy, and in this context *hospitality* (a host's conduct to his guest) means the right of a stranger not to be treated in a hostile manner by another upon his arrival on the other's territory. If it can be done without causing his death, the stranger can be turned away, yet as long as the stranger behaves peacefully where he happens to be, his host may not treat him with hostility. It is not the *right of a guest* that the stranger has a claim to (which would require a special, charitable contract stipulating that he be made a member of the household for a certain period of time), but rather a right to visit, to which all human beings have a claim, to present oneself to society by virtue of the right of common possession of the surface of the earth. Since it is the surface of a sphere, they cannot scatter themselves on it without limit, but they must rather ultimately tolerate one another as neighbors, and originally no one has more of a right to be at a given place on earth than anyone else. — Uninhabitable parts of this surface, the sea and the deserts, separate this community, but in such a way that the *ship* or the *camel* (the ship of the desert) makes it possible to come into contact with one another across these regions that belong to no one, and to use the right to the *surface,* which is common to the human species, to establish commerce with one another. The inhospitableness of the sea coastlines (for example, of the Barbary Coast), where ships in nearby seas are pirated or stranded sailors are made into slaves, or the inhospitableness of the sand deserts (of the Arabic Bedouins), where contact with the nomadic tribes is regarded as a right to plunder them, is contrary to natural right. The right of hospitality, that is, the right of foreign arrivals, pertains, however, only to conditions of the possibility of *attempting* interaction with the old inhabitants. — In this way, remote parts of the world can establish relations peacefully with one another, relations which ultimately become regulated by public laws and can thus finally bring the human species ever closer to a cosmopolitan constitution.

If one compares with this the *inhospitable* behavior of the civilized states in our part of the world, especially the commercial ones, the injustice that the latter show when *visiting* foreign lands and peoples (which to them is one and the same as *conquering* those lands and peoples) takes on terrifying proportions. America, the negro countries, the Spice Islands, the Cape, etc., were at the time of their discovery lands that they regarded as belong-

8:358

ing to no one, for the native inhabitants counted as nothing to them. In East India (Hindustan) they brought in foreign troops under the pretext of merely intending to establish trading posts. But with these they introduced the oppression of the native inhabitants, the incitement of the different states involved to expansive wars, famine, unrest, faithlessness, and the whole litany of evils that weigh upon the human species.

8:359

China* and Japan (*Nipon*), which have attempted dealing with such

*In order to call this great empire by the name it gives itself (namely, *China,* not *Sina,* or any other sound similar to this), one need only refer to Georgius's *Alphabetum Tibetanum,* pp. 651–54, note b in particular. Actually it uses no particular name to refer to itself, according to Professor *Fischer* from Petersburg;[9] the most common is the word *Kin,* which means gold (the Tibetans express this with *Ser*), which explains why the emperor is called the King of *Gold* (of the most magnificent land in the world). In the empire itself, however, this word probably sounds like *Chin,* which is pronounced by the Italian missionaries as *Kin* (due to their inability to pronounce the guttural consonant *ch*). — This leads one to conclude that the Land of the People of *Ser,* as it was referred to by the Romans, was China, but silk was transported via *Greater Tibet* to Europe (presumably through *Lesser Tibet,* Bukhara, Persia, and so on), which has led to many speculations about the age of this astonishing state in comparison to that of Hindustan by means of its association with *Tibet* and, through the latter, with Japan. The name *Sina* or *Tschina,* on the other hand, which neighboring territories give this land, leads to no such connection.– –Perhaps the ancient, although never widely known connection between Europe and Tibet also can be explained by what has been passed on to us by *Hesychius* regarding this, namely, the Hierophant's call (*Konx Ompax*) in the *Eleusinian Mysteries* (cf. *Journey of the Young Anacharsis,* part 5, p. 447 et seq.). For according to Georgius's *Alphabetum Tibetanum,* the word *concioa* means *God,* which bears a striking similarity to *Konx,* whereas *Pah-cio* (ibid., p. 520), which the Greeks may well have pronounced like *pax,* means *promulgator legis,* the divinity that suffuses all of nature (also called *Cencresi,* p. 177). — But *Om,* which La Croze translates as *benedictus* (*blessed*), applied to divinity, can hardly mean anything other than the *beatific* (p. 507). Yet given that Father Francisco Orazio, having often asked the Tibetan *Lamas* what they understood God (*Concioa*) to be, always received the following answer: "*It is the gathering of all blessed ones*" (i.e., of all the blessed souls that have returned to the deity through rebirth as the lama after many migrations through all manner of bodies, and thus as *Burchans,* souls transformed into beings worthy of adoration [p. 223]), the mysterious word *Konx Ompax* is likely to mean the *holy* (Konx), *blessed* (Om), and *wise* (Pax) highest beings existent throughout the entirety of the world (personified

guests, have therefore, wisely, limited such interaction. Whereas the former has allowed contact with, but not entrance to its territories, the latter has allowed this contact to only one European people, the Dutch, yet while doing so it excludes them, as if they were prisoners, from associating with the native inhabitants. The worst part of this (or, from the standpoint of a moral judge, the best part) is that they do not even profit from this violence, that all of these trading companies stand near the point of collapse, that the Sugar Islands, that seat of the cruelest and most premeditated form of slavery, do not yield any real return, but rather serve, only indirectly, a not very commendable purpose, namely, of training sailors for the navies, and hence ultimately serve the warfare in Europe, doing this for powers which make much ado about their piety, and who, while drinking injustice like water, consider their being the chosen ones to be a matter of orthodoxy.

8:360

The growing prevalence of a (narrower or wider) community among the peoples of the earth has now reached a point at which the violation of right at any *one* place on the earth is felt in *all* places. For this reason the idea of cosmopolitan right is no fantastic or exaggerated conception of right.

---

nature) and, as used in the Greek *Mysteries,* likely referred to the *monotheism* of the epopts in contrast to the *polytheism* of the people, even though Father *Orazio* (loc. cit.) detected a variety of atheism here.[10] — But how that mysterious word came to the Greeks via Tibet can be explained in the aforementioned manner and, conversely, make a case for Europe's early contact with China through Tibet (a connection perhaps even more likely than that with Hindustan).

9. Antonio Agostino Giorgi (1711–97), *Alphabetum Tibetanum missionum apostolicarum commodo editum* [Tibetan Dictionary Published for the Convenience of Apostolic Missions] (Rome, 1762), a Latin-Tibetan dictionary, based in part on works of Francesco Orazio (see below).

Johann Eberhard Fischer (1697–1771), *Quaestiones Petropolitanae* [Questions from St. Petersburg] (Göttingen, 1770).

10. Hesychius of Alexandria, fifth- or sixth-century grammarian who compiled a Greek dictionary.

Hierophant: in ancient Greece, leader of the Eleusinian cult.

Jean-Jacques Barthélemy, *Voyage du jeune Anacharsis en Grèce, dans le milieu du quatrième siècle avant l"ere vulgaire,* 5 vols. [Travels of the Young Anacharsis through Greece, in the Middle of the Fourth Century before the Beginning of the Common Era] (Paris, 1788).

Mathurin Veyssière de La Croze (1661–1739), Benedictine monk and historian.

Francisco Orazio (1680–1747), Capuchin monk who provided descriptions of life in Tibet, where he lived from 1716 to 1732.

Rather it is a necessary supplement to the unwritten code of constitutional and international right, for public human right in general, and hence for perpetual peace. Only under this condition can one flatter oneself to be continually progressing toward perpetual peace.

First Supplement:
On the Guarantee of Perpetual Peace

What *guarantees* perpetual peace is nothing less than the great artist *nature* (*natura daedala rerum*). The mechanical course of nature visibly reveals a purposive plan to create harmony through discord among people, even against their own will. Thus, if understood to be the compelling force of a cause whose laws of operation are unknown to us, this plan is called   8:361 *Fate*. But if, upon consideration of nature's purposiveness in the course of the world, it is understood as the underlying wisdom of a higher cause which is directed toward the objective final end of the human species and which predetermines this course of events in the world, this plan is called *Providence*.* To be sure, we do not actually *cognize* it as such based on the   8:362

*In the mechanism of nature, to which the human being (as a sensible being) belongs, a form is evident which is fundamental to its existence, and which we can make comprehensible in no other way than by attributing it to the design of an author of the world who determined it in advance. We call this predetermination (divine) *providence*. To the extent that it is ascribed to the *beginning* of the world, we call it *founding providence* (*providentia conditrix; semel iussit, semper parent,* — Augustine).[11] Insofar as it is understood to maintain this design through the *course* of nature in accordance with purposive universal laws, we call it *ruling providence* (*providentia gubernatrix*). Furthermore, with regard to particular ends which cannot be foreseen by human beings, but rather can only be presumed on the basis of the result, we call it *guiding providence* (*providentia directrix*). Finally, with regard to specific events as divine ends, we no longer call it *providence* but rather *dispensation* (*directio extraordinaria*). But to identify it as such is a foolish presumption of humankind (since it points to miracles, even though the events themselves are not called this). For to infer a particular principle of the effective cause from an individual event (i.e., to infer that this event itself is the end and not merely the side effect, by the mechanism of nature, of another end that is completely unknown to us) is illogical and displays self-conceit, however piously and humbly one may speak about it. — It is equally false and self-contradictory to distinguish between *general* and *particular* providence (considered *materially*) in terms of *ob-*

artifices of nature or *infer* its existence on the basis of such artifices, but rather (as in all relations in general between the form of things and ends) can and need only *add* it *in thought* in order to conceive of their possibility according to the analogy of human acts of artifice. To imagine the relation between these acts and their movement in concert toward the end that

---

jects in the world (e.g., to argue that providence takes care to preserve the species of creatures but surrenders individuals to chance). For the point of calling providence general is that no single thing be considered to be excepted from it. — Presumably one intended to distinguish providence (considered *formally*) according to the manner in which it seeks its ends, namely, between *ordinary* (e.g., the annual death and rebirth of nature after the change of the seasons) and *extraordinary* providence (e.g., the transport of wood by sea currents to Arctic coasts where it cannot grow, but where it is needed by the inhabitants there, who could not live without it). Although we can readily explain the physical-mechanical cause of these events (e.g., by the wooded riverbanks of the temperate lands, where trees fall into the water and are carried away by the Gulf Stream, for instance), we may not overlook the teleological cause, which points to the provisions of a wisdom that holds sway over nature. — But the conception widespread in the academic world of a divine *concurrence* or collaboration (*concursus*) with effects in the sensible world must be discarded. For to conjoin dissimilar kinds of things (*gryphes iungere equis* [coupling griffins with horses]) by saying that the one who himself is the complete cause of changes in the world would need to *complete* his own predetermining providence during the course of the world (which must therefore have been incomplete), e.g., to say that in addition to God the doctor healed the patient, that is, was present as assistant, is *first of all* self-contradictory. For *causa solitaria non iuvat* [a solitary cause does not help]. God is the originator of the doctor and all of his remedies, and therefore, if we wish to ascend to the highest but theoretically incomprehensible first cause, we must attribute the effect *fully* to him. Or we can ascribe the effect *fully* to the doctor, to the extent that we track the event in the chain of causes in the world as explicable according to the natural order. *Second,* this manner of thinking denies us any definite principles for judging effects. But from a *moral-practical* perspective (which refers exclusively to the transcendent world), e.g., in the belief that, if only our disposition is genuine, God will supplement our imperfect justice even by means incomprehensible to us, and that we therefore ought not flag in our striving toward the good, then the concept of divine concursus is quite fitting and even necessary. It is self-evident, however, that no one must try to *explain* a good action (as an event in the world) in these terms, since such an explanation would allegedly be theoretical cognition of the supersensible, which is an incongruous claim.

11. "It commands once and they obey forever." The quote may actually stem from

reason dictates to us immediately (the moral end) is an idea that is transcendent from a *theoretical* perspective. From a practical perspective, however (for example, in view of the concept of *perpetual peace* and the duty to work toward it by using that mechanism of nature), this idea is dogmatic and its reality is well established. — The use of the word *nature* is also, when speaking here merely of theory (not of religion), more appropriate for denoting the limits of human reason (as reason, regarding the relation of effects to their causes, must confine itself within the limits of possible experience) and *more modest* than the expression of a *providence* that is knowable to us. With an expression such as Providence one presumptuously fits oneself with the wings of Icarus, in order to approach the secret of its inscrutable intention.

Before we describe this guarantee in more detail it will be necessary first to examine the state in which nature has placed the actors on her vast stage which ultimately makes securing peace necessary, — only then will we look   8:363 at how this guarantee is provided.

Nature has made the following provisional arrangements:

1. She has made it possible for human beings to live in all the regions of the earth that they populate;
2. Through *war,* she has driven humankind in all directions, even into the most inhospitable regions, in order to populate them;
3. And through war she has compelled them to enter into more or less legal relations with one another.

It is remarkable that moss grows even in cold wastelands of the Arctic, which the *reindeer* digs out from under the snow, only to serve the Ostiaks or Samoyeds in turn as nourishment or as draft animal, or that the salty, sandy deserts are home to the *camel,* which seems virtually made for traversing the same, in order to not leave them unused. But nature's end becomes even more apparent when one becomes aware that in addition to the furry animals that live along the coastlines of the Arctic waters, seals, walruses, and whales provide the inhabitants of those regions, by means of their flesh and their fat, with nourishment and fuel. But the most astonishing sign of the provisions that nature makes is the driftwood that she brings to these barren regions (while it is unclear precisely where it comes from), without which the inhabitants would be able to build neither their car-

---

Seneca, instead of Augustine. Cf. Seneca, *De Providentia* 5.8, "*semper paret, semel iussit,*" which has a slightly different meaning: "he obeys forever, he commanded once."

riages and weapons nor their huts for dwelling in. Occupied enough with their struggle against the animals that live there, the inhabitants coexist peacefully. — What originally *drove* them *into* these regions, however, is presumably nothing other than war. But the first *tool of war* among the animals that humankind learned to tame and domesticate in the time that it has populated the earth, is the horse (the elephant came at a later time, a time of luxury for previously established states), just as the art of cultivating certain types of grass — the original composition of which is no longer knowable to us — known as *grains,* or the production and refinement of *species of fruit* by means of transplanting and grafting (in Europe this was done with perhaps only two species, crab apples and pears), was possible only with previously established states in which ownership of land was secure, — after humankind had earlier made its way from the lawless freedom of *hunting,** fishing, and shepherding to a life sustained by *agriculture,* and then *salt and iron* had been discovered, which perhaps became the first widely sought after articles of trade among the different peoples. It was trade that first brought them into *peaceful relations* with one another and thereby into relationships based on mutual consent, community, and peaceful interactions even with remote peoples.

8:364

By ensuring that human beings *could* live anywhere on earth, nature has also willed in a despotic fashion that they *ought* to live all over the earth, even against their own inclination, without any assumption that this *ought* implies a duty to do so in order to comply with a moral law. — Rather, nature has chosen war in order to attain this end. — We can observe peoples for whom the uniformity of their extraction can be established on the basis of the uniformity of their language, as is the case, for instance, with the Samoyeds of the Arctic Ocean, on the one hand, and a people with a similar language that lives two hundred miles away in the Altai Mountains, on the other. In this case another people, specifically the Mongolians, a mounted

---

*Of all ways of life, *hunting* is doubtless the most contrary to a civilized constitution. This is so because here the families must separate and they soon become estranged and, consequently, scattered about in extensive forests, *hostile* toward one another, since each of them requires a great deal of space in order to secure sustenance and clothing for themselves. — The *prohibition of eating blood* that was issued to Noah (Genesis 9:4–6), which, often reiterated, was imposed upon the heathens newly converted to Christianity by Jewish Christendom, albeit with a different intention (Acts 15:20, 21:25), seems to have originally been nothing other than a prohibition of the *hunter's way of life,* since the hunter must often eat raw meat, and the prohibition of eating raw meat would thus imply a prohibition of hunting.

and hence warlike people, has thrust itself in between and thus has scattered the one part of the tribe from the other into the most inhospitable, icy regions, where it certainly would not have ventured out of its own inclination.* — The same is true of the Finns that live in the northernmost region of Europe, the Lapps, with regard to the equally remote Hungarians, whose language is related to theirs, but from whom they are separated by   8:365
Gothic and Sarmatic peoples, who forced themselves between the two. And could there be any other explanation for the situation of the Eskimos (perhaps ancient European adventurers, a race fully distinct from all Americans) in the north, and that of the Pescharais in the south of America, down to Tierra del Fuego, than that nature has used war as the means to populate all of the regions of the earth? Yet war has no need of a particular motivating reason, but rather seems to have been embedded in human nature, and seems even to count as something noble, something which the human being is animated to pursue by the lust for honor without any self-serving motivation. This would explain why the *warlike spirit* (in the case of the native American savages as well as in the case of those in Europe during the age of chivalry) is judged to be of immediate and great value, not only *during* war (as is rightly expected), but also *in order that* there may be war. Often enough war has been started only in order to demonstrate this military courage, from which follows that an inner *dignity* is attributed to war as such. Even philosophers have been known to eulogize war as a form of ennobling humankind, disregarding the Greek saying: "What makes war such a bad thing is that it creates more evil people than it does away with." So much for what nature does to pursue *its own end* with regard to the human species as a class of animal.

The question now at hand concerns the essence with regard to perpetual peace: what nature does in this regard, or to be precise, with regard to the end that their own reason makes into a duty for human beings, and hence to

*One could ask: if nature has willed that these Artic coastlines should not remain uninhabited, what will become of its inhabitants, when nature stops supplying them (as is to be expected) with driftwood? For it is reasonable to assume that in the wake of the advance of culture the inhabitants of the temperate zones of the earth will make better use of the wood that grows on its river banks, not letting it fall into the rivers and float away into the sea. My answer to this question is as follows: those who inhabit the regions along the Ob, the Yenisei, the Lena, etc., will supply it to them by means of trade, in exchange for products from the animal kingdom, of which the sea in the Arctic regions has such a great wealth, but only after nature has first compelled them to establish peace among themselves.

further their moral aim; and how nature guarantees that that which human beings *ought* to do in accordance with the laws of freedom, but which they do not do, can be secured without injuring this freedom even through nature's compelling them to do so, and specifically with regard to all three types of public right, *constitutional right, international right,* and *cosmopolitan right.* — When I say that nature *wills* that this or that ought to happen, I do not mean that she imposes a *duty* upon us to act thus (for this can only be done by practical reason acting free of compulsion), but rather that she *does* it herself, regardless of whether we will it so or not (*fata volentem ducunt, nolentem trahunt*).[12]

1. Even if a people is not compelled by internal differences to submit itself to the compulsion of public laws, then war from outside would submit it to such a compulsion by means of that arrangement of nature mentioned above, according to which every people is confronted with another neighboring people that presses it, and against which it must form itself into a *state,* in order to be prepared, as a *power,* to defend itself against the other. The *republican* constitution is the only form thereof that is in perfect accordance with the right of humankind, but it is also the most difficult constitution to establish, and even more so to preserve, and to such an extent that many assert that it would have to be a state of *angels,* because human beings would be incapable of a constitution of such a sublime nature, given their selfish inclinations. But nature comes to the aid of that revered, but practically impotent general will that is rationally grounded, and does so by means of precisely the same selfish inclinations, such that what is of paramount importance in organizing the state well (an organization which lies with the capacity of humankind, to be sure) is that the state directs the forces within it against each other in such a way that the one hinders or nullifies the destructive effects of the other. Thus, the result for reason turns out as if neither existed and the human being, if not exactly a morally good person, is nonetheless forced to be a good citizen.

Establishing a state, as difficult as it may sound, is a problem that can be solved even for a nation of devils (if only they possess understanding). The problem is as follows: "To form a group of rational beings, which, as a group, require universal laws for their preservation, of which each member is, however, secretly inclined to make an exception of himself, and to organize them and arrange a constitution for them in such a way that, although they strive against each other in their private intentions, the latter

---

12. "The Fates lead the willing but drag the unwilling." Seneca, *Epistles* 107.11. Also quoted in TP 8:313.

check each other in such a way that the result in their public conduct is just as if they had no such evil intentions." It must be possible to *solve* such a problem. For it is not precisely how to attain the moral improvement of the human being that we must know, but rather only how to use the mechanism of nature on human beings in order to direct the conflict between their hostile intentions in a people in such a way that they compel each other to submit themselves to coercive laws and thereby bring about the condition of peace in which laws are in force. In the case of actually existing, however imperfectly organized states one can also observe this, in that in their external conduct they already closely approximate what the idea of right prescribes, although an inner morality is certainly not the cause of this conduct (and it should not be expected that a good state constitution would arise from an inner morality, but rather conversely that the good moral education of a people would follow the former). Hence reason can use the mechanism of nature, in the form of selfish inclinations, which by their nature oppose one another even externally, as a means to make room for reason's own end, legal regulation, and to thereby promote and secure, 8:367 insofar as it is within the power of the state to do so, both internal and external peace. — This is the essence of the matter: Nature wills irresistibly that right ultimately attains supreme authority. Whatever one neglects to accomplish in this regard will ultimately take care of itself, although with a great deal of trouble. "If you bend a cane too much, it will break; and if you attempt too much, you attempt nothing" (*Bouterwek*).[13]

2. The idea of international right presupposes the *separation* of several independent, neighboring states from one another. And although such a state of affairs in itself is already a state of war (if a federative union of these states does not prevent the outbreak of hostilities), even this state of war is, according to the idea of reason, better than the blending of these states into a power that overgrows the existing ones and ultimately turns into a universal monarchy. This is so because laws increasingly lose their force as the borders of a government are extended, and a soulless despotism, after having eliminated the seeds of good, ultimately declines into anarchy. Yet this is the aim of every state (or of its leader), to enter into a condition of lasting peace in this way, such that it might eventually rule the entire world. But nature *wants it* differently. She avails herself of two means of keeping peoples from intermixing and of separating them: differences in *languages*

13. Friedrich Bouterwek (1766–1828), philosopher and author of literary works. The source of the quote has not (yet) been determined.

and *religions.** These kinds of difference have the tendency to lead to mutual hatred and serve as a pretext for war, but in the wake of increasing culture and humankind's gradually coming within reach of an agreement regarding their principles, they lead to mutual understanding and agreement to peace. Yet this peace is not, as with the aforementioned despotism (in the graveyard of freedom), brought about and secured by the weakening of all energies, but rather by means of the liveliest competition among the same.

8:368

3. Just as nature has wisely divided the peoples from one another, whom the will of any state would seek to unite under it through deception or violence, even on the basis of international right, it also unites, by means of mutual self-interest, peoples whom the concept of cosmopolitan right would not have secured against violence and war. It is the *spirit of trade,* which cannot coexist with war, which will, sooner or later, take hold of every people. Since, among all of the powers (means) subordinate to state authority, the *power of money* is likely the most reliable, states find themselves forced (admittedly not by motivations of morality) to promote a noble peace and, wherever in the world war threatens to break out, to prevent it by means of negotiations, just as if they were therefore members of a lasting alliance. For the great alliances for the purpose of waging war, as is the nature of the matter, can arise only very rarely, and even more seldom can they succeed. — In this way nature guarantees perpetual peace through the mechanism of human inclinations itself. To be sure, it does this with a certainty that is not sufficient to *foretell* the future of this peace (theoretically), but which is adequate from a practical perspective and makes it a duty to work toward this (not simply chimerical) goal.

Second Supplement:
Secret Article Toward Perpetual Peace

In treaties of public right, a secret article is, objectively, that is, with regard to its content, a contradiction; but subjectively, that is, judged according to the position of the person who dictates it, a secret provision may well have a

---

*Difference of religions: a perplexing expression! As if we were also speaking of different *moralities.* There may certainly be different kinds of historical *confessions,* but this difference has nothing to do with religion itself, but rather only with the historical means used to promote religion and these are the domain of scholarly research. There may likewise be a variety of *religious texts* (*Zendavesta,*

place in such an article, since that person may find it beneath his dignity to publicly announce himself as its author.

The sole article of this kind is contained in the following clause: *the maxims of the philosophers concerning the conditions of possibility of public peace should be consulted by states prepared for war.*

But it seems belittling to the legislative authority of a state, to which we must naturally attribute the greatest wisdom, to seek instruction from its own *subjects* (philosophers) on the principles of its conduct with regard to other states; yet at the same time it seems very prudent to do so. The state will thus *call upon* the latter *quietly* (by making a secret of it) to do so, which means as much as: the state will *let them speak* freely and publicly about the general maxims of waging war and making peace (for they will do this of their own volition, as long as one does not forbid it), and the agreement among states on this point does not require any special arrangement to this effect on the part of the states, rather it is based already on the obligation by universal (moral-legislative) human reason. — I do not mean to say that the state must favor the principles of the philosopher over the pronouncements of the lawyer (as a representative of state authority), but rather only that one *listen* to the philosopher. The lawyer, who has made not only the *scales* of right, but also the *sword* of justice into his symbols, commonly avails himself of the latter, not simply in order to prevent any foreign influence on right, but rather, if the scale does not tip the way he wishes, also to add the sword's weight to the scale (*vae victis* [woe unto the defeated]), something which the lawyer, unless he is also a philosopher, at least in moral matters, is greatly tempted to do. This is so because his office requires only that he apply existing laws, but not that he examine whether these are in need of improvement. He considers his faculty to be among the "higher" ones, since it is coupled with power (as is the case with the other faculties, medicine and theology), whereas its rank is actually lower. — Compared to this allied power, the philosophical faculty has a very low rank indeed. It is said of philosophy, for example, that it is the *handmaiden* of theology (and this is said of the other two as well). — One is not able to see clearly, however, "whether she bears a flambeau in front of her lady or carries her train behind her."

One cannot expect that kings philosophize or that philosophers become kings. Nor is this desirable, for holding power unavoidably corrupts the free

8:369

---

the *Vedas, Koran,* etc.), but only one *religion* that is valid for all human beings and in all times. Those texts can contain nothing but the vehicles of religion, which are accidental and can vary according time and place.

judgment of reason. Yet both kings and king-like peoples (those which rule over themselves in accordance with laws of equality), should not allow the class of philosophers to diminish or fall silent, but rather should have them speak publicly, for this enlightens the business of government, and, because by its very nature it is incapable of forming mobs and clubs, this class is beyond suspicion of being mere *propagandists*.

8:370

Appendix

I. ON THE DISAGREEMENT BETWEEN MORALITY AND POLITICS WITH RESPECT TO PERPETUAL PEACE

Morality in itself belongs to the practical sphere, in the objective sense, as the totality of the unconditionally commanding laws according to which we *ought* to act. It is therefore obviously inconsistent, after having acknowledged the authority of this concept of duty, to want to say that one *cannot* carry out one's moral duties. For if this were so, the concept of duty would altogether disappear from the realm of morality (*ultra posse nemo obligatur* [no one is obliged beyond what is possible]). Therefore there can be no dispute between politics as the applied doctrine of right and morality as a theoretical doctrine of right (and hence no dispute between theory and practice), unless one were to regard morality as a universal *doctrine of prudence*, that is, to regard it as a theory of maxims according to which one selects the most effective means to attain ends to one's own advantage, that is, to deny that morality exists at all.

Politics says: *"Be ye as prudent as serpents,"* and morality adds to this, as a limiting condition, *"and as innocent as doves."* If both cannot coexist in a command, then there is really a conflict between politics and morality. If both coexist entirely, however, then the idea of their opposition is absurd, and the question as to how that conflict is to be resolved does not even present itself as a task to be pursued. Although the proposition that *"honesty is the best policy"* implies a theory which — unfortunately! — is often contradicted in practice, the equally theoretical proposition that *"honesty is better than any policy"* is infinitely superior to any refutation, and indeed is the necessary condition of the former.[14] The divine guardian of morality

14. *Translator's note:* Because the German word *Politik* can mean both "policy" and "politics," Kant's play on words here can not be rendered in English. When Kant writes that "honesty is the best policy" and "honesty is better than any policy" the implication is also that honesty is the best politics and honesty is better than any politics.

does not yield to Jupiter (the divine guardian of violence), for the latter is still subject to Fate, that is, reason is not enlightened enough to survey the entire series of predetermining causes that foretell with certainty the happy or unhappy consequences of humankind's activities in accordance with the mechanism of nature (although it does let us hope that these will be in accord with our wishes). But reason does provide us with sufficient enlightenment to know what one has to do in order to stay on the path of duty (in accordance with the rules of wisdom) and thus on the path toward our final end.   8:371

Now the practical person, for whom morality is mere theory, actually bases his miserable refutation of our well-intentioned hope on the following claim: that he can predict on the basis of human nature that no one will want to do what must be done in order to bring about the end that leads to perpetual peace, even while he concedes that it *can* and *ought* to be done. — Certainly the will of *all individual* human beings to live under a legal constitution in accordance with principles of freedom (the *distributive* unity of the will of *all*) is not sufficient to attain this end. For civil society to become a whole, it is also necessary that *all* individual human beings *together* want this condition (the *collective* unity of the general will), that they all want this solution of a difficult task. And since a unifying cause needs to be added to the differences among the particular wills of all in order to bring into being a common will, something of which no single individual, however, is capable, the *implementation* of this idea in practice can rely on nothing but *violence* to establish the juridical condition, and it is hence the coercive force of violence upon which public right will subsequently be based. One can expect that such public right will thus admittedly deviate vastly in lived experience from the (theoretical) idea of the juridical condition, since we cannot assume that the moral convictions of the legislator will move him to leave it up to the people that was newly created out of the disorderly masses to bring into being a juridical constitution through a common will.

At that point it would be said that whoever has attained power will not allow the people to dictate the laws to him. A state that has reached the point at which it is subject to no external laws will not subject itself to the judgment of other states with respect to the way that it seeks to defend its rights against them. And even a continent that considers itself superior to another will not fail, even if the latter otherwise in no way stands in its way, to plunder or even conquer it in order to increase its own power. In this way all of the plans of the theory for political, international, and cosmopolitan right vanish, turning into empty and unrealizable ideals, whereas a practice based on the empirical principles of human nature that does not consider it beneath its dignity to take instruction from the way of the world when formulating its own maxims, is the only practice that can hope to find solid

8:372   ground on which to build its edifice of political prudence.

Admittedly, if there is no freedom and no moral law based upon it, and everything that happens or could happen is a mere mechanism of nature, then politics (understood as the art of using this mechanism in order to govern humans) makes up the entirety of practical wisdom and the concept of right is an empty thought. Yet if we regard it as necessary to couple the concept of right with politics, and even to regard the former as a limiting condition of the latter, then one must concede that they are compatible with one another. I can imagine a *moral politician,* that is, one who interprets the principles of political prudence in such a way that they can coexist with morality, but not a *political moralist,* who fashions himself a morality in such a way that it works to the benefit of the statesman.

The moral politician will make the following into a basic principle: if a flaw that could not have been foreseen is found in the constitution of the state or in its relations with other nations, then it is a duty, in particular for heads of state, to focus on remedying it as soon as possible and bringing it into compliance with natural right, as the latter presents itself as a model to us in the idea of reason, even if this should require sacrifices of their egoism. Since severing the bond of a political or cosmopolitical union before a better constitution is prepared to replace it would be contrary to all political prudence that in this regard is in agreement with morality, it would be nonsensical to demand that such a flaw immediately and hastily be changed. But at a minimum one can demand that the ruler wholeheartedly endorses the maxim that such a change is necessary, so that the end of attaining the best constitution according to laws of right is constantly pursued. A state can *govern* itself in a republican manner, even if it still possesses a despotic *ruling power* according to its present constitution, until the people gradually become able to be influenced by the mere idea of the authority of the law (as if it exerted physical force) and hence are found capable of their own legislation (which is originally based on right). Even if the impetuosity of a *revolution* provoked by a bad constitution were to bring about a more lawful one illegitimately it should no longer be deemed permissible to return the people to the previous constitution, even though

8:373   under the old constitution any person who had violently or maliciously participated in that revolution would have rightly been subject to the punishment accorded rebels. But as concerns the relation to other states, one cannot demand of a state that it abandon its constitution, even if the latter is despotic (which indeed makes it a stronger one with regard to foreign foes), as long as the danger exists that it could be swallowed up by other states. It must therefore be permissible to delay the carrying out of such a change of constitution until a more fitting opportunity arises.*

It may well be that the despotizing moralists (those who fail in practice) defy political prudence in a variety of ways (by hastily taking or recommending measures), yet their experience with defying nature must gradually lead them to follow a better course; whereas moralizing politicians seek to gloss over unlawful principles of the state with the excuse that human nature is *incapable* of good in the way that the idea of reason dictates it, and the only effect that they have is to make progress *impossible* and to perpetuate the violation of right.

Instead of the practice [*Praxis*] that these politically prudent men boast about, they employ *practices* [*Praktiken*] intent on betraying the people and, if possible, the entire world, by flattering those in power in order to secure their own benefit. In so doing they are just like lawyers (those who practice law, not those who *legislate*) who presume to practice politics. For since it is not their business to argue about legislation itself, but rather only to carry out the current laws of the land, every already existing legal constitution, or if it is changed by a higher authority, the one that follows, is necessarily the best one in their eyes, and then everything follows in proper 8:374
mechanical order. But this skill at being able to turn their hand to anything deludes them into believing that they are also able to judge any *constitutional principles* whatsoever in accordance with principles of right (thus *a priori,* not empirically). And they make a great show of knowing human beings (which is certainly to be expected, since they have business with many of them), without, however, knowing *human nature* and what can be

---

*These are laws of permissibility. They allow for leaving in place a condition of public right that is tainted with injustice until everything has either itself developed to the point at which it is ripe for a complete change or been brought closer to ripeness by peaceful means. For any kind of *juridical* constitution, even if it is only to a small degree in conformity with right, is better than no constitution at all. The latter fate, anarchy, is precisely what a *hasty* reform would lead to. — Political wisdom will thus make it a duty to pursue reforms in accordance with the ideal of public right under existing circumstances, but will not use revolutions brought about by nature as excuses in order to engage in an even greater oppression, but rather take it to be an appeal of nature to bring about a lawful constitution based on principles of freedom, the only enduring kind of constitution, by means of thorough reforms.

made out of it (which requires a higher anthropological vantage point). If they nonetheless employ these concepts in their approach to civil and international right as reason would dictate it, they cannot but take this step in the spirit of chicanery, by using their familiar method of applying despotically given coercive laws in a mechanical manner, even where the concepts of reason provide only for a lawful coercion in accordance with the principles of freedom, the type of coercion which first makes possible a just and lasting constitution. The allegedly practical person believes that he is able to solve this problem by circumventing that idea, empirically, through his familiarity with how the constitutions that have survived the best to date, even though they were for the most part unlawful, were arranged. — The maxims of which he avails himself to this end (even though he may not speak them out loud) essentially come down to the following sophistic maxims:

1. *Fac et excusa* [act and make excuses]. Seize any promising opportunity to arbitrarily take possession of either the right that a state has over its people or over a neighboring people. The justification for it can be made much more easily and elegantly *after the fact* and the use of force more readily glossed over (particularly in the former case, where the supreme power in the state is also the legislative authority that one must obey without debate), than if one were to seek to offer convincing reasons in advance and wait for counter-arguments before acting. This brazenness itself gives the appearance of the inner conviction that the act is right, and the god of success (*bonus eventus*) is one's best advocate afterwards.

2. *Si fecisti, nega* [if you did it, deny it]. Deny that *you* are responsible for any misdeed that you have committed, one committed, for instance, in order to make your people desperate and thereby cause them to revolt. Claim instead that it is the unruliness of your subjects, or if you are seizing power over a neighboring people, claim that it is the fault of human nature that if one does not anticipate the violence of the other by resorting to violence oneself, then one can be assured of being subjugated by the other.

8:375

3. *Divide et impera* [divide and rule]. This means that if there are certain privileged figures among your people who have merely elected you to be their leader as *primus inter pares* [first among equals], then disunite them from one another and cause them to fall out with the people. Come to the aid of the people by holding up the prospect of greater freedom, and then everything will depend unconditionally on your will. And if you are dealing with foreign states, then sowing dissent among them is a quite reliable means of subjecting others to your will while appearing to come to the aid of the weaker.

No one is deceived by these political maxims, however, for they are all well known. And one need not be ashamed of them, as if their injustice were all too obvious. Great powers are never embarrassed by how the common masses might judge them, only by how other great powers might judge them, and, as concerns these principles, it is not their becoming evident, but rather their *failure* that is an embarrassment, since everyone is in agreement concerning the morality of the maxims themselves. For this reason the great powers can always count on *political honor,* which is to say the honor associated with the *augmentation of their power* in whatever way it may be attained.*

* * *

*When considering individuals who live together in a state, one might still doubt that it is a certain maliciousness rooted in *human nature* and suppose instead that it is apparently their lack of a sufficiently developed culture (i.e., their brutishness) which causes the illegal manifestations of their way of thinking. But in the case of the external relation of *states* toward one another this maliciousness becomes entirely apparent and undeniable. Within each state this maliciousness is concealed by the coercion of civil laws, because the inclination of citizens to use violence against one another is countered by a greater power, namely, that of the government. This not only gives a moral air to the whole (*causae non causae*),[15] but also provides much better for the development of the moral predisposition to immediate respect for right by erecting a barrier to outbreaks of inclinations that go against the law. — For everyone now believes of himself that he would hold sacred and follow faithfully the concept of right, if he could only be assured that everyone else would do the same, something which the government guarantees him in part. This would represent a great step *toward* morality (although not yet a moral step), toward a devotion to the concept of duty for its own sake, and not with a regard to reciprocity. — But since everyone, with his good opinion of himself, still presumes a malicious disposition in all others, they mutually come to the conclusion that they all are, in point of *fact,* worth very little. (We will not discuss at this point why this is so, since it cannot be blamed on the *nature* of humans as free beings.) But since respect for the concept of right, which the human being simply cannot escape, solemnly sanctions the theory that he can conform to it, everyone sees that he must act in accordance with it, however others may happen to act.

15. Probably from the *fallacia non causae ut causae,* the fallacy of presenting a noncause as a cause, in this case the fallacy of explaining the law-abiding conduct of the citizens as the result of their moral goodness, where in fact it is the result of the coercive power of the state.

From all of the turns and twists that an amoral doctrine of prudence makes in trying to show that the state of peace among human beings can be brought forth from the warlike state of nature, at least the following is clear:

8:376   that human beings are no more able to fully abandon the concept of right in their private relationships than they are in their public relationships, and that they would not dare to openly base politics on the machinations of prudence. They therefore cannot foreswear allegiance to the concept of public right (this is especially striking with regard to the concept of international right), but rather pay this concept all the honor due to it, even when they invent hundreds of excuses and deceptions in order to avoid it in practice and to ascribe to brute force the authority of being the source and unifying bond of all right. — In order to bring an end to this sophistry (if not to the injustices which it glosses over) and to compel the false *representatives* of those who wield power on earth to confess that they advocate might, not right (which is apparent from the tone that they adopt in doing so, as if they themselves had the authority to command), it will be good to expose the illusion with which they deceive themselves and others and discover the highest principle from which the end of perpetual peace is derived. Let us show that all of the evil that stands in the way of this end stems from the fact that the political moralist begins where the moral politician rightly leaves off, and by thereby subordinating the principles to the end (that is, putting the cart before the horse), thwarts his own intent to bring politics and morality into agreement with one another.

In order to bring practical philosophy into harmony with itself, one must first of all decide whether, in problems of practical reason, one should start

8:377   from the *material principle* of practical reason, the *end* (as the object of choice), or rather start from its *formal* principle, that is, the principle concerned solely with freedom in external relations, and which reads: act so that you can will that your maxim should become a universal law (whatever the end may be).

Without doubt this latter, formal principle must precede the material principle, for as a principle of right it is unconditionally necessary. The former, material principle necessitates only if one assumes that the empirical conditions that allow for the realization of the intended end are satisfied; and if this end (as with the end of perpetual peace) were also a duty, then this duty would itself have to be derived from the formal principle of the maxims governing external actions. — The former principle, that of the *political moralist* (the problem of *constitutional, international,* and *cosmopolitan right*) presents us with a merely *technical task* (*problema technicum*), whereas the second, as the principle of the *moral politician,* for whom it is a *moral task* (*problema morale*), differs vastly in its method of pursuing perpetual peace, which is in this case desired not merely as a physical good, but rather also as a condition that arises from the recognition of duty.

The solution of the first problem (that is, the problem of political expediency) requires a great deal of knowledge of nature, so that nature's mechanism can be employed to promote the desired end, and yet the result of all this with regard to perpetual peace is uncertain. This applies equally to all three types of public right. Whether the people can better be kept obedient and prosperous in the long-term through discipline or through appeals to their vanity, whether this is better achieved by means of the supreme authority of one individual, through an assembly of several leaders, perhaps also merely through an aristocracy of office, or by means of a self-government of the people, is uncertain. One has in history examples to the contrary for all the types of government (except for the genuinely republican form of government, which can come to mind only to the moral politician, however). — Even more uncertain is the status of alleged *international right* that is created on the basis of ministerial statutes, which is in fact only a word without substance and is based on treaties, where in the same act by which they are concluded the right to violate them is also secretly reserved. — By contrast, the solution of the second problem (that is, the problem of *political wisdom* in the state), impresses itself upon us automatically, so to speak, is apparent to everyone, and puts all artificiality to shame, leading as it does   8:378 directly to the end. But keeping prudence in mind, one should not seek to realize this end prematurely through use of force, but rather to approach it steadily, as circumstances become favorable for doing so.

Here it is said: "Seek ye first the kingdom of pure practical reason and its *justice*, and your end (the blessing of perpetual peace) shall be added unto you." For it is a unique feature of morality with regard to its principles of public right (and hence in relation to a political code that can be known *a priori*), that the more it makes conduct independent from the desired end, whether the intended advantage is physical or moral, the more it is in overall agreement with this end. This is so because it is precisely the general will (within a people, or in the relation of various nations among each other) that is given *a priori* which determines what is right among human beings. This unity of the will of all, however, if only one proceeds consistently in practice, can, in accordance with the mechanism of nature, also be the cause that brings about the desired result and makes the concept of right effective. — Thus it is a basic principle of moral politics, for example, that a people ought to unite itself into a state in accordance with the ideas of freedom and equality as the sole concepts of right, and this principle is not based on prudence, but rather on duty. Now political moralists may argue against this, however, by speaking of the natural mechanism of a mass of people who enter into society with each other, a mechanism which refutes these principles and thwarts their intent, or they may seek to disprove them by citing examples of badly organized constitutions from both ancient and modern times (for example, by citing democracies without a representative system), but their arguments do not deserve any attention. This is so primarily because such a pernicious theory itself leads to the evil that it foresees, putting the human being in a class together with the other living machines that are attributed only the awareness that they are not free beings, in order to make them in their own judgment the most miserable of all beings in the world.

8:379

The proposition *fiat iustitia, pereat mundus* ("let justice reign, even if it may cause all the rogues in the world to perish")[16] may seem to be an overstated proverb, but is nonetheless true, and is a solid principle of right that cuts off access to all the crooked paths laid out by deceit or force. One must only take care that it is not misinterpreted as permitting one to merely pursue one's own right with the greatest vigor (which would conflict with ethical duty), but rather understand it as the obligation of those who wield power to never refuse someone their right or diminish it out of disfavor or out of sympathy with others. The primary way of providing for this is an inner constitution of the state organized according to pure principles of right, but it also requires a constitution that unites this state with other neighboring or also distant states, in order to legally reconcile conflicts between them (in a way analogous to a universal state). — This proposition amounts to nothing other than the following: the political maxims must not be based on the welfare and happiness that an individual state can expect to derive from following such maxims, which is to say that they should not be based on the end that each of them will set for themselves (on what one *wants* to pursue), as the supreme (but empirical) principle of political wisdom, but rather should be based on the pure concept of the duty of right (on what one *ought* to pursue, the principle of which is given *a priori* by pure reason), whatever the physical consequences may be. The world will certainly not come to an end by there being fewer evil people. An immutable feature of moral evil is that it is self-contradictory and self-destructive in its

16. "Let justice be done even if the world should perish." Note that Kant's rendering of the saying is not a literal translation.

intentions (above all in the relationship to other like-minded persons), and it thereby makes room for the (moral) principle of the good, even if it does so in slow steps.

* * *

There is therefore *objectively* (in theory) no conflict at all between morality and politics. *Subjectively,* on the other hand (in the human being's propensity toward selfishness, a propensity which, however, need not be called practice, since it is not based on maxims of reason), this conflict will and may remain in force, because it serves as the whetstone of virtue. The true courage of virtue (according to the basic principle: *tu ne cede malis, sed contra audentior ito*)[17] in the present case does not so much consist in taking on the troubles and sacrifices which must be encountered, but rather in facing and conquering the deception of the far more dangerous, untruthful, and treacherous principle of evil within us that seeks to rationalize and justify all violations of right by appealing to the weakness of human nature.   8:380

The political moralist can in fact say that the people and their ruler, or one people and another, do *one another* no injustice by feuding with one another by means of force or deceit, even though they do commit the more general injustice of denying all respect to the concept of right, which is the sole possible basis for perpetual peace. For since the one transgresses in his duty to the other, who is just as wrongfully disposed toward the former, both parties get precisely what they deserve if they destroy each other, but in such a way that enough of this race remains to continue with this game until far into the future, so that their distant descendants will at some point take a lesson from their example. Providence is justified in so disposing the course of events in the world, for the moral principle in the human being is never extinguished, and reason, which is pragmatically able to realize ideas of right according to that principle, grows through the continuing progress of culture, but the guilt for those transgressions grows accordingly as well. Creation itself, that is, that such a brood of corrupt beings ever should have appeared on the face of the earth, seems impossible to justify if we assume that the human race never can or will be any better off. But this standpoint of judgment is much too high for us to attribute, for theoretical purposes, our concepts (of wisdom) to the most supreme, unfathomable power. — We are inevitably forced to come to such desperate conclusions if we do not

17. "Do not yield to misfortunes, but go and face them more boldly." Virgil, *Aeneid* 6.96.

assume that the pure principles of right in fact have objective reality, that is, that they can be realized, and that, for this reason, the people in a state and states among themselves must act in accordance with these principles, whatever empirical politics may have to say against this. True politics can take no steps forward without first paying tribute to morality, and although politics in itself is a difficult art, the union of politics and morality is no art at all. For morality cuts through the Gordian knot that politics is unable to untie whenever the two come into conflict with one another. — The rights of humankind must be held sacred, whatever it may cost those in power. One cannot pursue a half measure here and devise a hybrid, pragmatically conditioned right (between right and utility). Instead all politics must bend its knee before right but can hope to arrive at the point, however gradually, where it can shine perpetually.

8:381

II. ON THE AGREEMENT BETWEEN POLITICS AND MORALITY ACCORDING TO THE TRANSCENDENTAL CONCEPT OF PUBLIC RIGHT

If I abstract from all the *material* aspects of public right (regarding the various empirically given relations among individuals in a state or between states), as the teachers of law customarily conceive of it, then I am left with the *form of publicity,* the possibility of which is implied in any legal claim, since without it there would be no justice (which can only be thought of as *publicly proclaimable*), and thus no right, since right can be conferred only by justice.

Any legal claim must be capable of publicity. The capability of publicity can therefore, since one can quite easily judge whether it obtains in a given case, that is, whether or not it is consistent with the basic principles of the agent, provide an easily applicable criterion that is found *a priori* in reason. If it is not consistent with the agent's principles one can recognize through an experiment of pure reason, as it were, the falseness (opposition to the law) of any given claim (*praetensio iuris*).

In accordance with such an abstraction from all empirical elements contained in the concept of political and international right (including from the evil element of human nature that makes coercion necessary), one can cite the following proposition as the *transcendental formula* of public right:

"All actions that affect the rights of other human beings, the maxims of which are incompatible with publicity, are unjust."

This principle is to be understood as being not only *ethical* (as belonging to the doctrine of virtue), but also *juridical* (as concerning the rights of humans). If I may not *utter* my maxim explicitly without thereby thwarting my own aim, if it must rather be *kept secret* if it is to succeed, if I cannot *admit it publicly* without thereby inevitably provoking the resistance of all others to my plan, then the necessary and universal and hence *a priori* understandable opposition to me can be due to nothing other than the injustice with which my maxim threatens everyone. — Furthermore this principle is only *negative,* that is, it serves only as a means for recognizing what is *not right* with regard to others. — As with any axiom it is indemonstrably   8:382 certain and, moreover, it is easily applicable, as is clear from the case of the following examples of public right.

1. *In the case of the internal constitutional right* (*ius civitatis*) the following question arises, which many find difficult to answer, yet which the transcendental principle of publicity quite easily answers: "Is rebellion a rightful means for a people to cast off the oppressive authority of a so-called tyrant (*non titulo, sed exercitio talis* [not on the basis of the title but the practice (of a tyrant)])?" The rights of a people have been injured and it would be no wrong to him (the tyrant) to be dethroned, there is no doubt about that. Nonetheless it is wrong in the highest degree for the subjects to pursue their rights in this way, and they therefore would have no cause to complain of injustice if they were defeated in their endeavor and subsequently subjected to the most extreme punishment.

Now one may argue for and against this in a variety of ways if one wishes to resolve the question through a dogmatic deduction of the principles of right. Only the transcendental principle of the publicity of public right can avoid this circuitous route in addressing the question of right. In accordance with this principle, the people asks itself, before establishing a civil contract, whether it ought dare to make public the maxim of the intention to revolt on certain occasions. One can easily see that if in the process of creating a state constitution, one wanted to allow for the use of force against the head of state in certain cases, then the people must be claiming for itself a lawful power over the latter. But then the latter would not be the head, or, if both were to be made conditions of the establishment of the state, then no such establishment would be possible, although this had been the aim of the people. The injustice of revolt thus becomes apparent by virtue of the fact that its maxim, if one were to *admit to it publicly,* would thereby make one's aim impossible. One would therefore have to conceal it. — Such concealment by the leader of a state would not be necessary, however. He can say openly that he will punish any rebellion by killing its ringleaders, even if the latter believe that he was the first to violate the fundamental law. For if he is aware that he is in possession of *irresistibly* supreme authority in the state (which one must assume under any civil constitution, since whoever does not have sufficient power to protect each individual against others in the population does not have the right to give it orders), then he need not be concerned that the announcement of his maxim will thwart his aim. And it is fully consistent with this view that, if the revolt of the people succeeds, then that head of state will withdraw to the position of subject, and will thus likewise not be permitted to initiate any attempt to regain power, but also ought not fear being held accountable for his earlier government.

2. *As concerns international right:* only under the presupposition of some sort of juridical condition (that is, only under the external condition under which a person can really be accorded a right) does it make sense to speak of international right. This is so because as a form of public right the very concept of international right implies that a general will publicly assigns to each his rights, and this *status iuridicus* must proceed from some sort of contract, which may not (as in the case of the individual state) be based on coercive laws but can, if necessary, also be a contract establishing an *enduring and free* association, like the aforementioned one of the federation of distinct states. For without some kind of *juridical condition* that actively binds together the various (physical or moral) persons, that is, in the state of nature, there can be nothing other than private right. — And here there also arises a conflict of politics with morality (to the extent that the latter is taken as a doctrine of right), and here the criterion of the publicity of maxims can similarly be applied readily, yet only in such a way that the contract binds the states together only in their aim to preserve peace among each other and with other states, but by no means in order to make acquisitions. This brings us to the following antinomies between politics and morality, which are presented here together with their solutions.

a. "If one of these states has promised something to another, be it the provision of assistance, or the transfer of certain territories, subsidies, or the like, it can be asked whether it is permissible for the state to break its word in a case where its own welfare is at stake, by considering itself a double person, on the one hand as a *sovereign,* since it answers to no one within the state, and on the other hand merely as the highest *official of the state* who is in turn accountable to the state. The conclusion would then be that in the latter capacity he can absolve himself of responsibility for what he has obligated himself to in the former capacity." — But if a state (or its head) were to utter this maxim explicitly, then naturally everyone else would either flee from it or would unite themselves with others in order to resist its presumptuousness, which demonstrates that politics, with all its cleverness, would thwart its own aims if it operated in this way (by being open about them), and that that maxim must therefore be unjust.

b. "If a neighboring state that has grown to a formidable size (*potentia tremenda*) becomes cause for concern, can one assume that it will want to oppress others simply because it can, and does this give a less powerful state the right to an (allied) attack on the former, even without prior offense?" A state that would affirmatively state its maxim *out loud* in this regard would bring about the imagined ill even more quickly and certainly. For the greater power would anticipate the actions of the smaller powers, and as concerns the alliance of smaller powers, that would be a feeble reed against a larger state which knows how to avail itself of the tactic of *divide et impera* [divide and rule]. — This maxim of political prudence, declared publicly, thus necessarily thwarts its own aim and is therefore unjust.

c. "If a smaller state is situated in such a way that it divides the territory of a larger state, and the smaller territory is necessary for the preservation of the larger one, is the larger state not justified in subjugating the smaller one and appropriating it?" — One can readily see that the larger state may not declare such a maxim in advance, for either the smaller states would ally themselves early on, or other powerful states would fight over this booty. The public announcement of this maxim would therefore make it ineffective. This is a sign that this maxim is unjust and can indeed be unjust in a very great degree, for the fact that the object of an unjust action is small does not prevent the injustice done to it from being very great indeed.

3. As concerns *cosmopolitan right,* I will pass over this silently here, for due to its analogy with international right, its maxims can readily be stated and appreciated.

* * *

With this principle of the incompatibility of the maxims of international right with publicity we have a good indication of the *disagreement* between politics and morality (as a doctrine of right). But we must also inquire under what condition the maxims of politics are in fact in agreement with the right of peoples. For one may not draw the converse conclusion that those maxims that are compatible with publicity are for that same reason also just, since whoever has decisive authority need not make a secret of his maxims. — The condition of the possibility of international right as such is that a prior *juridical condition* exists. For without such a condition there is no public right, but rather any right which one may conceive of except public right (that is, in the state of nature) is merely private right. We have seen above that a federative condition of states, which has as its sole aim the

8:385

prevention of war, is the only *juridical* condition that is compatible with the *freedom* of those states. The agreement of politics with morality is hence possible only in a federal union (which is given *a priori* and necessary according to principles of right). And the legal basis of all political prudence is the establishment of such a federal union to the greatest extent possible, for without this end all of its sophisms are false wisdom and veiled injustice. This false politics has a *casuistry* that surpasses even the best of Jesuit schools. First, it uses the *reservatio mentalis:* in drawing up public contracts with expressions that one can interpret on occasion as one wants to one's own advantage (for example, the difference between the *status quo de fait* and *de droit*). Second, this politics also has its probabilism: it invents evil aims which it attributes to others, or makes claims with regard to the likelihood of their gaining predominance and takes these as legal grounds for undermining other peaceful states. Finally, it has the *peccatum philosophicum* [philosophical mistake] (*peccatillum, bagatelle*): it holds the swallowing up of a smaller state to be a readily pardonable and minor offense if a larger state gains thereby, to the purported advantage of the world as a whole.*

The duplicity of politics with regard to morality, in using one or the other branch to pursue its ends, promotes such sophistry. Both philanthropy and the respect for the rights of humankind are duties. The former is, however, only a *conditional* duty, whereas the latter is *unconditional* and absolutely obligatory, and one must first be fully certain that one has not violated the

---

*Examples of such maxims can be found in Hofrat Garve's treatise: "Über die Verbindung der Moral mit der Politik" [On the Connection between Morality and Politics], 1788. This worthy scholar confesses right at the outset that he is unable to give a satisfactory answer to this question. But to approve of this connection while admitting that one cannot adequately address the objections that can be raised against it seems to give more room to those who would be strongly inclined to misuse such a connection than it would seem to be advisable to do.[18]

18. Christian Garve (1742–98), well-known philosopher at the time, in his book, *Abhandlung über die Verbindung der Moral mit der Politik oder einige Betrachtungen über die Frage, inwiefern es möglich sei, die Moral des Privatlebens bei der Regierung der Staaten zu beobachten* [Treatise on the Connection between Morality and Politics or Some Observations on the Question to what Extent it is Possible to Observe the Morality of Private Life in the Government of States] (Breslau, 1788). At the beginning of the treatise, Garve states that a satisfactory answer to the question is beyond his scope. Kant also polemicised against Garve in the first section of TP, on the relation between theory and practice in morality.

latter if one wishes to surrender oneself to the sweet feeling of beneficence.   8:386
Politics is readily in agreement with morality in the first sense (as ethics), in
order to surrender an individual's rights to their leaders. But with regard to
morality in the second sense (as a doctrine of right), before which it must
bend its knee, politics finds it preferable to not enter into any contract at all,
and rather to deny it any reality at all and to interpret all duties as mere acts
of goodwill. This ploy of secretive politics would readily be thwarted,
however, if philosophy were to make the maxims of politics public, if only
politics would dare to allow the philosopher to make public his own.

With this aim I propose another, transcendental and affirmative principle
of public right, which would be formulated as follows:

"All maxims that *require* publicity (in order that they not miss their aim)
are in agreement with both politics and right."

For if they can attain their end only when that end is made public, then
they must also conform to the general end of the public (happiness), and it is
the proper task of politics to attain this harmony (to make the population
satisfied with its condition). But if this end can be reached *only* through
publicity, that is, by dispelling all mistrust toward the maxims of politics,
then these maxims must also be in harmony with the right of the public, for it
is in public right alone that the ends of everyone can be unified. — I must
postpone the further explanation and discussion of this principle for another
occasion, but the fact that it is a transcendental formula can be seen from the
removal of all empirical conditions (of the doctrine of happiness) as the matter of the law, and from the regard only for the form of universal lawfulness.

* * *

If it is a duty to realize a condition of public right, and if there is well-
founded hope that this can be attained, even if only in the form of an
endlessly progressing approximation of it, then the perpetual *peace* that
follows the peace treaties that have been concluded up to now (although
they have wrongly been designated so, since they actually are mere cease-
fires) is not an empty idea, but rather a task which, carried out gradually,
steadily moves toward its goal (since the periods in which equal advances
are made will hopefully grow shorter and shorter).

Metaphysics of Morals, Doctrine of Right, § 43–§ 62

EDITOR'S NOTE ON THE ORDER OF THE TEXT:

Bernd Ludwig has argued that the order of the text of the *Rechtslehre* is, in many instances, not the order Kant had in mind.[1] With regard to the parts translated here, Ludwig has proposed that Kant most likely intended the sequence of sections to read as follows: 44, 43, 45, 48, 46, 49, 47, 51, 52.

Ludwig proposes to divide § 49 into two, with the first part dealing with the executive branch and the second part with the judicial branch and the distinct functions of the three branches. He proposes to turn § 50 into Remark F and to place the remarks A through F after § 52.

Although there is still debate about the precise details of Ludwig's proposal, the reordering of the sections does indeed make the text more coherent and easier to understand, and it reestablishes the important argumentative connection between §§ 43–49 and §§ 51–52. Readers are advised to keep this in mind when they approach the text.

Given that the Akademie edition is used as the source for this translation and that its page numbers are used as reference in the secondary literature, the text below is published in its original order. It seems easier to read the sections in a different order than to deal with a new set of section numbers that do not match those in the secondary literature and with page numbers that are not continuous.

1. Cf. his edition of the *Rechtslehre:* Immanuel Kant, *Metaphysische Anfangsgründe der Rechtslehre,* ed. Bernd Ludwig, 2nd rev. ed. (Hamburg: Meiner, 1998) and, for more details, Bernd Ludwig, *Kants Rechtslehre* (Hamburg: Meiner, 1988).

Second Part of the Doctrine of Right: Public Right

First Section of Public Right: Constitutional Right

§ 43

The sum total of those laws that require a general pronouncement in order to bring about a juridical condition is known as *public right.* — The latter is thus a system of laws for a people, that is, a number of human beings, or for a number of peoples, which, because they mutually influence one another, require a juridical condition under a will that unites them, a *constitution* (*constitutio*), if they are to participate in what is in accordance with right. — This condition among the individuals in a people is known as the *civil* condition (*status civilis*) and, as the whole in relation to its own members, as the *state* (*civitas*). The latter, due to its form, constituted as it is by the common interest of all its members in existing in a juridical condition, is called the *commonwealth* (*res publica latius sic dicta*). In its relation to other peoples, however, it is known simply as a *power* (*potentia*), hence the word *potentates,* but it is also known, due to (supposed) inherited union, as a nation (*gens*). There is hence cause to conceive, subordinate to the concept of public right, not only constitutional right, but also *international right* (*ius gentium*). Since the earth is not an endless surface but a finite, contained surface, the two together inevitably lead to the idea of *right of a state of peoples* (*ius gentium*) or *cosmopolitan right* (*ius cosmopoliticum*). If the principle that limits external freedom by means of laws is lacking in only one of three possible forms of juridical condition, then the artifice of all others is inevitably undermined and must ultimately collapse.

§ 44

Experience teaches us of the maxim of the violence and maliciousness of human beings, who, before external compulsive legislation is in force, feud with one another. But it is not experience, and hence not some fact, that makes public coercion through laws necessary. However good-natured and righteous one might imagine them to be, implicit a priori in the idea of reason of such a (nonjuridical) condition is the notion that, before a public legal condition can be established, individual people, peoples, and states cannot be secure against violence from one another, due specifically to the right of each to do *what he believes is right and good* and not be dependent on the opinion of others. Hence the first principle that one must decide upon if one is not to renounce all concepts of right is the following: one must emerge from the state of nature in which each follows only his own thoughts and unite oneself with all others (with whom one cannot avoid interacting) in subjecting oneself to public external coercion through laws, and hence enter into a condition in which what is to be recognized as his own is *legally* established and secured by sufficient *power* (a power that is not his own, but rather an external one), which is to say, that one should, above all, enter into a civil condition.

The state of nature was not for this reason necessarily a state of *injustice* (*iniustus*) in which confrontation with others was governed by the mere measure of one's power. But it was a state in which *justice was absent* (*status iustitia vacuus*) where, when one's right was *disputed* (*ius contro-versum*), there was no competent judge to pronounce a judgment with the force of law. Anyone may compel the other with force to exit this condition and enter a juridical condition since, although something external can be acquired by seizure or contract according to everyone's *concepts of right,* such acquisition is only *provisional* as long as it does not possess the sanction of a public law, as it is not established by public (distributive) justice and is not secured by a force executing this right.

If one wished to recognize no acquisition prior to entering into the civil condition, not even as provisionally legal, then the civil condition 6:313   itself would not be possible. For, with regard to their form, the laws of "mine" and "yours" in the state of nature imply precisely the same as what is prescribed in the civil condition, to the extent that the civil state is conceived according to concepts of pure reason. In the latter, however, the conditions are stated under which the rights of "mine" and "yours" can be exercised (in accordance with distributive justice). — There would there-fore be no duties of right with regard to acquisition, and hence no com-mandment to emerge from the state of nature, if there were not, at least *provisionally,* an external "mine" and "yours" in the state of nature.

§ 45

A state (*civitas*) is a union of a number of people under laws of right. To the extent that these are laws that are a priori necessary, that is, as long as these follow from the concepts of external right per se (i.e., are not statutory), the form of this state is the form of the state as such, that is, the state according to the *idea* of how the state should be according to pure principles of right, and which serves as the guiding standard (*norma*) and internal measure of every actual union in a commonwealth.

Each and every state contains three *powers,*[2] that is, it contains the general, unified will in the form of three persons (*trias politica*): the *sovereign power* (sovereignty) resides in the person of the legislator, the *executive power* resides in the person of the ruler (in accordance with the law), and the *judicial power* (as conferring to each what is his by law) in the person of the judge (*potestas legislatoria, rectoria et iudiciaria*), similar to the three propositions in a practical syllogism: the major premise contains the *law* of the sovereign will, the minor premise contains the *command* to act according to the law, that is, the principle of subsumption under the will of the sovereign, and the conclusion contains the *adjudication* (the judicial sentence), which determines what is right in the case at hand.

§ 46

The legislative authority can reside only in the united will of the people. For since all right is to issue from it, this authority must not be *able* to do any injustice to anyone by its law. It is certainly always possible that someone can commit an injustice against *another* by ordering something against him, but this can never be done in that which one decides with regard to oneself (for *volenti non fit iniuria* [no injustice is done to the willing, i.e., to someone who consents]). Thus only the united and consenting will of all,   6:314 when each decides for all precisely the same as all decide for each, can legislate, therefore only the general, united will of the people can legislate.

The members of such a society, who are united for the purpose of legislation (*societas civilis*), in other words the members of a state, are known as *citizens* (*cives*), and the legal attributes of the same, which are inseparable from their being as such, are the following: lawful *freedom* to obey no other law than one to which one has given one's assent; civil *equality,* to recognize no one among the *people* as one's superior whom one does not have the moral capacity to legally bind as much as the latter has the capacity to legally bind him; and third, the attribute of civil *independence,* to owe one's existence and preservation not to the will of any other among the people, but only to one's own rights and powers as a member of the commonwealth, hence civil personhood, which consists in being entitled to be represented by no one else in legal matters.

Only the ability to vote qualifies one for citizenship. Yet this ability assumes the independence of the citizen among the people, who is not

2. *Gewalten* could also be translated as "authorities" but is translated here as "powers" because the term *Gewaltenteilung* is commonly translated as "separation of powers."

merely part of the commonwealth but a member thereof, which is to say, wishes of his own volition to be an acting part of the same in community with others. The latter quality makes the distinction between the *active* and the *passive* citizen necessary, even though the latter concept seems to stand in contradiction with the explanation of the concept of the citizen as such. — The following examples can serve to address this difficulty: the journeyman of a merchant or artisan, the servant (who does not stand in service of the state), minors (*naturaliter vel civiliter*), all women, and anyone at all whose existence is preserved (through food and protection) not by their own means but through arrangements of others (except that of the state), do not possess civil personhood, and their existence is mere inherence, as it were. — The woodcutter whom I employ on my property; the smith in India who goes to different houses with his hammer, anvil, and bellows to work iron, in contrast to the European carpenter or ironsmith, who can put up the products of his work as wares for public sale; the private tutor, in contrast to the schoolteacher; the sharecropper in contrast to the tenant farmer are all mere laborers for the commonwealth because they must be told what to do or protected by other individuals and hence do not possess civil independence.

6:315

This dependence on the will of others and inequality in no way stand in opposition to the freedom and equality of them *as human beings,* who together constitute a people. On the contrary, only under the conditions of freedom and equality can a people become a state and enter into a civil constitution. Yet not all are entitled by the same right to the ability to voice consent in this civil constitution, that is, to be a citizen and not merely a fellow subject of the state. For the right to manage the state as *active* members, the right to organize it, and the right to participate in the introduction of certain laws do not follow from their due claim to be treated by all others in accordance with the laws of natural freedom and equality as *passive* parts of the state. Rather, from the latter follows only that, whichever kind of positive laws they might give their assent to, these must not contradict the natural laws of freedom and the equality, appropriate to this freedom, of all individuals among the people. Namely, such laws must not contradict the right to work one's way out of the passive condition into the active condition.

§ 47

All three of the authorities in the state are offices of dignity and, as essential ones that necessarily issue from the idea of the state as such for its founding (constitution), are *state offices of dignity.* They imply the relation of a general *sovereign* (who, considered with regard to laws of freedom, can be none other than the united people itself) to the individuals among the people as *subjects,* that is to say, the relation of *commander* (*imperans*) to the one who *obeys* (*subditus*). — The act by which a people constitutes itself as a state, but properly speaking only the idea thereof, according to which alone one can conceive the lawfulness of the state, is the *original contract* according to which all (*omnes et singuli*) within the people relinquish their external freedom in order to take it up again immediately as members of a commonwealth, that is, as members of a people regarded as a state (*universi*). One cannot say that the state or the human being within the   6:316 state has sacrificed *part* of his innate external freedom for some end. Rather, he has emerged from the state of wild, lawless freedom in order to find his freedom as such undiminished in a legal dependence, that is, in a juridical condition, because this dependence arises from his own, legislating will.

§ 48

The three authorities in the state are, *first, coordinate* to one another as so many moral persons (*potestates coordinatae*), which is to say that each complements the others (*complementum ad sufficientiam*) and makes the state constitution complete. But, *second,* they are also *subordinated* to one another (*subordinatae*), such that one cannot usurp the function of the others which it lends help to. Each has, rather, its own principle. That is, it commands in the quality of a particular person, yet it does so under the condition of the will of a person superior to it. *Third,* through the unification of both of these relations each subject is granted his right.

It can be said of these authorities [or powers], considered in their dignity: that the will of the *legislator* (*legislatoris*) is *irreproachable* (*irreprehensibel*) with regard the external "mine" and "yours," the executive power of the *supreme commander* (*summi rectoris*) is *irresistible* (*irresistibel*), and the judgment of the *highest judge* (*supremi iudicis*) is *irrevocable* (*inappellabel*).

§ 49[3]

The *regent* of the state (*rex, princeps*) is the (moral or physical) person to whom the executive power (*potestas executoria*) is attached: he is the *agent*

---

3. Section 46 discussed the legislative authority; section 49 discusses first the executive and then the judicial authorities.

of the state, who appoints the magistrates and dictates to the people the rules by which each person in the state can acquire something in accordance with the law (by subsumption of a case under the law) or preserve what is his own. Viewed as a moral person he is called the *directorate,* the government. His *orders* to the people and the magistrates and their superiors (ministers), whose duty is the *administration of the state,* are ordinances, *decrees* (not laws), for they concern decisions in particular cases and are given revocably. A *government* that also legislates would be designated a

6:317   *despotic* government, in contrast to a *patriotic* one (*regimen civitatis et patriae*), by which is meant not a *paternalistic* government (*regimen paternale*), which is the most despotic of all (in treating citizens as children), but rather one in which the state itself (*civitas*) treats its subjects as if they were members of a family, but also as citizens, that is, according to laws of their own independence, and in which each is in possession of himself and not dependent on the absolute will of another either next to him or over him.

The sovereign of the people (the legislator) thus cannot be the same as the *regent,* for the latter is subject to the law and consequently is obligated to *another,* the sovereign. The former can also strip the latter of his power, remove him from office, or reform his administration, but may not *punish* him (and precisely this is the meaning of the expression heard in England: the king, the supreme executive authority, can do no wrong). For that would in turn be an act of executive authority, which is entitled above all to the ability to *coerce* in accordance with the law, but which would be itself simultaneously subject to coercion, which would be a self-contradiction.

Finally, neither the sovereign nor the ruler can *act as adjudicator;* they can only appoint judges as magistrates. The people passes judgment on itself through those fellow citizens who, chosen freely, act as representatives of the same, and are appointed to such positions with specific regard to each act. For adjudication (the judicial sentence) is an individual act of public justice (*iustitiae distributivae*) through a state administrator (a judge or court) with regard to a subject, that is, to someone who belongs to the people and hence holds no public office, in order to confer on (to grant) him what is his. Since each person among the people is merely passive in this relation (to authority), either of the other two authorities would be able to do wrong to him by passing judgment on what is his in a controversial case, since not the people itself would be deciding it and judging whether or not one's fellow citizen is *guilty* or *not guilty.* Once the facts in the suit have been established, however, the court has the judicial authority to apply the law and confer on each what is his by means of the executive authority. Hence only the *people* can judge one of their own, although only indirectly,

through representatives that it appoints (the jury). — It would also be beneath the dignity of the head of state to play judge, that is, to subject oneself   6:318
to the possibility of doing wrong and thereby end up having one's judgment
appealed (*a rege male informato ad regem melius informandum* [from a
king badly informed to a king who should be better informed]).

There are thus three different authorities [or powers] (*potestas legislatoria, executoria, iudiciaria*), by means of which the state (*civitas*) has its
autonomy, that is, constitutes and preserves itself in accordance with laws
of freedom. — The *well-being* of the state consists in their being united
(*salus reipublicae suprema lex est*).[4] But the well-being of the state is not
the same as the *welfare* and *happiness* of its citizens, for its happiness can
perhaps (as Rousseau[5] also asserts) be attained more readily and agreeably
in the state of nature, or even under a despotic government. The well-being
of the state is rather the condition of the greatest harmony of the constitution with principles of right, a condition which reason dictates, *through a
categorical imperative,* that we strive to attain.

General Remark on the Legal Consequences That Follow
from the Nature of a Civil Union

A.

The origin of the supreme authority is, as a matter of practical concern,
not open to examination by the people that is subject to it. That is to say, the
subject *ought not* occupy itself with *musing* about this origin as if it were a
right about the obedience of which one should have misgivings (*ius contro-
versum*). For since the people must, in order to pass judgment with the force
of law on the supreme authority of the state (*summum imperium*), be regarded as already united under a general, legislating will, it can and may
judge in no way other than the current head of state (*summus imperans*)
wills it. — Whether subjugation under the head of state was preceded by the
historical fact of an actual contract (*pactum subiectionis civilis*) or the
authority came first, only to be followed later on by the law, or even whether
it were supposed to have followed in this sequence — these are for the
people, since it is already under civil law, mere musings that are pointless yet nonetheless dangerous for the state. For if the subject who had

4. "The well-being of the commonwealth is the supreme law" Cf. Cicero, *De legibus*
3.3: "*Salus populi suprema lex esto.*" Cf. also A 7:331 and TP 298.

5. See Kant's discussions of Rousseau in IUH, CB, and A.

6:319   envisaged the latter origin wished to resist the authority currently in power, he would, in accordance with the laws of the latter, that is to say, completely rightfully so, be punished, killed off, or be banished as an outlaw (*exlex*). — A law that is so holy (inviolable), that it is a crime to even *practically* doubt it and thus suspend its effect for a moment is conceived as coming not from human beings but rather from a supreme, flawless legislator. This is the meaning of the proposition "All authority comes from God," which expresses not a *historical cause* of the civil constitution, but rather the practical principle of reason that one ought to obey the existing authority, whatever its origin may be.

From this follows the proposition that the sovereign in the state has no (compulsory) duties with regard to subjects, only rights. — Furthermore, even if the organ of the sovereign, the *regent,* were to act in contradiction to the laws, for example, against the law of equality in the distribution of the burdens of the state through the imposition of taxes, the recruitment of soldiers, etc., the subject is permitted to respond to this injustice by lodging a *complaint* (*gravamina*), but not by resisting.

Indeed there even can be no article contained in the constitution whereby some authority in the state would be enabled to resist and thereby restrict the commander in chief in the case of the latter's trespassing against constitutional laws. For the one who is supposed to restrict the authority of the state must have more, or at least the same amount of power as the one who is restricted and, as the legitimate commander who orders his subjects to resist, must also be able to *protect* them and render judgment with the force of law in any given case, and hence be able to order the resistance publicly. But in such a case not the commander in chief, but the one restricting the commander in chief is the commander in chief, which represents a self-contradiction. The sovereign here acts by means of his minister also as the regent and hence despotically. The deception by means of which the people imagines a limiting authority through its deputies cannot so hide the despotism that it does not become apparent in the means employed by the minister. The people, which is represented by its deputies in parliament, has in these guarantors of their freedom and rights individuals who have a vested interest in positions for themselves and their families such that, to the extent they are dependent on the minister, as for army, navy, and civilian positions, these deputies are much sooner prepared to play into the hands of

6:320   the government than to resist the presumptiveness of the government. (In any case, a public declaration of such resistance would require a previously established unanimity among the people, a unanimity that cannot be allowed in a time of peace). — The so-called moderate state constitution, as a constitution of internal right in the state, is thus preposterous and, rather than being part of right, is merely a principle of cleverness used not to impede the powerful transgressor of the rights of the people with its arbitrary influence on the government, but rather to cloak this influence as much as possible in the appearance of an opposition that the people is allowed.

There is therefore no lawful resistance of the people against the legislating head of the state, for a juridical condition is possible only through subjecting oneself to a general, legislative will. There is thus no right of *sedition* (*seditio*), even less a right to *active rebellion* (*rebellio*), and least of all a right to *assault* the individual person of the head of state (monarch) under the pretense of his abuse of power (*tyrannis*), indeed, to take his life (*monarchomachismus sub specie tyrannicidii*). The slightest attempt in this direction is *high treason* (*proditio eminens*), and a traitor of this kind can, as one who attempts to *assassinate his fatherland* (*parricida*), be punished with no less than death. — The reason for the duty of the people to endure even what is taken as an intolerable abuse of the highest authority is the following: its resistance against the highest legislation must be conceived as nothing other than against the law, indeed, as nullifying the entire legal constitution. For to be authorized to do so requires a public law that would allow this resistance of the people, that is to say, the supreme legislation would contain a condition whereby it was not the highest and make the people as subject sovereign in one and the same judgment over the one to whom it is subject. This is a self-contradiction and one which becomes apparent in light of the question who should be judge in the dispute between the people and the sovereign (for these are still, considered legally, two distinct moral persons). It becomes evident here that the former wishes to be judge of its own case.*

* The *dethronement* of a monarch can also be thought of as the *voluntary* abdication of the crown and surrender of power and return of the latter to the people, or as a relinquishment of power without an assault on the highest person, whereby the latter would return to the status of a private person. For this reason the crime of the people that forced the relinquishment would have at least the pretense of the *right of necessity* (*casus necessitatis*) for itself, but it would never have the least right to punish him, the head of state, for its previous administration, since everything that he did in his capacity as head of state would have to be regarded as externally lawful since he, regarded as the source of the laws, cannot do wrong. Among all the atrocities of the overthrow of a state by means of revolt, even the *murder* of the monarch is not the worst, for one can imagine that the people commits it for *fear* that he could, if he remains alive, regain his strength and let the people suffer its just punishment. It would therefore be not an enactment of penal justice

6:321   A change in a (faulty) state constitution, which may become necessary from time to time — can thus be carried out only by the sovereign itself by

6:322   means of *reform,* not by the people, by means of *revolution,* and when it occurs it can affect only the *executive power,* not the legislative. — In a state constitution that is made such that the people can legally *resist* the former

---

but rather an act of mere self-preservation. It is formal *execution* that horrifies the soul that is filled with ideas of human right and this feeling returns each time when one thinks of such events, like the fate of Charles I or Louis XVI. But how does one explain this feeling, which is not aesthetic (based on sympathy, an effect of the imagination, in which one places oneself in the position of the one suffering), but rather moral, due to the complete inversion of all concepts of right? It is regarded as a crime that remains eternally and can never be expiated (*crimen immortale, inexpiabile*) and seems similar to the crime that the theologians call the sin that can be forgiven neither in this world nor in the afterworld. The explanation of this phenomenon in the human spirit seems to issue from the following reflections on oneself, and these also throw light on the principles of constitutional right.

Each and every transgression of the law can and must be explained in no way other than that it arises from a maxim of the transgressor (making such a misdeed into a rule). For if one derived this transgression from a sensual impulse, it would not have been committed by the transgressor, as a *free* being, and could not be attributed to him. It simply cannot be explained how it would be possible for the subject to form a maxim against the clear prohibition of legislative reason, for only events in accordance with the mechanism of nature are capable of explanation. The transgressor can commit his misdeed either according to a maxim of a presumed objective rule (as universally valid), or as an exception to the rule (as giving oneself dispensation from the rule on occasion). In the *latter* case *he only deviates* from the law (although intentionally). He can also detest his transgression and, without formally renouncing his obedience of the law, only wish to circumvent it. In the *former* case, by contrast, he rejects the authority of the law itself, the validity of which he cannot, however, reasonably deny, and he makes it into a rule that he act against it. His maxim is thus opposed to the law not merely as *lacking* (negatively), but rather as *contrary* to it or, as one says, *diametrically* opposed to it, as a contradiction (hostile to it, as it were). As far as we understand, the commission of such a transgression of a formal (completely fruitless) malice is impossible for human beings and yet not to be ignored in a system of morality (even though as the mere idea of the most extreme evil).

The reason for the horror at the thought of the formal execution of a monarch *by his people* is thus that the *murder* must be conceived as only an *exception* to the rule which the people takes as its maxim, whereas the *execution* is the complete *inversion* of the principles of the relation between sovereign and people (making the latter, which has the

through its own representatives (in parliament) and the representative of the former (in the person of the minister) — which is then called a limited constitution — , there is nonetheless no active resistance allowed (the people's arbitrarily joining in order to compel the government to a certain course of action, thus itself committing an act of executive authority), but rather only a *negative* resistance, which is to say a *refusal* of the people (in parliament) to always comply with the former in the demands that it claims as necessary for the administration of the state. If the latter were to occur, it would be the surest sign that a people was corrupt, its representatives venal, and the head of the government despotic through its minister, and the latter himself a traitor of the people.

Incidentally, when a revolution has succeeded and a new constitution is established, the unlawfulness of its beginning and implementation cannot release the subjects from the obligation to submit to the new order of things as good citizens. And they cannot refuse to honor and obey the authority that now is in power. The dethroned monarch (who survives the toppling of government) cannot be held accountable for his earlier administration, much less be punished for it, if he, returned to the status of a citizen, prefers his peace and that of the state to daring to take leave of it, in order, as a pretender, to recklessly attempt to recover his office, be it by means of secretly instigated counterrevolution or with the aid of other powers. But if he prefers the latter, his right to that office remains, since the revolt that took it from him was unjust. It is then a question of international right whether other powers have the right and the calling to join with this unsuccessful ruler in an alliance of states, merely so that the crime committed by the people not remain unpunished, or so that it not be allowed to stand as a scandal for all states and thereby return by force every state in which a constitution has come about through *revolution* to its old condition.

6:323

---

legislation of the former to thank for its existence, into the ruler of the former). Violence is thus brazenly and resolutely raised above the holiest right, and the act, like an abyss which irretrievably consumes everything, seems to be a suicide committed on him by the state and a crime incapable of expiation. One thus has reason to assume that agreement with such executions is not motivated by a presumed principle of right, but rather out of fear of revenge against the people by a state which might arise again. And the formality of the execution is assumed only to give the deed the appearance of a punishment and hence a *legal procedure* (which murder would not be). This concealment is faulty, however, for such a presumption on the part of the people is even worse than murder, for it is based on a principle that would make even the reestablishment of the toppled state impossible.

B.

Can the ruler be considered the supreme proprietor (of the land), or must he be considered only the supreme commander of the people through laws? Since land is the supreme condition under which alone it is possible to have external things as one's own, the possible possession and use of which constitutes the first right that can be acquired, all such rights must thus be derived from the sovereign as *prince of the land,* or, better, as supreme proprietor thereof (*dominus territorii*). The people, as the mass of subjects, also belongs to him (it is his people), but not as its owner (as a right regarding things), but as supreme commander (as a right regarding persons). — Yet this supreme proprietorship is only an idea of the civil union needed to make conceivable the necessary unification of the private property of all among the people under one public and general possessor for the purpose of determining particular property, not according to principles of *aggregation* (which proceeds empirically from the parts to the whole), but rather according to the necessary, formal principle of *division* (of the land) according to concepts of right. According to these concepts the supreme owner can have no private property on any part of land (for he would otherwise make himself a private person), rather this only belongs to the people (not collectively, but rather distributively). A nomadic people is an exception to this, in which case there is no private ownership of the land at all. — The supreme commander can have no *domains,* that is, no estates for his private use (for maintaining his court). For since it would otherwise be at his own discretion how expansive they should be, the state would run the risk of seeing all ownership of the land in the hands of the government and all its subjects as *bondsmen of the land* (*glebae adscripti*) and possessors of that which is always only property of another, and hence robbed of all freedom (*servi*). — One can say the following of the sovereign prince: *he possesses nothing* (of his own), except himself. For if he had something of his own next to someone else, then a disagreement with the latter could be possible for which there would be no judge to arbitrate. But one can also say that that *he possesses everything,* since he has the right of command over the people, to whom all external things (*divisim*) belong (and he can thereby let each obtain what is his own).

It hence follows that there could be no corporation in the state, no rank, and no order which could, as owner, hand down land to subsequent generations for their exclusive use (into eternity) according to certain statutes. The state can lift such statutes at any time, under the condition that the survivors are compensated. The *knightly order* (as a corporation, or even as a mere rank of individual, especially honored persons) and the *clerical order,*

6:324

known as the Church, can never acquire, by means of these privileges that they are favored with, ownership of the land that is transferable to its successors, but rather only temporary use of it. The estates of the knightly order, in the one case, can be revoked without reservation if public opinion has changed with regard to the use of the *military honor* in protecting the state from apathy concerning its defense, and the church estates, in the other case, can be revoked if the opinion changes with regard to the use of masses, prayers, and a whole host of clergymen to save the people in the state from eternal fire (but under the condition mentioned above). Those who thus are subjected to reform cannot complain that their property was taken from them, for the reason of their prior possession lay only in the *opinion of the people* and was valid as long as this persisted. But as soon as this opinion changed, even only in the judgment of those who have earned the greatest claim to commanding this people, the purported ownership had to end, as if it had been lost by its appeal to the state (*a rege male informato ad regem melius informandum*) [trans. above, p. 117].

6:325

The right of the supreme commander, as supreme proprietor (or as prince of the land), to *levy taxes* on the private owners of the land rests on this originally acquired ownership of the land. This right enables him to demand land taxes, excises, customs, and services (such as the provision of troops for military service). The only way that this happens in accordance with laws of right is that the people levies taxes on itself through its corps of deputies, yet it is also permissible that it takes the form of a compulsory loan (one which deviates from previously established law) in accordance with the right of majesty if the state is in danger of dissolution.

This right of the supreme commander to manage the state's economy, its finances, and the police rests on this same principle. The police ensures public *safety, comfort,* and *decency* (because if the sense of decency [*sensus decori*], as a negative taste, is not deadened by begging, public noise-making, foul smells, and public prostitution [*venus volgivaga*], all of which constitute injuries to the moral sense, this facilitates the government's task of directing the people through laws).

There is a third part to the preservation of the state, namely, the right of *inspection* (*ius inspectionis*). No association which can have an influence on the *public* welfare of society (*publicum*) can be kept secret (by political or religious illuminati), but rather it must not refuse revealing their constitution when asked to do so by the police. The searching of the private quarters of an individual is only an emergency measure for the police, and something for which it must always be authorized by a higher authority in each particular case.

C.

6:326

Indirectly, that is, to the extent that he assumes the duty of the people, the supreme commander has the right to levy taxes on the people for its own preservation (the people's), for example, through *aid for the poor, foundling houses,* and *churches,* what are otherwise known as charitable or pious foundations.

The general will of the people has united itself into a society that is to be preserved into perpetuity and, to this end, has subjected itself to an internal authority of the state in order to preserve those members of this society that are not able to do so themselves. It thus follows for reasons of the state that the government has the right to require the wealthy to provide the means of subsistence for those who cannot provide themselves even the most basic needs of nature. Since their existence is also an act of subjecting oneself to the commonwealth for the protection and care required for their survival, they have obligated themselves to the commonwealth. This is the basis for the state's right to compel them to contribute their part for the preservation of their fellow citizens. This can be done in the following ways: through the taxation of the property of the citizens or of their commerce, or the establishment of funds and their interest, not for the needs of the state (for it is rich), but rather for the needs of the people, but not merely through *voluntary* contributions (for we are speaking here of a *right* of the state vis-à-vis the people), since some among them are for profit (for example, lotteries, which produce more poor and are a greater danger to public property than would otherwise exist, and which should therefore not be allowed), but rather through compulsory contributions, as political burdens. This leads to the question of whether the poor ought to be cared for by means of *current contributions,* so that each era provides for its own, or by means of *resources* collected gradually or by *pious* foundations in general (such as widows' homes, hospitals, etc.). In any case, these contributions ought not to be obtained through begging, which is closely related to robbery, but rather by means of a legal levy. — The first arrangement must be regarded as the only one appropriate to the right of the state, from which no one can withdraw who has to live. This is so because it does not (as would be the concern with pious foundations), if such contributions increase with the number of the poor, make poverty into a livelihood for lazy people and thereby constitute an *unjust* burden on the people by the government.

As concerns the preservation of children who are abandoned out of desperation or shame or even murdered for that reason, the state has the right to impose on the people the duty to not knowingly allow this, albeit unwanted, addition to the state to perish. Whether this can rightly happen by means of taxing old bachelors and spinsters (by which *wealthy* singles are 6:327 meant), as persons who are after all partly to blame for this, or whether by means of foundling houses erected for the purpose, or by other means (another means of preventing it is hardly to be found), is a task for which no solution has yet been found that does not either infringe on rights or morality.

The *church,* which must be carefully distinguished from *religion* (an inner conviction that lies completely outside the realm of civil authority), as an institution for public *religious worship* for the people (whatever source this worship may have, be it in opinion or conviction), becomes a true state need, [namely, people need to] regard themselves also as subjects of a supreme *invisible* power which one must pay homage to, a power which can often come into a very unequal conflict with the civil authority. The state thus does not have the right to arrange the inner constitution and church affairs according to its own view of what seems advantageous and to prescribe or command the faith and rituals of worship (*ritus*) (for this must be left entirely to the teachers and chairmen that the people has chosen), but, rather, the state has only the *negative* right to keep the influence of the public [religious] teachers away from the *visible,* political commonwealth, which could be detrimental to public peace; hence the state has the right in internal conflicts or conflicts among the various churches not to allow civil harmony to be endangered, which is thus a right of the police. To decide that a church is to have a certain faith or which one it is to have, or that a church preserve it unchanged and not reform itself are interventions on the part of the state authority that are *beneath its dignity* because it puts itself, as in a schoolyard quarrel, at the level of equality with its subjects (the monarch becomes a priest), who can bluntly tell it that it understands nothing about the matter, above all what concerns the latter, namely, the prohibition of internal reforms. — For what the entire people cannot decide about itself, the legislator can also not decide about the people. No people can decide to never progress in its insights with regard to its faith (enlightenment), and hence to never reform itself with regard to church affairs, for this would be opposed to the humanity in its own person and hence to the supreme right of the people. Thus no civil authority can decide this for the people. — But concerning the costs of maintaining the 6:328 church, these cannot, for the precisely same reason, come at the expense of the state, but rather must come at the expense of the part of the people which adheres to one faith or the other, that is, only at the expense of the congregation.

D.

The right of the supreme commander in the state also includes (1) the distribution of *offices* that entail employment for compensation; (2) the distribution of *offices of dignity* that entail a distinction of rank without pay, that is to say, awarding a superior rank based only on honor, for the purpose of commanding an inferior rank, which, although free and bound only by public law, is nonetheless determined in advance to obey the former, — and (3) beyond these (rather beneficent) rights, *penal right.*

When one considers civil offices, the following question arises: does the sovereign have the right to relieve, at his own discretion, someone of an office that he has given him (without the latter having committed a crime)? I answer, "No!" For what the united will of the people will never decide about its civil servants, the head of state can also not decide about them. The people (who is supposed to bear the costs incurred by the employment of a civil official) wishes without doubt that the latter is equal to the duty bestowed upon him. This is possible only through a sufficient period of preparation and training, a period which could have otherwise been spent learning another occupation to provide one's livelihood. If summary dismissals were allowed, such offices would generally be filled with people who lack the necessary skill and had not acquired mature judgment through practice, and this would run counter to the intention of the state. The intention of the state also requires that each official can rise from a lower to a higher office (which would otherwise fall into the hands of unqualified persons), and that each can count on a lifelong livelihood.

Offices of dignity are not simply those which fill a political office, but also those offices which make the officeholder into a member of a higher class without his performing any special services. This is the difference between *nobility* and the class of common citizens, to which the people belong. Nobility is inherited by male descendants and is, through them, also acquired by females of unnoble birth. Only the nobly born woman does not pass noble rank on to her unnobly born husband; rather she herself returns to the class of common citizens (of the people). — The question is now whether the sovereign has the right to establish a class of nobility as a *hereditary* intermediate class between himself and the other citizens. This is not a question of whether it is prudent on the part of the sovereign for either his own advantage or for that of the people, it is rather a question of whether it accords with the right of the people to have a class of persons above it, who are, though subjects themselves, *born* commanders (or at least privileged) vis-à-vis the people. — The answer to this question follows, just as above, from the following principle: "What the people (the entire mass of subjects) cannot decide about itself and its fellows, the sovereign can also not decide about the people." Now, *hereditary* nobility is a rank that is acquired before it has been merited and gives no occasion to think that it will be earned. To think otherwise is pure fancy and lacking any reality. For if the ancestor had merited it, he would not have been able to bequeath this merit to his descendants. The latter would rather have had to earn it for themselves, since nature does not arrange things such that the talent and will that make meritorious political service to the state possible can be *inherited.* Since one cannot assume of any human being that he will discard his freedom, it is impossible that the general will of the people will agree to such a baseless prerogative, and hence the sovereign cannot assert it. — If however such an anomaly has crept into the machinery of the government in days past (from the feudal system, which was almost entirely directed at waging war), with subjects who claim to be more than common citizens, namely, born state officials (such as a hereditary professor), the state can correct its mistake of having wrongly given hereditary privileges in no way other than gradually, by reducing positions when vacated or letting them remain vacant, and therefore has the provisional right to allow an office of honor to continue to exist in name until the division into sovereign, nobility, and people will have given way in public opinion to the natural division into sovereign and people.

No one can be a person in the state without any dignity at all, for one always has at least the dignity of the citizen, except when he has lost it through his own *crime,* since he will then be kept alive but is made into the   6:330 mere tool of the will of another (either of the state, or of another citizen). Whoever is the latter (which he can only become through judgment and right), is a *serf (servus in sensu stricto)* and is part of the *property (dominium)* of another, who therefore is not just his master (*herus*), but rather also his *owner (dominus)*, who can sell him as a thing and use him as he sees fit (only not for ignominious ends) and *dispose of his abilities,* although not of his life and limbs. No one can contractually bind himself to such a dependency, by which he would cease to be a person, for only as a person can he make a contract. Now it may seem that a person could obligate himself through a work contract (*locatio conductio*) to certain duties for another (for wages, food, or protection), which are specified with regard to type but remain *unspecified* with regard to amount, and thereby become a mere subject (*subiectus*), not a serf (*servus*), but this is all false appearance. For if his master is authorized to utilize the abilities of his subject as he sees fit he can also (as is the case with the negroes on the Sugar Islands) exhaust them to death or desperation, and he has really given himself to his master as property, which is impossible. — He can thus obligate himself only to complete work that is specified with regard to both type and quantity, either as a day laborer or as a resident worker. In the latter case he might, in part, render services to his master for the use of his master's land in place of receiving wages, and, in part, pay certain fees (a rent) for his own use of the land in accordance with a lease. This contract would not thereby make him a *land serf* (*glebae adscriptus*), whereby he would lose his personhood, so he could make a lease that is either limited with regard to time or is hereditary. He may have made himself a *personal* subject by means of his crime, but such a servile status cannot be *inherited,* since he has become such only due to his own fault. In just the same way the offspring of a serf cannot be claimed as property because of the cost of raising it, since rearing is an absolute natural duty of parents and, in the case that these were serfs, this duty falls on the masters, who, with the possession of the subjects, also assumed the duties of the same.

6:331

E.

ON PENAL RIGHT AND THE RIGHT OF PARDON

I.

Penal right is the right of the commander vis-à-vis his subject to inflict pain on him for his crime. The highest authority in the state can thus not be punished, rather one can only withdraw oneself from his rule. — That trespass of public law that makes him who commits it unable to be a citizen is known simply as a *crime* (*crimen*), or as a public crime (*crimen publicum*). The former (a private crime) is therefore subjected to civil justice, the latter to criminal justice. — *Embezzlement,* that is, misappropriation of money or wares entrusted in commerce and fraud in sale and purchase committed before the eyes of the other are private crimes. Counterfeiting or false bills of exchange, theft, robbery, etc. are, on the other hand, public crimes, since the commonwealth, and not merely a single person, are thereby endangered. — These crimes can be divided into those of the *base* character (*indolis abiectae*) and those of the *violent* character (*indolis violentae*).

Judicial punishment (*poena forensis*), which is distinguished from *natural* punishment (*poena naturalis*) insofar as vices punish themselves and the legislator takes no account of the latter, can never be imposed merely as a means to promote another good for the criminal himself or for civil society, but must be imposed on him only *because he has committed a crime.* For the human being can never be treated merely as a means to the ends of another and thus be joined with the objects of the right regarding things, against which his innate personhood protects him, even though he can be condemned to lose his civil personhood. He must be found *punishable* before one can think of drawing some advantage from this punishment for himself or his fellow citizens. Penal law is a categorical imperative, and woe to him who creeps along the twisting paths of the doctrine of happiness in order to find something that, for the advantage it promises, frees him even in the slightest degree from his punishment, according to the Pharisaic motto: "It is better that *one* man should die than that the entire people perish." For if justice comes to an end, there is no value anymore in mankind's existence on Earth. — What ought one to think of the proposal that a criminal's life be spared if he agreed to have dangerous experiments performed on him, so that the doctors could obtain new knowledge that would be fruitful for the commonwealth, and he were to be fortunate enough to survive? A court of law would scornfully turn down the medical faculty that would make such a proposal, for justice ceases to be justice at all if it gives itself away for any price.

6:332

But what kind and what degree of punishment does public justice make its principle and standard? None other than the principle of equality (in the position of the pointer on the scales of justice), in not tending more toward one side or the other. Hence: whatever undeserved evil you cause another among the people, you do unto yourself. If you curse him, you curse yourself; if you steal from him, you steal from yourself, if you strike him, you strike yourself, if you kill him, you kill yourself. Only the *law of retribution* (*ius talionis*) can determine the quality and quantity of punishment, albeit, let it be well understood, in the chambers of a court (not in your private judgment). All other determinations tip the scales to and fro and cannot, due to other interfering considerations, give a judgment equal to that of pure and strict justice. — Now it duly seems that the difference between the classes does not permit the principle of retribution (repaying like with like). But even though it cannot be possible according to the letter, it can nonetheless be valid with respect to its effects if the sensibilities of the higher class are accounted for. — A punishment of money, for example, due to a verbal injury, bears no relation to the insult, for whoever has a lot of money can permit himself the insult for mere fun. But maligning someone's love of honor can come close to injury of one's pride. The verdict and right may require not only public apology, but also that one, even though the other is of a lower class, also kiss his hand. The same would be true when a violent person of distinguished class, because of the blows that he delivers to the innocent citizen of lower class, is sentenced not only to apologizing but also to a solitary and troublesome confinement, since, beyond the inconvenience, the vanity of the culprit is also painfully attacked, and like is

6:333

appropriately repaid with like through humiliation. — Yet what does it mean to say: "If you steal from him, you steal from yourself"? Whoever steals makes the property of all insecure. He steals from himself (according to the right of retribution) the security of all possible property. He has nothing and can also acquire nothing, yet wishes to live, while this is in no way possible other than that others provide for him. But since the state will not do this for free, he must lend his abilities to work to its bidding (convict labor) and comes for a certain amount of time or, if deemed necessary, forever into the state of slavery. — But if he has murdered, he must *die*. Here there is no surrogate for satisfying justice. There is no *similarity* between a life, however filled with misery, and death, and there is also no equality between the crime and retribution unless the murderer receives a sentence of death from the court, although this death must be free from any abuse that could make the humanity in the suffering person into a disgrace. — Even if civil society were to dissolve with the agreement of all its members (for instance, if a people that inhabited an island were to decide to disperse itself and scatter to all corners of the world), the last murderer to be found in its prison would have to be executed first, so that everyone receive what his deeds merit and so that the bloodguilt not adhere to the people that did not press for this punishment. It would adhere to the people because it can be regarded as a participant in this public injury of justice.

This equality of punishment, which is possible only through the judge's pronouncement of the death sentence in accordance with the strict law of retribution, is evidenced by the fact that only the death sentence for all is proportionate with the *inner maliciousness* of the criminals (even if the case does not concern a murder, but rather another political crime only to be expiated with death). — Let us suppose that, as in the last Scottish rebellion, where various participants in the rebellion (such as *Balmerino*[6] and others) believed in their revolt to be only acting on a duty owed to the House of *Stuart,* while others pursued private intentions, the highest court handed down the following verdict: everyone should have the freedom to choose between death and servitude. I propose that the honest man will choose death, while the rogue chooses servitude. This follows from the nature of the human spirit. For the former knows something that he values more highly than life itself, namely, *honor.* The other holds even a shame-ridden life to be more valuable than not existing at all (*animam praeferre pudori.*

6:334

---

6. Arthur Elphinstone, sixth Baron Balmerino (1688–1746), Scottish nobleman who aided the 1745 attempt to put the Scottish prince Charles Edward Stuart on the British throne. The attempt failed and Balmerino was decapitated.

Iuven.).[7] The former is without argument less punishable than the second, and thus they are proportionally punished by the death to which they all are subjected, the former mildly in conformity with his kind of sensibility and the latter severely in conformity with his kind of sensibility. If all had been punished with servitude, however, the first would have been punished too severely, and the latter would have been punished too mildly for his maliciousness. Thus, even in a judgment concerning a number of criminals in a plot, *death* is the best equalizer before public justice. — Moreover, one has never heard that anyone sentenced to death for murder has complained that his punishment is too great and thus wrong. Anyone would laugh in his face if he were to claim this. — One would otherwise have to assume that, although the criminal does not receive unjust treatment before the law, the legislative authority in the state is not authorized to impose this kind of punishment and, if it does so, it is in contradiction with itself.

Thus anyone who is a murderer, that is, who commits a murder or has ordered it or has taken part in one, must also suffer death. Justice, as an idea of judicial authority according to general a priori grounded laws, wills it to be this way. — But let us assume that the number of accomplices (*correi*) in such a deed is so great that the state would nearly have no subjects left if it were to rid itself of such criminals, and that it wishes not to be dissolved, which would mean to enter into the much worse state of nature, which lacks all external justice whatsoever. In order to avoid such consequences, above all deadening the feeling of the people with the spectacle of the slaughter, the sovereign must have it within his power to act as (to assume the role of) judge himself in this emergency situation (*casus necessitatis*) and to pronounce a judgment that imposes a punishment other than the death penalty on the criminals which preserves the population. Deportation would be such a punishment, for instance, yet this judgment would be handed down not according to a public law, but rather by decree, that is, through an act of the right of majesty, which, as a pardon, can only ever be used in individual cases.

By contrast the Marquis of *Beccaria* has, out of a sympathetic sentimen-   6:335

7. Juvenal, *Satires* 8.83, "to prefer life to honor." The full sentence in which the phrase occurs is the following: "Be a stout soldier, a faithful guardian, and an incorruptible judge; if summoned to bear witness in some dubious and uncertain cause, though Phalaris himself should command you to tell lies and bring up his bull and dictate to you a perjury, count it the greatest of all sins to prefer life to honor, and to lose, for the sake of living, all that makes life worth having" (trans. G. G. Ramsay). Phalaris was a tyrant of Agrigentum, said to have roasted his victims in a metal bull.

tality of an affected humanitarianism (*compassibilitas*), put forth his assertion that all instances of the death penalty are *wrongful*.[8] The reason for his assertion is that the death penalty could not have been contained in the civil contract, since otherwise every person would have had to assent to losing his life if he were to murder another (of the population). Such assent is, however, impossible, since no one can dispose of his own life. Such an argument is pure sophistry and a distortion of right.

A person suffers punishment not because he wills *it,* but rather because he wills a *punishable action.* For it is no punishment to have happen to oneself what one wills, and it is impossible to want to be punished. — To say "I want to be punished if I murder someone" means only the following: "I subject myself together with all others to the laws, among which, naturally, if there are criminals among the people, will also be penal laws. I, as co-legislator who dictates the *penal law,* cannot possibly be the same person who is punished as a subject according to the law. For as such, that is, as a criminal, I can have no voice in legislation (the legislator is holy). Thus if I write a penal law against myself as a criminal, it is pure reason within me legislating in accordance with right (*homo noumenon*) that subjects me, as one capable of a crime, and hence as another person (*homo phaenomenon*) together with all others in the civil union, to the penal law." In other words, it is not the people (each individual therein) but rather the court (public justice), and hence someone other than the criminal, who dictates the death penalty. Thus, the social contract does not at all contain the promise that one may punish oneself and thus dispose of oneself and one's life. For if the authorization to punish were based on a *promise* by the evildoer to *want* to have himself punished, it would also have to be left to him to find himself deserving of punishment, and the criminal would thus be his own judge. — The central point of the error (πρῶτον ψεῦδος) to this sophism is that one regards the judgment of the criminal (which one must necessarily attribute to one's *reason*) that one must lose one's life, as a resolution of the *will* to take it oneself. The execution and the adjudication of justice are thereby presented as unified in one and the same person.

There are, however, two crimes that are punished with death, with regard to which it is questionable whether the *legislation* is authorized to punish them with the death penalty. Both are caused by a pursuit of honor. The first concerns the *honor of womanhood,* and the second concerns *mili-*

8. Cesare, Marchese di Beccaria Bonesana (1738–94), known for his proposals to reform the criminal justice system.

tary honor. Both are cases of true honor, and it is the duty of every member of both classes of human being to pursue them. The first of these crimes is maternal *infanticide (infanticidium maternale)*, the second is the *murder of a fellow soldier* in a *duel (commilitonicidium)*. — Legislation cannot remove the shame of a birth out of wedlock, and it can do just as little to wipe away the taint that arises from the suspicion of cowardice to which a subordinate military commander is subject if he does not answer a disparaging affront with an authority that shows he is beyond the fear of death. It thus seems that persons in these cases find themselves in the state of nature and that *killing (homicidium)*, which need not even be called *murder* then *(homicidium dolosum)*, is certainly punishable in both cases, yet cannot be punished by the supreme authority with death. The child that was born illegitimate is outside of the law (for that is implied by the concept of marriage) and is thus born outside of its protection. It has slipped into the commonwealth, as it were (as a forbidden ware), so that its existence (since it ought not have come into existence in this way) and hence also its destruction can be ignored, while the disgrace of the mother, if her illegitimate birth becomes known, cannot be erased by any ordinance. — Similarly, a soldier with the rank of a junior officer who is insulted finds himself required by public opinion of the fellows in his rank to seek satisfaction and, as in the state of nature, the punishment of the insulter, not through the law before a court but rather through a *duel,* in which his own life is endangered. This is done in order to prove his military valor, on which the honor of his rank rests, even if this is to be won through the *killing* of his opponent in this struggle, which is carried out, although reluctantly, publicly and with the assent of both involved. This killing cannot actually be called *murder (homicidium dolosum).* — What then does right dictate in each of these cases (which both belong to criminal justice)? — Here penal justice runs into difficulties: one must either declare the concept of honor (which is no mere delusion here) null through the law and therefore punish with death, or remove the seemingly appropriate death penalty, and thus be either cruel or too lenient. The resolution of this conundrum is as follows: the categorical imperative of penal justice remains (the unlawful killing of   6:337 another must be punished with death), but the legislation itself (and hence also the civil constitution), as long as it remains barbaric and undeveloped, is at fault for the motivation of honor in the people (subjectively) not coinciding with the standards that (objectively) are appropriate to its intention, such that the public justice that issues from the state becomes *injustice* with regard to the justice that issues from the people.

II.

The *right of pardon* (*ius aggratiandi*) for the criminal, either as mitigation or complete remission of the punishment, is likely the most slippery of all rights of the sovereign. He can use it to display the splendor of his majesty but in doing so cause great injustice. — With regard to the crimes committed among his *subjects* he simply has no place to exercise it. For here impunity (*impunitas criminis*) is the greatest wrong to the latter. He can make use of the right of pardon only in the case of a harm *to himself* (*crimen laesae maiestatis*). But even here he cannot pardon if impunity could cause danger to befall the people itself. — This right is the only one that deserves the name "right of majesty."

ON THE LEGAL RELATION OF THE CITIZEN TO HIS OWN COUNTRY AND TO FOREIGN COUNTRIES

§ 50

The *country* (*territorium*), whose inhabitants are fellow citizens of one and the same commonwealth purely by virtue of the constitution, that is, without having to exercise a particular legal act (thus merely by birth) is called *fatherland*. A country where they are not citizens but for the above condition, is known as a *foreign country*, and, when this country is at all part of the dominion of the government, it is known as the *province* (with the meaning the word has in the use of the Romans). The province, because it is not an incorporated part of the empire (*imperii*) where fellow citizens *reside*, but rather are only a *possession* of the empire as if a *lower house* of it, must honor the land of the ruling state as *motherland* (*regio domina*).

1. The *subject* (considered also as a citizen) has the right to emigrate, for the state cannot hold him back as its property. Yet he can take with him only his movable belongings, not his fixed belongings, which would nevertheless happen if he were allowed to sell the land he had owned to date and take the money for it with him.

2. The *ruler of the country* has the right to promote the *immigration* and settlement of foreigners (colonists), even though his subjects might not take a liking to this, as long as the latter are not deprived of any of their private property in land.

3. In the case of a crime on the part of a subject that makes any association with him a danger for the state, the ruler has the right of *banishment* (that is, *deportation*) to a province in a foreign country where he will not enjoy any of the rights of a citizen.

4. He also has the right to *remove him from the domain entirely* (*ius exilii*), to send him into the world at large, that is, out of the country entirely (called *Elend* [misery] in Old German). Since the ruler thereby withdraws all protection from him, this means as much as making him an outlaw within his own borders.

§ 51

The three authorities in the state that issue from the concept of a *commonwealth* in general (*res publica latius dicta*) are only so many relations of the unified will of the people, which originates a priori in reason. These are a pure idea of a head of state, and this idea has objective practical reality. Yet this head of state (the sovereign) is only a *thought-entity* (representing the entire people), insofar as there is lacking a physical person who represents the supreme state authority and lends effectiveness to this idea on the will of the people. Now the relation between the former and the latter can be conceived in three different ways: either that *one* commands all in the state, or that *some,* who are equal to one another, command all others in the state, or that *all* together command over every one, and thus also over themselves. That is, the *form of the state* is either *autocratic, aristocratic,* or *democratic.* (The expression *monarchist* in place of autocratic is not appropriate to the concept intended here, for the *monarch* is the one who possesses the *highest* authority, while the *autocrat* or *self-ruler* is the one who holds *all* authority. The autocrat is the sovereign, the monarch only represents it. — One readily recognizes that the autocratic form of state is the *simplest,* namely, a relation of one (the king) to the people, whereby only one is the legislator. The aristocratic form of state is already *composed* of two relations, namely, of the nobility among themselves (as legislators), constituting the sovereign, and then the relation of this sovereign to the people. The democratic form of state is the most complex of all, uniting first the will of all in order to make a people, then uniting the will of the citizens in order to build a commonwealth, and then to place over this the sovereign, which is this united will itself.* As concerns the *administration* of right in the state, the simplest is surely also the best, but, with regard to *right* itself, it is the most dangerous considering the despotism which it so invites. Simplification is indeed the reasonable maxim in the machinery of uniting the people through coercive

6:339

---

* I will not discuss the adulteration of these forms that arise from unauthorized persons that force their way to power (*oligarchy* and *ochlocracy*) or any of the so-called *mixed* state constitutions, since that would lead too far afield.

laws, as long as everyone among the people is passive and obeys the one who is above them. But this does not result in subjects as *citizens*. As concerns the false consolation with which the people must content itself, namely, that monarchy (here actually autocracy) is the best constitution of the state *when the monarch is good* (that is, he has not merely the will for it, but also the insight): this is a tautological truism and says nothing other than that the best constitution is the one through which the state administrator is made into the best regent, that is, the one which is the best.

§ 52

It is *futile* to try to track down the *historical document* of this mechanism, which is to say that one cannot arrive at the point in time at which civil society began (for savages do not draw up any document of their subjugation to the law, and it is to be presumed from the mere nature of undeveloped human beings that they began it with violence). But to pursue this inquiry with the intention of perhaps changing by force the currently existing constitution is punishable. For this change would have to occur through the people that revolts for that end and hence not through legislation. Yet mutiny within an already existing constitution is an overthrow of all civil-legal relations and hence of all right. It is thus not a change of the civil constitution, but rather a dissolution of the same, and then the transition into the better constitution is not a metamorphosis, but rather a palingenesis, which demands a new social contract on which the previous one (now nullified) has no influence. — It must, however, be possible for the sovereign to change the existing constitution if it is not compatible with the idea of the original contract while still preserving the form that is essential to the people constituting a state. This change cannot, however, consist in the state changing its constitution from one of these three forms to one of the two others, for example, in aristocrats agreeing to subject themselves to an autocracy or merging into a democracy, or vice versa, as if it were based on the free choice and at the discretion of the sovereign which constitution he wished to subject the people to. For even in the case that he decided to change into a democracy he would be able to do wrong to the people, since it could even detest this constitution and find one of the other two more beneficial to it.

The forms of state are only the *letter* (*littera*) of the original legislation in the civil condition and may therefore remain as long as they — as belonging to the machinery of the state constitution —, are held to be necessary

6:340

through long, old habit (thus only subjectively). But the *spirit* of that original contract (*anima pacti originarii*) contains the obligation of the constituting authority, namely, the obligation to adapt the *mode of governing* to that idea and thus, if it cannot happen at once, to gradually and continually change that mode of governing so that it is, *in its effect,* in agreement with the only lawful constitution, namely, that of a pure republic. Those old empirical (statutory) forms, which served merely to bring about the *subjugation* of the people, thereby dissolve into the original (rational) form, which makes only *freedom* its principle, indeed makes it the condition of all *coercion.* It is coercion under the condition of freedom that is required for a legal constitution of the state in the strict sense of the word, and which will ultimately lead to a form of state according to the letter as well. — This is the   6:341
only lasting state constitution, where the *law* itself rules and is tied to no particular person. It is the ultimate end of all public right, the only condition in which each can be *peremptorily* allotted what is his. In the meantime, however, as long as those forms of state, according to the letter, bestow so many different moral persons with the supreme authority, only a *provisional* internal right exists, and not a condition of civil society that is absolutely in conformity with right.

Yet every true republic is and can be nothing other than a *representative* system of the people, meant, in the name of the people, and through all citizens in their unity, to ensure its rights by means of its representatives (deputies). But as soon as a head of state as a person (be it the king, aristocratic class, or the entire people, the democratic union) also lets itself be represented, the united people does not merely *represent* the sovereign, rather it *is* itself the sovereign. For in it (the people) is found the origin of the supreme authority from which all rights of individuals as mere subjects (particularly as officers of the state) must be derived. The now established republic no longer needs to let the reins of government from its hands and surrender them again to those who led it before, and who could now destroy all new arrangements by means of an absolute use of power.

It was therefore a great mistake in judgment on the part of a powerful ruler of our time that he sought to escape an embarrassing situation with respect to state debts by leaving it up to the people to assume and distribute this burden as it saw fit, for it thereby naturally acquired not only the legislative authority with regard to the taxation of the subjects, but rather also with regard to the government in general. The people was thus able to hinder the government from incurring new debts through waste or war, whereby the ruling authority of the monarch completely disappeared (was not merely suspended) and went to the people,[9] to whose legislative will the "mine" and "yours" of every subject was now subjugated. One can also not say that in this case one should assume an implicit yet contractual promise by the national assembly not to constitute oneself as the sovereign, and only rather to administer the government's affairs for it and then to hand the reins of the regime back over to the monarch after business was done. Such a contract is in itself null and void. The right of the supreme legislative authority in the commonwealth is no alienable right, but rather the most personal of rights. Whoever has it can dispose over the people only by means of the general will of the people, but he cannot dispose over the general will itself, which is the original ground of all public contracts. A contract that would obligate the people to surrender its authority would not be consistent with its legislative authority and yet would obligate it, something which, in accordance with the proposition "no one can have two masters," is a contradiction.

6:342

9. Note that on Kant's reconstruction of the events, the French "revolution" was not a real revolution, as Kant here implies that the king voluntarily gave up essential parts of his powers.

Second Section of Public Right: International Right   6:343

§ 53

The human beings who constitute a people[10] can be conceived as natives of the land in accordance with the analogy of being born of a common set of *ancestors* (*congeniti*), even if they in fact are not. They are born, however, in the intellectual and legal sense, of one common mother (the republic), and constitute, as it were, a family (*gens, natio*) whose members (citizens) are all equal and do not interbreed with those whom they consider unnoble and who may exist near them in the state of nature, even though the latter (the savages) in turn consider themselves noble due to the lawless freedom that they have chosen, and constitute populaces, although not states. The law of *states* in relation to one another (which in German is not entirely correctly called right of *peoples* [*Völkerrecht*], but which rather should be called right of states [*ius publicum civitatum*]) is that which we are to consider under the name of international right. This is where a state, as a moral person, in the condition of natural freedom, which is consequently considered the condition of constant war, in part has the right *to wage* war, in part has rights *in* war, and in part has rights *after* the war, that is, has the right to compel the other to emerge from this condition of war, and thus makes a task of creating a constitution which establishes an enduring peace. The only feature that distinguishes the state of nature among peoples from the state of nature of individual human beings or families (in their relation among another) is that in international right one is concerned not merely with the relation of one state to another in the whole, but also with the relation of individual persons belonging to one to individual persons of   6:344 another, as well as to the entire other state itself. The difference between the rights of states and the rights of individuals in the mere state of nature requires only such qualifications as can easily be derived from the concept of the latter.

§ 54

The elements of international right are: (1) that states, considered in their external relations with one another (like lawless savages), are by nature in a nonjuridical condition; (2) that this condition is a *condition* of war (where might is right), even if not an actual war and actual perpetual feuding (hostility), feuding which (in that both do not want to have it better),

10. "People" is here used not in the nationalist but in the political sense of the term.

although none is treated wrongly by the other, is in itself wrong in the highest degree; and that the states which neighbor one another are obligated to emerge from this state of war; (3) that a league of states according to the idea of an original social contract is necessary, not to intervene in the domestic differences of one another, but to protect one another against attacks from the outside; (4) that the association must imply no sovereign power (as in the civil constitution), but rather only a *cooperation* (federalism), an alliance that can be broken off at any time, and thus must be renewed from time to time, — this is a right that is subsidiary to another, original right, namely, the right to prevent the fall into the condition of real war between the states (*foedus Amphictyonum*).[11]

§ 55

In light of that original right for free states to wage war against one another in the state of nature (in order, for instance, to create a condition approaching a juridical one) the following question arises first: what right does the state have *vis-à-vis its own subjects* to use them in war against other states, to expend their goods, even their life, or to risk them, and to risk them in such a way that it does not depend on their own judgment whether they wish to go to war or not, but rather on the supreme command of the sovereign which can send them off to it?

This right seems to be easily demonstrated, namely, on the grounds that one has the right to do with one's own (property) as one pleases. What someone has *made* oneself in its substance is indisputably one's property. — Here is the deduction as a mere lawyer would present it.

6:345

There are various kinds of *products of nature* in a country which must nevertheless, as concerns the *quantity* of a certain kind, also be considered *artifacts* (*artefacta*) of the state, since the country would not produce them in such quantities if there were not a state and an orderly, ruling government and the inhabitants had remained in the state of nature. — Domestic chickens (the most useful species of poultry), sheep, pigs, cattle, etc. would, either due to lack of fodder or due to predators, be found not at all or at most very seldom in the country where I live, if there were not a government there that ensures the livelihoods and possessions of the inhabitants. — The same is true of the number of human beings, which, just as in the American

11. An amphictyonic league was an association of neighboring cities in ancient Greece, established for the protection of a religious center. The most important one was the one related to the Temple of Apollo at Delphi.

deserts, even if one were to credit them with the greatest diligence (which they do not possess), can only be small in number. The inhabitants would be only very thin on the ground, since none of them would able to spread out widely on land with his household, since the land is always at risk of being devastated by humans or wild animals or predators. A sufficient livelihood could thus not be found for such a large quantity of human beings as currently live in a country. — Just as one can say of plants (for example, of potatoes) and of domestic animals, since they, as concerns their quantity, are a *product* of human beings, that one can use them, use them up, and consume them (have them killed), so, it seems, one can say of the supreme authority in the state, the sovereign, that he has the right to lead his subjects, who for the most part are his own product, into war as if on a hunt, and lead them to a battle as if on a pleasure outing.

This basis of a right (which presumably is also vaguely in the mind of the monarchs) is valid to be sure with regard to animals, which can be the *property* of human beings, but simply cannot be applied to the human being, especially as a citizen, who must be considered a co-legislating member of the state (not merely as a means, but rather also at the same time as an end in itself), and who must freely assent, not just to the waging of war in general, but rather to every particular declaration of war by means of his representatives. Under this limiting condition alone can the state have at its disposal his service in the face of danger.

6:346

We will thus have to derive this right from the *duty* of the sovereign vis-à-vis the people (not vice versa), whereby the people must be regarded as having given its assent and, as such, although it is passive (lest something be done to it), it nonetheless also acts on its own and represents the sovereign itself.

§ 56

In the natural condition of states, the *right to wage war* (to engage in hostilities) is the allowed manner for a state to pursue its right vis-à-vis another state. That is, when it believes itself to be harmed, it uses its own *force,* since this pursuit cannot occur in this condition by means of a *lawsuit* (the sole means by which disputes in a juridical condition can be reconciled). — Causes for such a pursuit include, beside active injury (the first aggression, which is different from the first hostility), also the *threat.* This includes either being the first to start *arming* for war, which provides the grounds for the right to *prevent* (*ius praeventionis*), or even merely (through acquisition of lands) a *terrifying* growth in the *power* (*potentia tremenda*) of another state. The latter is a harm to the less powerful merely due to the condition of the *more powerful,* before any *action,* and in the state of nature a preventive attack is lawful. This is the basis of the right of balance between all states which come actively into contact with one another.

As concerns *active injury,* which gives grounds for the *right to wage war,* this includes self-acquired satisfaction for the insult of the one people by the people of the other state, that is, *retribution (retorsio),* without seeking compensation (by peaceful means) from the other state. This bears a similarity in form with the outbreak of war without a prior breaking off of peace (*announcement of war*), since, if one wants to find a right in the state of war, something analogous to a contract must be assumed, namely, the *acceptance* of the declaration of the other party that both parties intend to pursue their right in this way.

§ 57

Right in war is precisely that part of international right where one has the most difficulty in even conceiving what it is to mean and to think of a law in this lawless condition (*inter arma silent leges*)[12] without contradicting oneself. It would have to be the following: to wage war according to those principles according to which it still remains possible to emerge from the natural condition of states (in their external relations vis-à-vis one another) and to enter into a juridical one.

No war between independent states can be a *punitive* war (*bellum punitivum*). For punishment takes place only in the relation between commander (*imperantis*) and subject (*subditum*), which is not the relation of states with regard to one another. — But also neither a war of *eradication* (*bellum internecinum*) nor a war of *subjugation* (*bellum subiugatorium*) is allowed, which would be the moral extermination of a state (its people would either be merged with that of the conqueror into a mass or be forfeited to servitude). It is not that this emergency means of the state to attain a condition of peace in itself contradicts the rights of a state. It is rather that the idea of international right implies only the concept of antagonism according to principles of external freedom in order to protect what is one's own, but not as a means of acquisition of the kind that would result in the expansion of the power of one state becoming a threat to another.

The state on which war is waged is permitted to employ all means of defense, except for those the use of which would make the subjects of that

12. "Amidst weapons the laws are silent," Cicero, *Pro Milone* 10.

state unable to be citizens. For otherwise the state in turn would make itself incapable of being regarded as a person in the relations among the states according to international right (which, as such, participates in equal rights with other states). To be excluded are: using one's own subjects as spies, using them or foreigners as treacherous murderers, using them as poison mixers (also belonging to this class are probably the so-called sharpshooters, who lie in wait to ambush individuals), or using them to spread false news. In a word, states shall not avail themselves of such malicious means which would destroy the trust that is required for the future establishment of a lasting peace.

It is allowed in war to demand exactions and contributions from the defeated enemy, but one may not plunder the people, that is, take forcibly from individuals what is their own (for that would be robbery, since it was not the defeated people, but rather the state that rules the people, which waged war *through the people*). This is to be done in such a way that *receipts* are given in return for the impositions, so that the burden is proportionally distributed across the country or province during the time of peace that follows.

6:348

§ 58

Right *after a war,* that is, at the point in time of the peace treaty and with respect to the consequences of the latter, consists in the following: the victor determines the conditions to which the defeated party is to agree and about which *treaties* are usually drafted that customarily lead to the conclusion of peace. The victor does so not in accordance with some protective right that is due to it for some alleged injury inflicted by its opponent, but rather, by leaving this question unanswered, it rests its case on its power.

The victor can therefore not put it to the defeated party that the latter should reimburse it for the cost of the war, since it would otherwise have to assert that the war of his opponent was unjust. As much as he might think of this argument, he may not use it, since he would otherwise declare the war a war of punishment and thereby would in turn offend his opponent. Part of right after war is the exchange (without payment of ransom) of prisoners of war without regard to equality in the numbers exchanged.

The defeated state, or its subjects, do not lose their freedom as citizens through the conquest of their country; the state does not become a colony, and its subjects are not degraded to the status of serfs, for otherwise the war would have been a punitive war, which contradicts itself. — A *colony* or a province is a people that has its own constitution, legislation, and land, and on this land those who belong to another state are only foreigners, even if the latter state has supreme *executive* authority over this people. This state with supreme executive authority is called the *mother state*. The daughter state is ruled by the mother state but is governed by itself through its own parliament, possibly under the leadership of a viceroy (*civitas hybrida*). Such was *Athens* in relation to various islands, and so is Great Britain with respect to Ireland.

6:349   Even less can *serfdom* and its lawfulness be derived from one people's conquest of another through war, since one would have to presume a punitive war for this. Least of all would hereditary slavery be possible, the general idea of which is absurd, since guilt for someone's crime cannot be inherited.

That the conclusion of peace is tied to an *amnesty* is part of the concept of the former.

§ 59

The *right of peace* includes: (1) the right to stay at peace when there is war nearby, or the right to *neutrality;* (2) the right to have the duration of the concluded peace ensured, that is, the *guarantee* of peace; and (3) the right to mutual *alliance* (a confederation) between several states, which is the right to a common *defense* against any external or internal attacks, not an alliance for attack or internal expansion.

§ 60

The right of a state vis-à-vis an *unjust enemy* knows no limits (not with respect to quantity, that is, degree, although there are limits with respect to quality). That is to say that the injured state may not use *all* means, but may use any means permissible in themselves to the degree that it is able, in order to assert what is its own. — But what is an *unjust enemy* according to concepts of international right, in which, as generally in the state of nature, each state is judge of its own case? It is the enemy whose publicly declared will (be it through words or deeds) betrays a maxim which, if it were made into a general rule, would make peace among the peoples impossible and would instead perpetuate the state of nature. An example of this is the breach of public contracts, which, one can presume, is a matter that concerns all peoples to the extent that their freedom is thereby threatened. Thus all peoples are thereby called upon to unite against such mischief and take power from such a state. — But one can*not* do so *in order to divide its land*

and to make a state disappear from the earth, as it were, for that would be an injustice against the people of the state, which cannot lose its original right to unite itself into a commonwealth. Rather one does so in order to let it accept a new constitution, one which according to its nature is unfavorable to the inclination to wage war.

Incidentally, the expression "an unjust enemy in the state of nature" is 6:350 *redundant,* for the state of nature is itself a state of injustice. A just enemy would be one whom I would do wrong if I were to resist, but such a person would then not be my enemy.

§ 61

Since one ought to emerge from the state of nature among peoples in order to enter into a legal condition just as much as one ought to do so in the state of nature among individuals, therefore, before this happens, all right of peoples and all that can be acquired through war or preserved as external "mine" and "yours" among states are merely *provisional,* and only in a general *union of states* can this become *peremptorily* valid (analogous to the union through which a people becomes a state) and can a true *condition of peace* be attained. But since too great an expansion of such a state of peoples over vast regions would ultimately make governance of the same, and hence the protection of each member, impossible, whereas a number of such corporations would in turn lead to a condition of war, *perpetual peace* (the ultimate end of all of international right) is admittedly an idea that cannot be realized. Yet the political principles that aim at this idea, namely, those that direct us to enter into such relations as serve a continual *approach* toward perpetual peace are indeed, to that extent that they are a task grounded in duty and hence in the right of human beings and states, realizable.

One can call such a *union* of several *states* for the purpose of preserving the peace a *permanent congress of states,* a congress which any neighboring country reserves the right to join. An example of this (at least as concerns the formal aspects of international right with regard to preserving peace) was to be found in the first half of the eighteenth century in the assembly of the states-general in The Hague. Here the ministers of most of the European courts and even of the smallest republics lodged their complaints with respect to the hostilities that one was subjected to by the other, and in this way they thought of all of Europe as a single, federal state, which they took to be the arbitrator in their public disputes. Instead, afterwards international right endured only in books, having disappeared from the cabinets, or, after violence had already been practiced, was entrusted in the form of deductions to the darkness of the archives.

6:351 By *congress* I mean here only a voluntary assembly of various states that can be *dissolved* at any time and not an organization which (as that of the American states) is based on a state constitution and is thus is indissoluble. — Only through such a congress can the idea of a public right of peoples be realized that should be established in order to decide their disputes in a civil manner, through legal proceedings, as it were, and not in a barbaric manner (in the manner of savages), that is, through war.

6:352

Third Section of Public Right: Cosmopolitan Right

§ 62

This rational idea of a *peaceful,* if not yet friendly and universal community of all peoples on earth who can come into active relations with one another is not a philanthropic (ethical) one, but rather a principle of *right.* Nature has placed them all together (due to the spherical shape of the place where they live, as *globus terraqueus*) within finite boundaries. And since the possession of land on which the earth's inhabitant can live can always only be thought of as the possession of a part of a certain whole and thus a part to which everyone originally has a right, all peoples *originally* stand in a community of the land, but it is not a *legal* community of possession (*communio*) and thereby of use, or ownership of the same. Rather it is a community of possible physical *interaction* (*commercium*), that is, of a universal relation of one to all others to *present* oneself for possible *commerce* [*Verkehr*] with each other. They have a right to try to enter into it, without the foreigner being justified in confronting him as an enemy for that reason. — This right, to the extent that it concerns the possible unification of all peoples with the intention of establishing certain universal laws governing their possible commerce, can be called *cosmopolitan* right (*ius cosmopoliticum*).

Oceans may seem to prevent peoples from entering into a community with one another, and yet due to navigation they provide the most auspicious means for their commerce. Such can be all the more lively the more 6:353 *coasts* are in proximity to one another (as in the Mediterranean), although visiting such coasts, but more so settling on them in order to establish a connection with the home country, provides the occasion for afflictions and violence in one part of the globe to be felt in all parts. This possible abuse cannot, however, nullify the right of a citizen of the earth to *attempt* to enter into community with all others and, to this end, to *visit* all regions of the world, even though this is not a right to *settle* on the land of another people (*ius incolatus*), which would require a special contract.

Yet the question arises whether a people can *settle* in newly discovered lands (*accolatus*) and take possession of land near a people that has already established itself in the area, without first seeking the assent of the latter.

If such settlement occurs at such a distance from the site where the latter lives that no infringement on the latter's use of land takes place, then the right to do so is unquestionable. But if they are herding or hunting peoples (as the Hottentots, the Tongas, and most of the American peoples), whose livelihood depends on large, barren expanses of land, then this would be able to happen not with violence, but rather only by contract, and even this without exploiting the ignorance of the inhabitants with regard to the relinquishment of such land. This is so even though there seem to be a sufficient number of reasons justifying violence as means for bettering the world: for one, bringing culture to undeveloped peoples (as in the pretense with which even *Büsching*[13] wants to excuse the bloody introduction of the Christian religion into Germany), for another, purging one's own land of depraved individuals with the hope that they or their offspring will improve in another part of the world (as in New Holland). All of these purportedly good intentions cannot wash away the stain of injustice in the means used to attain them. — One might object here that such doubts about using violence to begin to establish a legal condition would perhaps leave the entire planet still in a lawless state. But this is just as unable to nullify the conditions of right as is the pretense of state revolutionaries that, if constitutions are corrupted, the people has the right to reform them by means of violence and to be unjust once and for all, so that afterwards they can establish justice all the more certainly and cause it to thrive.

Conclusion

6:354

If someone cannot prove that a thing exists, he may always try to prove that it does not. If he is not able to do either (which often is the case), then he can ask the question whether he has an *interest* in *assuming* one or the other (by means of a hypothesis), from either a theoretical or a practical point of view, that is, in order merely to explain a certain phenomenon (as for example retrograde motion and standstill of the planets), or in order to attain a certain

13. Anton Friedrich Büsching (1724–93), historian, theologian, and geographer.

end, which in turn can be either *pragmatic* (purely technical) or *moral,* that is, an end that duty requires us to adopt as a maxim. — It is self-evident that what is made into a duty here is not the *assumption* (*suppositio*) of the realizability of that end, which is a purely theoretical and also problematic judgment, for there is no obligation to do so (to believe something). What is our duty is, rather, to act in accordance with the idea of that end that is our duty, even if not the least theoretical probability exists that it can be realized, for its impossibility also cannot be demonstrated.

Now moral-practical reason in us pronounces its irresistible veto: *There shall be no war,* neither between me and you in the state of nature, nor between us as states, which, although internally in a legal condition, are externally (in relation to one another) in a state of lawlessness. — For this is not the manner in which everyone ought to seek his rights. It is thus no longer a question whether perpetual peace is real or unreal and whether we deceive ourselves in our theoretical judgment if we assume that it is real. Rather we must act as if it is real, which it may not be, and work toward establishing it and the constitution that seems the most suitable to that end (perhaps republicanism of all states together and separately), to bring it about and to bring an end to the hopeless waging of war, which all states without exception have heretofore aimed their internal institutions toward as their main end. And even if the latter, as concerns the completion of this aim, might remain a pious wish, we still would certainly not deceive ourselves by adopting the maxim to work relentlessly toward it. For this is duty. To assume, by contrast, that the moral law in us itself is deceptive would bring about the abhorrent wish to dispense with all reason and regard oneself, as far as one's principles are concerned, as thrown in together with the other classes of animals as part of the same mechanism of nature.

One can say that this general and enduring establishment of peace is not merely part, but rather the entire final end of the doctrine of right within the bounds of mere reason. For only the condition of peace is a condition where "mine" and "yours" is secured under *laws* among a number of people that live in proximity and hence are together under a constitution. The rule of this constitution must not be taken from the experience of those who have hitherto found it to their greatest advantage, as a norm for others. This rule must be taken, rather, a priori through reason from the ideal of a legal union of human beings under public laws in general, since all examples (which can only illustrate, but not prove) are deceptive. For this reason a metaphysics is required, the necessity of which even those who mock it carelessly concede themselves when they, as they often do, say, for instance: "The best constitution is one where the laws, not the human beings, are in power." For what can be more metaphysically sublimated than precisely this idea? Yet it has, according to their own assertion, the most proven objective reality, which can also easily be demonstrated in particular cases. This idea should not be brought about in a revolution, in one leap, that is, through a violent overthrow of a previously existing faulty constitution — (for then a moment would occur in the meantime where the entire juridical condition was nullified). Rather it must be attempted and carried out through gradual reform, according to fixed principles, and only it can direct us to a continual approach toward the highest political good, perpetual peace.

The Contest of the Faculties, Part 2

Part Two. The Contest of the Faculty of Philosophy with the Faculty of Law[1]

The Question Renewed: "Is Humankind Continually Improving?"

1. What do we *want* to know here?

One is asking for a piece of human history, but one of future history and not past, hence a *predictive* history which, when it is not determined by known laws of nature (as are solar and lunar eclipses), is called *divinatory* but still natural; but which, when it can be given in no other way than by supernatural revelation and the extension of one's view into the future, is called *visionary* (prophetic).* — Incidentally, when we ask the question of whether the human *species* (as a whole) is improving steadily, we are concerned not with the natural history of the human being (with the question, say, of whether new races of human beings could come into being in the future), but rather with a *moral history* of the human being. Yet this moral history is not one given according to the *concept of the human species* (*singulorum*), but rather is concerned with the *whole* of humankind, as it is socially united on earth yet divided into distinct peoples (universorum).

2. How *can* we know it?

By telling a divinatory history of that which is to come in the future, thus by giving a portrayal of events to come that is possible a priori. — But how is a history possible a priori? — Answer: when the one divining the events himself *brings about* and arranges the events that he announces in advance.

Jewish prophets had an easy time prophesying that their state sooner or

---

* Whoever plays at prophecy (with neither knowledge nor honesty), from the Pythia to gypsies, can be called a *false prophet*.[2]

1. This is the second of three independently written essays. The connection of this essay with the general theme of a conflict between faculties is quite loose.

2. The Pythia is Apollo's priestess, the oracle at Delphi.

later would be subject not merely to decline, but rather to complete dissolution, for they themselves were the agents of this fate. — As leaders of their people they weighed down their constitution with so many ecclesiastical burdens and civil burdens ensuing from these, that their state became completely unfit for existence in its own right, and, most of all, for coexistence with other, neighboring peoples. The jeremiads of their priests, of course, necessarily went unheard, since they stubbornly insisted on their intention of an unsustainable constitution that they themselves had created. They could thus infallibly predict the outcome themselves.

Our politicians proceed in just the same way, and, as far as their influence extends, are just as successful with their predictions. — One must, they say, accept people as they are, not expect them to be as some unknowing pedant or good-natured dreamer imagines they ought to be. But "*how they are*" should be described thus: the way we *have made* them by means of unjust coercion, by means of treacherous plans that we have suggested to the government, namely, obstinate and with a tendency to rebel. Given this tendency, the prophecies of those purportedly clever statesmen come true when one begins to relax the reins and tragic results ensue.

Even clergy occasionally prophesy the complete decline of religion and the imminent coming of the Antichrist while doing precisely what is required to make it so. This they do by not being concerned with imparting moral principles to their congregation that would lead directly to moral improvement, but rather with making observances and historical faith into an essential duty that is intended to bring this improvement about indirectly. From this arises a mechanical unanimity as in a civil constitution, but none in moral conviction. They nonetheless complain of an irreligiosity that they have created themselves and could therefore also predict without any particular gift of foresight.

3. Classification of the concept of what one seeks to know for the future.   7:81

There are three possible propositions here with predictive content. The human race either is continually *regressing* toward the worse, is constantly *progressing* toward the better as far as its moral vocation is concerned, or is in a perpetual *standstill* at the current stage of moral worth among the members of creation (which is precisely the same as an eternal circling around the same point). The *first* proposition can be called moral *terrorism,* the *second eudaemonism*[3] (which, when considering the aim of the progress

---

3. "Theory of happiness."

from far away, can also be called *chiliasm*).[4] But the *third* can be called *abderitism*[5] because, since a true standstill in the moral realm is not possible, a constant alternation between inclines and equally frequent and equally deep declines (an eternal fluctuation, as it were) results in nothing at all, just as if the subject remained in the same location in a standstill.

a. On the terrorist conception of human history.

Regression toward the morally worse in the human race cannot continue indefinitely, for the latter would at a certain stage destroy itself. Faced with mounting human atrocities and their accompanying afflictions, one therefore says "It cannot get any worse than this, the Day of Judgment is nigh," and the pious zealot already dreams of the re-creation of all things and a newly born world after this one has gone down in flames.

b. On the eudaemonist conception of human history.

7:82   One may always concede that the quantity of good and evil that attaches to our nature always remains the same and can neither increase nor decrease in one and the same individual. For how should this quantity of good in one's native constitution be increased, given that this is to happen by means of the freedom of the subject, which in turn would require an even greater measure of goodness than it possesses? — The effects cannot exceed the capacity of the effective cause. Hence the measure of good that coexists with evil in human beings cannot exceed a certain quantity, beyond which they could work themselves up and thereby constantly progress toward the even better. Eudaemonism with its sanguine hopes thus seems untenable and promises little in support of a prophetic human history with regard to the perpetual progression on the path of goodness.

c. On the hypothesis of abderitism in the determination in advance of the history of humankind.

This opinion may well be shared by the majority. Bustling foolishness is the characteristic of our species: one steps quickly onto the path of the good, but does not remain there, rather, in order not to be bound to a single end, reverses the plan of progress, even if just for the sake of change, one builds

4. Chiliasm: millenarianism.

5. Abdera was an ancient Greek city with a reputation of foolishness. Christoph Martin Wieland, the influential editor of the journal *Der Teutsche Merkur,* had written a successful series of satirical essays in the *Merkur,* republished together in 1774 as *Geschichte der Abderiten* [History of the Abderites].

up only to tear down and to subject oneself to the hopeless toil of rolling the boulder of Sisyphus uphill, only to let it roll back down. — The principle of evil in the natural constitution of the human race seems not to be amalgamated (merged) with the good, but rather both seem to neutralize one another, from which inactivity would follow (which would be called a standstill here). This empty bustling, letting good and evil alternate by moving forward and backward, would require regarding the entire play of interaction of our species with itself on this planet as a mere prank, which can lend it no greater worth in the eyes of reason than that of other animal species that engage in this game with far lesser costs and without the use of intellect.

4. The problem of progress is not to be resolved immediately through experience.

7:83

If the human race, considered as a whole, were found to be moving forward and in the process of progressing even for a great length of time, one could still not be certain that the epoch of regression is not setting in precisely at this point in time by virtue of the physical constitution of our species. And conversely, if it is moving backward in an ever-speedier decline toward the worse, one must not despair that this is not precisely the point in time where the turning point (*punctum flexus contrarii*) could be found, whereby the course of the human race, due to the moral constitution of our species, turns again toward the better. For we are speaking here of freely acting beings, beings who can be *told* in advance what they *ought* to do, but for whom it cannot be *predicted* what they in fact *will* do, and who, when truly bad circumstances prevail, know to derive from the feeling of the afflictions that they have brought upon themselves an even stronger motivation to make things better than they had been before this state. — But "poor mortals (says the Abbot *Coyer*),[6] nothing among you is constant other than inconstancy!"

Perhaps it is due to the incorrect choice of perspective from which we view the course of human events that the latter seems so irrational. The planets, seen from Earth, appear to move backward, then to stand still, then to move forward. If viewed, however, from the position of the sun, something which only reason can do, they continually move, according to the Copernican hypothesis, in their regular orbit. Some who are otherwise not unwise like to insist on their explanation of phenomena and the perspective

6. Gabriel François Coyer (1707–82). The quote is taken from his book, *Bagatelles morales* [Moral Bagatelles] (1754), which had appeared in German translation in 1761.

they have chosen, even if they thereby catch themselves up in Tychonic cycles and epicycles[7] to the point of absurdity. — But it is exactly our misfortune that we are not capable, as concerns the prediction of free acts, to assume this perspective. For that would be the perspective of *providence,* which lies beyond the grasp of all human wisdom and which also extends to the *free* actions of human being. While such actions can be *seen* by human wisdom, they certainly cannot be *foreseen* by it (there is no difference here for the eye of God), since for doing so human beings require the context of natural laws, yet, with regard to future *free* actions, he must do without the direction and counsel of these.

7:84

If one may assume that human beings possess an innate and unalterably good, albeit limited, will, then he would be able to predict with certainty this progress of his species toward the better. This he could do because it would concern a matter that he himself can bring about. But given a mixture of evil and good in his constitution, the measure of which he does not know, he does not know himself what effect he can expect from it.

5. The divinatory history of the human race must be nonetheless connected with some kind of experience.

There must exist some experience in the human race which, as an event, indicates that the latter has a makeup and capacity to be both the *cause* of human progress toward the better and (since this is supposed to be the act of a being endowed with freedom) the *agent* thereof. But a given cause allows one to predict an event as an effect if those circumstances that contribute to it prevail. That the latter must prevail at some point can be predicted in a general manner, just as the calculation of probabilities in a game, but it cannot be determined whether this will occur in my lifetime and whether I will have the experience that would confirm the prediction. — Hence an event must be sought which indicates, indefinite with respect to time, the existence of such a cause and the act of its causation in the human race, and which would allow the inference that progress toward the better is inevitable. This inference could then be extended to the history of time past (that is, that it has always been progressing), but in such a way that that event must not itself be considered to be the cause of this progress, but rather only to be indicative, as a historical sign (*signum rememorativum, demonstra-*

7. Tycho Brahe (1546–1601), astronomer who combined elements of the Ptolemaic and Copernican systems. He held that most of the planets revolved around the sun, while this system itself revolved around the earth.

tivum, prognostikon),[8] and thereby prove the *tendency* of the human race as a *whole,* that is, not as a number of individuals (for that would result in a never-ending enumeration and calculation), but rather as it is found on earth, divided into peoples and states.

6. On an event in our time which proves this moral tendency of the human race.

This event does not consist for instance in important deeds or misdeeds of human beings whereby what was great is made small among human beings or what was small made great and, as if by magic, old and splendid states disappear and in their place others arise as if from the depths of the earth. No, nothing of the sort. It is simply the spectators' mind-set, which reveals itself *publicly* in the face of this show of large-scale transformations and which makes known such a universal and yet unselfish sympathy with the players on the one side against those on the other, even at the risk that this partiality could become quite detrimental to them. This mind-set (due to its universality) demonstrates a character of the human race as a whole and also (due to its unselfishness) a moral character of the latter, at least a capacity for it, a character that not only lets one hope for progress toward the better but rather already is itself such progress, to the extent that the capacity for such progress is sufficient for now.

The revolution of a spirited people that we have witnessed in our times may succeed or fail. It may be so filled with misery and atrocities that any reasonable person, if he could hope, undertaking it a second time, to carry it out successfully, would nonetheless never decide to perform the experiment at such a cost. — Nevertheless, in the hearts of all its spectators (who themselves are not involved in the show), I assert, this revolution meets with a degree of *sympathy* in wish that borders on enthusiasm, a sympathy the expression of which is itself associated with danger. This sympathy can thus have no other cause than a moral capacity in the human race.

This contributing moral cause is twofold. First that of *right:* that a people must not be hindered by other powers in giving itself a civil constitution that it itself regards as good. Second that of the *end* (which is also a duty): that only such a constitution of a people is *in accordance with right* and morally good in itself which, in its nature, is made such that wars of aggression are

8. "A sign that reminds, demonstrates, and foretells." Cf. the part on "Signum et Signatum" in Baumgarten's *Metaphysica,* §§ 347–50.

avoided as a matter of principle. This can be none other than the republican constitution, at least in its conception.* Thus the end is to submit to the restriction whereby war (the source of all afflictions and ruin of morals) is prevented and the human race, in all its frailty, is ensured negatively of progress toward the better, of at least not having its progress disturbed. 7:86

This and the *affective* sympathy with the good, *enthusiasm,* even though it is not to be approved of, since all affect as such is deserving of rebuke, nonetheless, through this history, gives cause for the following remark of importance for anthropology: that true enthusiasm is aimed solely at the *ideal* and, indeed, at the purely moral, to which the concept of right belongs, and cannot be attached to selfishness. The opponents of the revolutionaries could not be animated by payments of money to the zeal and greatness of spirit that the mere concept of right brought forth in the revolutionaries. Even the concept of honor of the old martial nobility (analogous to enthusiasm) vanished when faced with the weapons of those who had in mind the rights of the people to whom they belonged** and whose protectors they

---

* This is not meant to say that a people with a monarchical constitution purports to have the right, or even has a secret wish, to have it changed. For perhaps its possession of extended territories in Europe recommends this constitution as the only kind through which it can maintain itself amidst powerful neighbors. Even the grumblings of the subjects are not due to the government's domestic policies, but rather to its policy toward foreign nationals when it, for instance, hinders foreigners in forming a republic, and are in no way proof of a people's dissatisfaction with its own constitution. Indeed, they demonstrate an affection for the latter, since they are all the safer against threats the more that other peoples take on a republican constitution. — Nevertheless libelous sycophants, in order to make themselves important, have attempted to portray this innocent chatter as innovationism, Jacobinism, and conspiracy that threaten the state. Yet there is not the least cause for this pretense, especially not in a country that lies more than a hundred miles from the site of the revolution.

** The following can be said of such enthusiasm for the assertion of right for the human race: *postquam ad arma Vulcania ventum est, — mortalis mucro glacies ceu futilis ictu dissiluit.* [When it came up against the weapons of Vulcan, the mortal sword broke like brittle ice.][9] — Why has no ruler ever dared to say openly that he recognizes no *right* of the people against him? Or to say that the people has only the *beneficence* of the government to thank for the happiness it grants them, and that any presumption on the part of the subject to a right against the government is absurd (because this implies the concept of a permitted resistance) and even punishable? — The reason is that such a public declaration would cause all his

considered themselves to be. The outside, viewing public then sympathized   7:87
with this feeling of exaltation without the least intention of participating.

7. A divinatory history of humankind.

In this principle there must be something *moral* which reason recognizes
as pure, but also, due to its great and epoch-making influence, as something
to which the human soul acknowledges an attendant duty. What is more,
what is moral in this principle concerns the human race in the entirety of its
unity (*non singulorum, sed universorum*),[10] for it revels at its hoped-for
success and the attempts at attaining this success with such widespread and
unselfish sympathy. — This event in question is not the phenomenon of
revolution, but rather (as Erhard[11] describes it) of the *evolution* of a constitution of *natural right*. This admittedly is not yet itself attained through
wild struggles — for both civil and foreign war destroys all *statutory* order   7:88

---

subjects to rise up against him, even if they, like obedient sheep, led by a kind and
understanding master, well fed and strongly protected, would have nothing to
complain about concerning their welfare. — For the enjoyment of life's comforts is
not sufficient for beings endowed with freedom, since these could also be had from
others (in this case from the government). What matters to a being endowed with
freedom is the *principle* by which it attains such comforts for itself. Yet welfare has
no principle, neither for the recipient nor for the giver (one person may conceive of
his welfare in one way and another person in another), since what is at issue here is
the *material* of the will, which is empirical, and hence not capable of the universality of a rule. A being endowed with freedom thus can and should, being conscious of his advantage over animals, which possess no reason, demand, according
to the *formal* principle of his will, no government for the people other than one in
which the people co-legislates. That is, the right of human beings who are supposed to obey must necessarily precede all regard for their well-being, for their
right is sacred and elevated above any price (of usefulness). It is something which
no government, however beneficent it may be, may infringe on. — But this right is
always only an idea whose implementation is restricted by the condition that its
means are consistent with morality, which the people must never contravene, and it
may not be realized by means of revolution, which is always unjust. — Autocratic
rule and yet republican *governance*, that is, in the spirit of and analogous to
republicanism, are what makes a people content with its constitution.

9. The quotation is from Virgil, *Aeneid* 12.739–41.

10. "Not individually, but collectively." Cf. A 7:328.

11. Johann Benjamin Erhard (1766–1827), *Über das Recht des Volkes zu einer Revolution* [On the Right of the People to a Revolution] (Jena and Leipzig, 1795).

that has hitherto prevailed — , but it still leads to striving for a constitution which cannot be keen on war, namely, the republican constitution. This constitution might be republican with regard to the *form of the state,* or merely with regard to the *mode of government,* in which a single head of state (the monarch) would administer the state in analogy to the laws that a people would give itself according to universal principles of right.

In light of circumstances and signs prevalent at present I propose that the human race shall attain this end and herewith also predict, even without the gift of the prophet's vision, a progression of the human race from then on toward the better that can not be completely reversed. For such a phenomenon in human history *will not be forgotten,* since it has uncovered a predisposition and power in human nature the likes of which no politician would have been able to cleverly deduce from the course of events to date. Only nature and freedom, unified in the human race according to internal principles of right, can promise it, but the time of its occurrence remains indeterminate and an event of chance.

But even if the end intended in the case of this event is not presently attained, even if the revolution or reform of the constitution of a people fails in the end or if, after lasting for some time, everything returns to its previous state (as politicians now prophesy falsely), this philosophical prediction loses none of its force. — For that event is too great, too bound up with the interest of humanity, and too widespread in its influence throughout the world, that favorable conditions would not occasion peoples to remember it and make renewed attempts of this kind. Since it is such an important matter for the human race, the intended constitution would, at some point, ultimately have to attain that level of permanence which the lessons of repeated experience would not fail to bring about in the hearts of everyone.

That the human race has always progressed and will further progress toward the better is thus not merely a well-intentioned proposition and one to be recommended from a practical perspective, but rather is justifiable even for the most rigorous of theories, whatever unbelievers might say. When one considers not merely what can occur within one people, but rather what can happen among all the peoples on earth, which might gradually participate in this progress, a perspective into an unbounded future time is opened, provided that, for instance, the first epoch of a natural revolution which swallowed up the animal and plant kingdom prior to humankind's emergence will not be followed (according to Camper and Blumenbach)[12]

7:89

12. Petrus Camper (1722–89), anatomist; Kant here probably refers to Camper's book, *Über den natürlichen Unterschied der Gesichtszüge* [On the Natural Differences in

by a second whereby the human race is submitted to the same fate, so that other creatures may take the stage, and so on. For humankind is a mere trifle for the omnipotence of nature, or, rather, for the omnipotence of its highest cause, which remains inaccessible to us. But it is no trifle that the rulers of humankind would take members of the species to be trivial and treat them as such by yoking them as animals, as a mere tool for their ends, or by setting them against each other in their disputes in order to slaughter one another. This would be an inversion of the *final end* of creation itself.

8. On the difficulty of the maxims aimed at the world's progress toward the better with regard to their publicity.

Popular enlightenment is the public instruction of the people in its duties and rights with regard to the state to which it belongs. Since the rights at issue here are natural and those that arise from common human understanding, those among the people who are naturally fit to pronounce and interpret such rights are not the teachers employed by the state, but rather free teachers of right, that is, the philosophers. Due to the freedom that they permit themselves, the latter are objectionable to the state, which always desires only to rule, and have the reputation, as *"enlighteners,"* of posing a threat to the state, even though their voices are not directed in a *familiar* manner to the people (which takes little note of them or their writings), but rather are directed *deferentially* to the state, which is implored to take heed of the legal needs of the people. This can happen in no way other than by publicity, if an entire nation is to present its grievance (*gravamen*). The *prohibition* of publicity therefore hinders the progress of a people toward the better, even with regard to that which concerns the mere minimum of its demands, namely, its natural rights.

Another concealment that is imposed through laws on a people, albeit   7:90
one that is easy to detect, is that of the true makeup of its constitution. It would be an affront to the majesty of the British nation to say that it is an unlimited *monarchy*. Rather, one wants to describe it as a constitution which *limits* the will of the monarch by means of the two houses of parliament, representatives of the people, even though everyone well knows that the monarch's influence on these representatives is so great and so infallible that nothing is passed by these houses without his willing and proposing it through his ministers. And he very likely also occasionally proposes mea-

---

Facial Traits] (Berlin, 1792). Johann Friedrich Blumenbach (1752–1840, biologist, anatomist) wrote *Handbuch der Naturgeschichte* [Manual of Natural History] (Göttingen, 1779 and many later editions).

sures of which he knows and also *brings about* that he will meet with resistance (e.g., because of the slave trade),[13] in order to give seeming proof of the freedom of parliament. — This way of regarding the matter is deceptive in such a way that one no longer seeks to establish a true and right constitution, since one presumes to have already found one, and an untruthful publicity deceives the people with the false pretense of a *monarchy limited** by a law that originates from the people, while its representatives, bought out with bribes, subject the people to an *absolute monarch*.

* * *

7:91 The idea of a constitution that is consistent with the natural rights of human beings, the idea, namely, that those who obey the law should also, united, be legislators thereof, underlies all forms of state. And the polity, which, conceived in accordance with this idea and through concepts of pure reason, is a platonic *ideal* (*republica noumenon*), is no mere figment of the imagination, but rather the eternal norm for all civil constitutions, and disposes with all war. A civil society that is organized in accordance with this idea is its representation in accordance with the laws of freedom by means of an example in experience (*republica phaenomenon*) and can only be attained with great difficulty through numerous feuds and wars. But its constitution, when it has once been achieved in large part, qualifies it as the best possible one to hold off war, the destroyer of all that is good. It is hence a duty to enter into such a constitution. In the meantime, however,

---

* A cause, the makeup of which one does not immediately understand, reveals itself through the effect that inevitably follows from it. — What is an *absolute* monarch? It is the one whose command that there should be war immediately brings about war. — What is a *limited* monarch in contrast? It is the one who must ask the people in advance whether or not there should be war, and if the people says there should be no war, then there is no war. — For war is a condition in which *all* the resources of the state must be at the disposal of the head of state. Now the British monarch has waged quite a bit of war without seeking this consent. This king is thus an absolute monarch, something that he is not supposed to be according to the constitution. But he can circumvent the constitution because he can ensure for himself the agreement of the representatives of the people through precisely those resources of the state, namely because he has the power to bestow all public offices and titles. This system of bribery may not, of course, be a public one, in order to succeed. It thus remains under a very transparent veil of secrecy.

13. This refers to the struggle for power between George III (1738– 1820) and the British parliament.

since such a constitution will not soon come into being, it is the duty of the monarchs, even though they may rule in an *autocratic* way, to nonetheless govern in a *republican* way (not a democratic way). That is to say that the people ought to be treated according to principles in line with the spirit of the laws of freedom (as a people with mature reason would dictate to itself), even if, by the letter, the people is not asked for its consent.

9. What will the progress toward the better yield for the human race?

Not an ever-increasing quantity of *morality* in its disposition, but rather an increase in *legality* through actions performed in accordance with duty, whatever the actual motivations for these actions might be. That is to say, the yield (the result) of this cultivation of humankind toward the better will take the form of an increase in the good *deeds* of humans, hence in the phenomena of the moral quality of the human race, which shall become ever more numerous and better. — For we have only *empirical* data (experiences) on which to base this prediction, namely, on the physical cause of our actions insofar as they occur, which are themselves thus phenomena. We cannot base this prediction on the moral cause, which contains the concept of duty with regard to what ought to happen, and which can be conceived only a priori by pure reason.

Violence on the part of the powerful will gradually diminish and obedience with regard to the laws will increase. There will be more beneficence and less squabbling in legal proceedings, more reliability in keeping one's word, and so on, in the commonwealth in part out of love of prestige, and in part out of a consciousness of one's own advantage. This will ultimately also extend to peoples in their external relations among one another, all the way to the cosmopolitan society, without the moral basis of the human race thereby being allowed to be increased, for this would require a kind of new creation (supernatural influence). — For we must not expect too much of human beings in their progress toward the better, in order that we not earn with reason the derision of the politician, who is keen on holding the hope of this progress to be the dream of an exaggerating mind.*

7:92

---

* It is certainly *pleasant* to think up state constitutions that correspond to the demands of reason (especially in matters of right). But it is *inappropriate* to propose them seriously, and it is *punishable* to incite the people to do away with an existing constitution.

Plato's *Atlantis,* More's *Utopia,* Harrington's *Oceana,* and Allais's *Sevarambia* have all eventually been put on stage but have never been tried in reality (with the exception of *Cromwell's* failed monstrosity of a despotic republic).[14] — The cre-

10. In what arrangement alone can the progress toward the better be expected?

Not by the path of things *from the bottom up,* but rather *from the top down,* is the answer. — To expect that education of the youth in intellectual and moral culture, reinforced by religious teachings, through both domestic instruction and schooling, from the lowest to the highest grades, will not only make them good citizens in the end, but rather also educate them to become good in a way that can continually progress and perpetuate itself, is a plan that can hardly be hoped to deliver the desired results. For it is not enough that the people believes that the cost of educating the youth should fall not on them, but rather on the state, while the state, for its part, has no money left for paying the salaries of competent teachers who will perform their duties with pleasure (as *Büsching*[15] complains), since it needs everything for war. The entire machinery of this education lacks in coherence if it is not designed according to a considered plan and intention of the supreme authority in the state, implemented, and then maintained in a consistent manner. This might imply that the state would reform itself from time to time and, attempting evolution rather than revolution, make progress toward the better. But since it is also *human beings* who do the work of educating and therefore have had to be educated themselves, and given the frailty of human nature and the fortuitousness of the circumstances that facilitate such an effect, it is only in a wisdom from on high (which, when it is invisible, is called providence) that hope in the progress of humankind can be found. Such wisdom is the positive condition for the promotion of this end. Yet, concerning what can be expected and demanded of *human*

7:93

---

ation of these states is much like the creation of the world: no one was present when it happened, nor could anyone be present, for otherwise he would have to have been his own creator. To hope that a state constitution of the kind of which we are speaking here could ever, after however much time, be completed, is a sweet dream. But to continually approach such a state is not only *thinkable,* but rather, to the extent that it is consistent with the moral law, a *duty,* not for the citizen of the state, but for the head of the state.

14. Plato's *Atlantis,* the story of the lost continent that appears in the *Timaeus* and *Critias;* Thomas More (1478–1535), *Utopia* (1516); James Harrington (1611–77), *The Commonwealth of Oceana* (1656), which was dedicated to (but prohibited by) Cromwell; Denis Varaisse d'Allais, *Histoire des Sevarambes* (1677–79), a German edition of which appeared in 1783.

15. Anton Friedrich Büsching (1724–93), historian, theologian, and geographer, director of the Gymnasium (high school that prepares for university entrance) in Berlin.

beings, it is only negative wisdom, namely, that they will begin to find it necessary to make the greatest hindrance to moral progress, namely, *war,* which always contravenes this end, gradually more humane, and then more rare, and finally to eliminate wars of aggression altogether and enter into a constitution which, in accordance with its nature, based on genuine principles of right, can make continual progress toward the better without thereby growing weaker.

CONCLUSION

A doctor who falsely consoled his patients day by day that their recovery was near, one of them that his pulse was improving, another that his stool and yet another that his perspiration promised improvement, and so on, received a visit by one of his friends. "How are you doing, my friend, with your illness?" was the first question. "Well, how do you think? I'm *dying of sheer recovery!*" — I cannot blame anyone who, faced with so many political ills, despairs of the salvation of the human race and its progress toward the better. Yet I rely on the heroic medication that *Hume* speaks of and which might lead to a quick cure. — "When I now see," he says, "the nations caught up in war with one another, it is as if I saw two drunks beating up on each other in a porcelain shop. For it is not enough that the wounds they inflict on each other will take long to heal, they will also have to pay afterward for all the damage that they have caused."[16] *Sero sapiunt Phryges.*[17] But the after-pains of the current war can force the political diviner to admit an imminent change in the human race for the better, one which is already in sight.

7:94

16. A loose paraphrase of Hume's remark in "Of Public Credit": "I must confess, when I see princes and states fighting and quarrelling, amidst their debts, funds, and public mortgages, it always brings to my mind a match of cudgel-playing fought in a *China* shop." In David Hume, *Essays, Moral, Political and Literary,* 2nd ed., ed. Thomas Hill Green and Thomas Hodge Grose (London, 1882; repr. Scientia Verlag, Aalen, 1992), vol. 1, p. 371.

17. "Too late do the Phrygians become wise." Cf. Cicero, *Epistulae ad familiares* [Letters to His Friends] 7.16.1: "*Sero sapiunt,*" which is there presented as a quote from a text called *The Trojan Horse.* The Trojans, also called Phrygians, had obstinately refused to deliver Helena.

Anthropology from a Pragmatic Point of View, Part 2, Section E

E. The Character of the Species

Giving a description of the character of a certain species of beings requires both showing that it can be brought under one concept together with other species that are familiar to us, and also that that which renders them different from one another be given and used as the peculiar property (*proprietas*) to distinguish it. — But if we compare a species of beings that is known to us (A) with another species that is unknown to us (non A), then how can we expect or demand of ourselves that we describe the character of the first, if we lack the mediating concept of comparison (*tertium comparationis*)? — Even if our highest concept of a species is that of an *earthly* rational being, we shall be unable to describe its character, since we have no knowledge of rational, *extraterrestrial* beings that would allow us to state their peculiar property and characterize the earthly ones among the rational beings in general. — It therefore seems that it is simply an impossible task to describe the character of the human species, since this task could only be accomplished by a comparison of two *species* of rational beings through *experience,* a comparison which the latter does not make available to us.

In order to assign the human being his class within the system of living nature and thereby characterize it, we are left with no option but the following conclusion: that the human being has a character that he himself creates, by means of his ability to perfect himself in accordance with ends that he sets himself, a quality by virtue of which he, as an animal endowed with the *capacity of reason* (*animal rationabile*) is able to turn himself into a *rational animal* (*animal rationale*). — In accordance with this, the human being works first to *preserve* itself and its species, and second trains, teaches, and *educates* its species for domestic society, and third *governs* its species as a systematic whole (that is, organized according to principles of reason) suitable for society. The distinguishing characteristic of the human species, however, in comparison with the idea as such of possible rational beings on earth is the following: that nature has sown in it the seeds of *discord* and has intended that it create, through its own reason, *harmony* out of this discord, or at least continually approximate such harmony. In the *idea* this harmony is the *end,* but in its *execution* this discord is the *means* of a supreme wisdom inscrutable to us, which intends to bring about the perfection of the human being through the continuous progress of culture, even though this entails many sacrifices of the pleasures of life.

Among the living *inhabitants of the earth,* the human being is clearly distinguished from all other natural beings by his *technical* predisposition to manipulate objects (that is, mechanical manipulation connected with consciousness), by his *pragmatic* predisposition (that is, his skill at using other human beings to further his own ends), and by his *moral* predisposition (that is, to act according to the principle of freedom under laws applying both to himself and to others). Indeed, any one of these three levels alone is sufficient to distinguish the human being's character from that of other inhabitants of the earth.

I. *The technical predisposition.* A series of questions raises itself with regard to the technical predisposition: whether the human being was originally destined to walk on all fours (as Moscati[1] proposed, perhaps merely as an idea for a dissertation thesis) or upright; — whether the gibbon, the orangutan, and the chimpanzee, among others, were destined in such a way (Linnaeus and Camper[2] disagree on this matter); — whether he is a fruit-eating or (since he has a membranous stomach) carnivorous animal; — whether, since he possesses neither claws nor tusks, and hence has no weapons (aside from reason), he is by nature a beast of prey or a peaceful animal. — The answers to these questions are no cause for concern. In any case, the following question can also be raised: whether he is by nature a *sociable* animal or hermit-like and averse to company, of which the latter is more likely the case.

The idea of nature's provision for the survival of the species is difficult to bring into agreement with the notion of the first pair of human beings, fully developed, being placed by nature in front of its means of sustenance, if

1. Pietro Moscati (1739–1824), anatomist in Pavia, Italy. Kant discusses this proposal in his 1771 review of the German translation of a lecture by Moscati, "Von dem körperlichen wesentlichen Unterschiede zwischen der Structur der Thiere und Menschen" [On the Essential Bodily Difference between the Structure of Animals and That of Humans]. See Ak 2:421– 25.

2. Petrus Camper (1722–89) stressed the similarities between humans and other animal species; Carolus Linnaeus (1707–78) was famous for his new system for classifying different species.

nature does not also give it a natural instinct, albeit one which no longer

7:323   exists in us in our current natural condition. The first human being would have drowned in the first pond that he encountered, for swimming is a skill that one must learn. Or he would have eaten poisonous roots and fruits and thereby have been in constant danger of death. Yet if *nature* had *implanted* this instinct in the first pair of human beings, how is it possible that they did not pass it on to their children, something that clearly never happens now?

Songbirds teach their young certain songs and thereby propagate them through tradition. An isolated bird that had been taken from its nest when still blind and reared elsewhere has no song, but only a certain inborn sound of its vocal organs. But where did the first song come from?* For it is not learned, and if it had arisen merely through instinct, then why was it not inherited in the young?

The characterization of the human being as a rational animal lies already in the shape and organization of his *hand, fingers,* and *fingertips,* in part through their construction, in part through their fine sensitivity. Nature has by this means designed him not for merely a single manner of manipulating objects, but rather generally for all forms of manipulation, and has thus designed him for the use of reason and thereby marked the technical predisposition of his species or the predisposition of his species for skill in manipulation as that of a *rational* animal.

II. *The pragmatic predisposition.* The pragmatic predisposition to civilization through culture, primarily through the cultivation of his social qualities, and the natural propensity of the species to emerge in the context of society from the brutishness of mere private force and become a civilized (although not yet moral) being destined for harmony, together constitute a higher level. — The human being is capable of and requires education in the

---

* Let us here assume the validity of Sir Linné's [Linnaeus's] hypothesis concerning the archaeology of nature: that what first emerged from the all-encompassing ocean that first covered the earth was a subequatorial island in the form of a mountain. On this mountain all of the various climatic gradations of temperature and the plants and animals particular to these climatic regions developed gradually, from the tropical heat near its lower shoreline to the arctic cold at its peak. With regard to the species of birds that appeared in this way, the songbirds imitated the inborn sounds of the vocal organs of many diverse voices and, to the extent that their vocal organs permitted, connected each of them. Each species thereby created its own song, which was later passed on by one member to another by means of instruction (similar to the passing down of tradition). One sees evidence of this in the degree of variation in sounds produced by finches and nightingales from different countries.

form of both instruction and discipline. The question at hand is (either in agreement with or opposed to Rousseau):[3] whether the character of the species is, according to its natural predisposition, better found in the *brutishness* of his nature, or in the *artifices of culture,* to which no end can be foreseen. First and foremost it must be noted that in the case of all other animals, when they are left to their own devices, each individual fully attains its entire vocation, whereas in the case of the human being only the *species* attains this. The human species can work its way up toward its vocation only through the *progress* of a series of an indeterminately large number of generations. The goal always remains in the distance. While the *tendency* toward the final end can often be hindered, it can never be fully reversed.

III. *The moral predisposition.* The question at hand is the following: whether the human being is *good* by nature or *evil* by nature, or equally susceptible to both, depending on who is responsible for his upbringing (*cereus in vitium flecti,*[4] etc.). In the latter case, the *species* itself would possess no particular character. — But this case is inconsistent with itself, since a being equipped with the capacity of practical reason and with consciousness of the freedom of his faculty of choice (a person) recognizes himself, even if in the most obscure terms, as subject, by virtue of this consciousness, to a law of duty and in possession of a feeling (which is the moral feeling), that *he* is treated and himself treats *others* either justly or unjustly. This is precisely the *intelligible* character of humanity in general, and to this extent the human being is, with regard to his innate predisposition (by nature), *good.* Yet experience shows that there exists in the human being a tendency to actively desire that which is forbidden, even though he knows that it is forbidden. This tendency toward *evil* takes form so inevitably and so early on as to be evident as soon as the human being even begins to make use of his freedom, and can therefore also be considered to be innate. Thus the human being must also be judged, in his *sensible* character (by nature) to be *evil.* This does not, however, present a contradiction when speaking of the *character of the species,* since one may assume that the natural vocation of this character consists in continuous progress toward the better.

The sum of pragmatic anthropology with regard to the vocation of the human being and the characteristics of its development is the following: the human being is destined by virtue of his reason to exist in society with other

3. See below, note 5.

4. Horace, *Ars Poetica,* 163, "soft as wax for moulding to evil," trans. H. Rushton Fairclough.

7:325 humans and to *cultivate* himself through art and sciences, to *civilize* himself, and to *become moral* in this society, however great his animal tendency may be to *passively* submit to the lure of leisureliness and good living, which it calls happiness, and instead to *actively* make itself worthy of humanity by struggling against the impediments that come with his brutish nature.

The human being must thus be *educated* to be good. The one who educates him is, however, also a human being, one who also therefore is subject to the same brutish nature and is supposed to bring about that of which he himself is in need. This is the source of the constant deviation from his vocation, while it repeatedly turns back towards it. — I intend to now discuss the difficulties involved in solving this problem as well as the impediments to solving it.

A.

The first physical aspect of the vocation of humankind consists in the human drive to preserve the species as an animal species. — But already here the periods of its natural development do not coincide with the periods of its social development. According to the *former,* he is *driven* by the *sexual instinct* and *capable* of reproducing and thereby preserving his species by the age of fifteen at the latest. According to the *latter,* he can barely manage this (on average) before twenty. For although a youth is capable from an early enough age of satisfying his and a woman's inclinations as a citizen of the world, he is still far from capable of sustaining his wife and child as a citizen of the state. — He must first learn a trade and find a clientele in order to start a household with a wife, and in the more refined classes he may be twenty-five before he is mature enough for his vocation. And with what does he then fill the intervening time in which he is compelled to an unnatural abstinence? With hardly anything but vices.

B.

The impulse to pursue scientific knowledge, as a form of culture that ennobles humankind, bears no correlation for the species as a whole to the span of an individual's lifetime. The scholar, when he has advanced in culture to the point where he advances the field, is called away by death, and his position is taken up a young pupil who, shortly before his own death,

7:326 and after he has made a similar advance, in turn surrenders his place to another. — What accumulation of knowledge would have resulted, what new methods would have been discovered and been made available, if a person such as Archimedes, Newton, or Lavoisier with his diligence and talent had been given a lifespan of centuries with no decline in his vital energy? But progress of the species in the sciences is always fragmentary (along the time axis) and does not guarantee that one is safe from the threat of regression presented by the barbarism of revolution against the state.

C.

The species seems equally unable to attain its vocation with regard to *happiness,* which nature constantly drives it to pursue, but which reason restricts to the condition of worthiness to be happy, that is, morality. — The hypochondriac (ill-humored) account that *Rousseau* gives of a human species daring to emerge from the state of nature as extolling a return to the state of nature and into the forests, should not be understood as his real opinion. With this account Rousseau expressed the difficulty that our species has in entering upon the path that continuously approaches its vocation. Such an account need not be invented from nothing: experience from times past and present must make any thinking person uncertain and doubtful whether our species will ever be any better off.

Rousseau wrote three essays on the damage caused by (1) the emergence of the human species from the state of nature into *culture,* namely, fading strength; (2) the process of *becoming civilized*, namely, inequality and mutual repression; and (3) the process of supposedly *becoming moral,* namely, unnatural education and malformations in manner of thinking. These three essays,[5] which portray the state of nature as a state of *innocence* (the return to which is prevented by the fiery sword of a gatekeeper to paradise), are only intended to serve as the guiding idea for his *Social Contract,* his *Émile,* and his *Savoyard Vicar,*[6] an idea with which they can find a way out of the

---

5. Jean-Jacques Rousseau (1712–78). The full title of the First Discourse is: "A Discourse That won First Prize at the Academy of Dijon. In the Year 1750. On the following question proposed by the Academy: Has the revival of the Sciences and Arts contributed to improving morality?" The full title of the Second Discourse is: "Discourse on the Origin and Foundations of Inequality Among Mankind" (1755). In Jean-Jacques Rousseau, *The Social Contract and The First and Second Discourses,* ed. Susan Dunn (New Haven: Yale University Press, 2002). Original French titles: "Discours qui a remporté le prix a l'académie de Dijon en l'année 1750. Sur cette question proposée par la même Académie: Si le rétablissement des sciences et des arts a contribué à épurer les mœurs," 1750. The French title of the second Discourse is: "Discours sur l'origine et les fondements de l'inégalité parmi les hommes," 1755. The third essay mentioned by Kant is probably *Julie ou la nouvelle Héloise* [Julie or the New Heloise], 1759.

6. The books mentioned are *Émile ou de l'éducation* [Émile: Or, On Education] and *Du contrat social ou Principes du droit politique* [Of the Social Contract or Principles of Political Right], both published in 1762. *Profession de foi du Vicaire Savoyard* [The Profession of Faith of a Savoyard Vicar] originally appeared in *Émile.*

madness of ills with which our species has surrounded itself through its own fault. — Rousseau did not ultimately wish that the human being *go* back to the state of nature, but rather that it should *look* back upon the state of nature

7:327   from the vantage of its current state. He assumed that the human being is by *nature* (as this can be passed on) good, but in a negative way, namely, that it is not innately or deliberately evil, but rather only in danger of being infected and corrupted by evil or inept leaders and examples. But since this in turn requires good human beings, who must have been thus educated for this themselves, of which likely none will exist who are not themselves corrupt (either innately or by having contracted it), the problem of moral education remains unsolved for our *species,* and not merely as a matter of degree, but indeed with regard to the quality of the principle, since an innate tendency toward evil can very well be criticized and at best be tamed by common human reason, but cannot be eradicated by it.

* * *

Under a civil constitution, which embodies the highest degree of the artificial elevation of humankind's predisposition to the good and is directed to the final end of its vocation, the expressions of *animality* emerge earlier and are fundamentally more powerful than those of pure *humanity,* and only by being *weakened* does the tame cattle become more useful to the human being than the wild beasts. One's own will is always prepared to resist one's fellow human beings and constantly strives, with a claim of unconditional freedom, not only to be independent, but even to become master over other beings who are by nature his equals. One observes this

7:328   even in the youngest child,* because nature strives to lead it from culture to

---

* The crying of a newborn child is not the expression of distress, but rather of indignation and infuriated anger. The newborn cries not because it is in pain, but rather because it is irritated, presumably because it wants to move and experiences its inability to do so as a confinement that robs it of its freedom. — What was nature's intent in having the child come into the world screaming, even though *in the brutish state of nature* this is extremely dangerous for the mother and the child itself? For a wolf, even a hog, would thereby be enticed into devouring it, if the mother were absent or weakened by childbirth. There is no animal beside the human being (as it now exists) that *loudly announces* its presence upon birth, and this seems to be a precaution on the part of the wisdom of nature to preserve the species. One must therefore assume that in the early period of natural history with respect to this class of animal (namely, in the time of brutishness) this loud-mouthed entrance into the world did not yet occur, but that it only began in a later, second period, when both parents had already arrived at the level of culture required for *domestic* morality, and not (as reason actually dictates) beginning with morality and its law to a culture suited to and purposive in accordance with morality. This inevitably gives rise to a misguided tendency that turns it against its end, as when, for example, religious instruction, which necessarily ought to be a *moral* culture, starts with *historical* knowledge, which is merely a culture of memory, and vainly attempts to deduce morality from it.

If we consider the education of humankind as the *entirety* of its species — that is, taken *collectively* (*universorum*), and not as the education of each individual (*singulorum*), in which case the mass forms not a system, but rather an aggregate of component members — , an education which consists in the pursuit of a civil constitution based on the principle of freedom but also on the principle of legal coercion: the human being can expect this education only from *providence,* that is, from a wisdom that is not *his* own, but which is nevertheless the impotent *idea* of his own reason (and which is impotent through his own fault). This education from above is, I say, salutary, but harsh and strict, a treatment of humankind by nature that is coupled with hardship and verges on the destruction of the entire race. The aim of nature is, namely, to bring about, out of *evil,* which is always in a state of internal strife with itself, the *good,* unintended by humankind, but which, once it exists, continues to preserve itself. Providence means precisely the same wisdom we marvel at in the preservation of species of organized natural beings, the wisdom which works constantly to destroy them and yet always protects them, even though we do not presume any higher principle at work in this providential care than we already do in the case of the preservation of plants and animals. Moreover, the human race ought to and *can* be the master of its own good fortune. But that it *will* be this cannot be 7:329 deduced a priori from the natural predispositions of humankind that are known to us. Rather, we can only have an expectation of this on the basis of experience and historical knowledge, an expectation that is as well justified as is necessary in order that we not despair of progress toward the better and instead work to promote (each to the extent possible) the approximation of this goal with all due prudence and moral insight.

---

life. We do not know, however, how and by what effective means nature brought about this development. This observation could have far-reaching implications, such as the notion that this second period in natural history might be followed by a natural revolution that heralds a third such period, in which an orangutan or chimpanzee develops the organs required for walking, manipulating objects, and speaking into a human limb structure, the inside of which contains an organ for the use of the intellect, and which would gradually develop through the culture of society.

One can therefore declare: the fundamental character feature of the human species is the capacity of a rational being to endow itself with a character in the first place, both for itself as an individual and for the society in which nature places it. But this already presupposes a favorable natural predisposition and propensity to the good, since evil, in strife with itself and not yielding any internal permanent principle, actually possesses no character.

The character of a living being is that which allows one to know its vocation in advance. — The following can, however, be understood as a principle with regard to the ends of nature: nature intends that every creature attain its vocation by developing all the predispositions of its nature in a manner purposive to attaining that destiny, such that, even though not every *individual* fulfills the end of nature, the species does. — In the case of nonrational animals this individual attainment does indeed occur, and herein lies the wisdom of nature. But in the case of humankind only the species attains this vocation. We know only one species of rational beings on earth, the human species, and see in it merely a tendency of nature toward this end, namely, to ultimately bring about, by its own activity, the development of the good out of evil. This is a prospect which, unless natural revolutions bring it to a sudden halt, can be expected with moral *certainty* (that is, with a certainty sufficient to the duty of working toward that end). — For it is human beings, that is, rational beings who are malicious, but also endowed with inventiveness and simultaneously with a predisposition to morality, who, in the course of the progress of culture, feel increasingly the harms that they selfishly inflict on each other and, since they see no other means against it available to them other than to subject the private spirit (of individuals) to the public spirit (of all united), and although they are reluctant to do so, to subject it to a discipline (of civil coercion), albeit one to which they subject themselves only according to laws they give themselves. Through their awareness of this they feel ennobled, namely, to the extent that they belong to a species suited for the vocation of the human being as reason represents it to him in the idea.

7:330

FUNDAMENTALS OF AN ACCOUNT OF THE CHARACTER OF THE HUMAN SPECIES

I. The human being was not intended to belong to a herd as is livestock, but rather, as a bee, to belong to a hive. — The *necessity* of being a member of some civil society. The simplest, least artificial way of establishing a civil society in this "hive" is to have one leader (monarchy). — But many such hives of bees next to each other will soon feud with one another as predators (war), but not, as human beings do it, in order to increase their own hive by means of uniting it with the other one — here the comparison ends —, but rather merely in order to use, through cunning or force, the diligence of the *other* to *its own* ends. Every people seeks to strengthen itself by subjugating neighboring peoples, whether it is the lust for expansion or the fear of being swallowed up by the other if one does not beat the other to it. For this reason, the internal or external warfare in our species, however great an ill it may be, is simultaneously the force that motivates the transition from the brutish state of nature into the state of *civil* society, a mechanism of providence in which the friction between forces that strive against one another brings harm to them, yet which are kept in regular motion for a long time by the push or pull of other driving forces.

II. *Freedom* and *law* (the latter of which restricts the former) are the two hinges upon which civil legislation turns. — But so that law is effective and not mere empty verbiage, a middle term must be added,* namely, *force,* which, coupled with freedom and law, can guarantee the success of the latter principles. Four combinations of force with these two are possible:

A. Law and freedom without force (anarchy).
B. Law and force without freedom (despotism).
C. Force without freedom and law (barbarism).
D. Force with freedom and law (republic).

7:331

One can see that only the last of these deserves to be called a true civil constitution, although by *republic* one does not mean one of the three forms of state (democracy),[7] but simply a state as such. The old declaration *Salus civitatis* (not *civium*) *suprema lex esto*[8] does not mean: the sensuous well-being of the community (the *happiness* of its citizens) shall serve as the supreme principle of the constitution of the state. For this kind of well-being, or what each individual imagines the object of his personal inclinations to be, whatever this may be, is not at all suited to serve as any kind of objective principle, which is necessary if such a principle is to be universal. This maxim says nothing other than: *intellectual well-being,* the preserva-

* Analogous to the *medius terminus* in a syllogism, which, connected with both the subject and predicate of the judgment, results in the four syllogistic figures.

7. The other two forms of state are aristocracy and autocracy. Cf. also PP 8:352–53 and MM 6:338–42.

8. "The well-being of the state (not: of the citizens) is the supreme law." Cicero, *De legibus* 3.3: "*Salus populi suprema lex esto.*"

tion of the *constitution of the state* once one exists, is the supreme law of a civil society, since the latter can only exist by means of the former.

The character of the species, as evident based on the collected historical experience of all times and among all peoples, is the following: that they, taken collectively (as the human race as a whole), are a mass of persons that exist next to one another and after one another and who cannot *do without* peaceful coexistence and yet cannot *avoid* constant strife amongst one another, and who therefore consider themselves to be destined by nature to a coalition that forms a *cosmopolitan society (cosmopolitismus)*, through mutual coercion under laws that they themselves originate, a society which is constantly threatened by divisiveness yet progresses overall. This idea, unattainable in itself, is, however, not a constitutive principle (that is, of the expectation of a peace that actually exists amidst the most vigorous actions and reactions among human beings), but rather a regulative principle, an idea to be diligently pursued as the vocation of the human race under the reasonable assumption of a natural tendency to this idea.

If one asks whether the human species (which can also be called a *race*, if one compares it as a species of rational *inhabitants of the earth* to inhabitants of other planets and conceives of it as a mass of creatures that arose from one demiurge) is to be regarded as a good or bad race, then there is, I must confess, little to boast about. It is true that someone who considers the behavior of human beings not only in ancient history, but also in contemporary times, will often be tempted to be misanthropic in his judgment, like *Timon,*[9] but far more often and more aptly to complain, like *Momus,*[10] of foolishness, not maliciousness, as the most striking feature of the character of our species. Yet since foolishness, combined with a touch of maliciousness (which would then be called folly), is unmistakably part of the moral physiognomy of our species, it can be clearly seen, already merely on the basis of the concealment of a large part of our thoughts, which every prudent person finds to be necessary, that each member of our race finds it advisable to be cautious and not let others catch sight of one *entirely* as one is. This alone betrays the tendency of our species to be ill-disposed toward one another.

It could be the case that there are rational beings on another planet that can only think out loud, both while awake and while asleep, who, irrespective of whether they are together with others or alone, can have no thoughts

9. Timon: legendary Athenian misanthrope.

10. Momus: in Greek mythology: god of ridicule. The term is also used for a carping critic.

that they do not immediately *utter.* How would their behavior differ from that of our human species? If they were not all as *innocent as angels,* then it is difficult to see how they could manage to get along with one another, to have even some degree of mutual respect for one another and tolerate one another. — It is thus an essential part of the makeup of both the individual human being and the human species that it can try to explore the thoughts of others while withholding one's own thoughts, a characteristic which inevitably progresses gradually from *play-acting* to intentional *deception,* and finally to *lying.* This would lead to a caricature of our species, and one not intended merely to be *laughed* at in good humor, but rather one which would justify both *contempt* with regard to the character of our species and also the confession that this race of rational beings were not deserving of any honorable place beside the other rational inhabitants of the world (which are unknown to us),* — if it were not precisely this very condemna-   7:333 tion that revealed a moral predisposition in us, an innate appeal of reason, to work against that tendency, and to present the human species not as evil, but rather as a race of rational beings that strive continually to make progress, against obstacles, from evil to the good. Its will would be good in general,

---

* Frederick II[11] once asked the excellent Sulzer, whose accomplishments he held in high esteem and whom he entrusted with the management of the educational institutions in Silesia, how his work was going. Sulzer answered: "It has been going much better ever since we have begun to build on Rousseau's principle that the human being is good by nature." "Ah, mon cher Sulzer (said the king), vous ne connaissez pas assez cette maudite race à laquelle nous appartenons." [Ah, my dear Sulzer (said the king), you do not know well enough the accursed race to which we belong.] — A further part of the character of our race is the need, in striving for a civil constitution, for discipline through religion, so that what cannot be attained by *external* coercion can be effected through the *internal* coercion (of conscience), by lawmakers making political use of the moral predisposition of the human being, a tendency that is part of the character of the species. But if morality is not prior to religion in this discipline of the people, then religion becomes the master over morality, and statutory religion becomes a political instrument of state authority under *religious despots.* This is an ill that inevitably leads to a perverted character and tempts one to rule by means of *deception* (known as political prudence). That great monarch, though *publicly* declaring himself to be merely the highest servant of the state, was not able, with a sigh of resignation in his private confession, to hide the opposite view, but he excused his own person by attributing this corruption to the wicked *race* known as the human species.

11. Frederick II ("the Great") (1712–1786), king of Prussia from 1740 to 1786. Johann Georg Sulzer (1720–79), philosophy professor in Berlin.

but carrying it through is hindered by the fact that reaching the end cannot be expected simply on the basis of a free agreement of *individuals*. Rather, reaching that end can only be expected from the progressive organization of the citizens of the earth within and into the species as a system that is interconnected in a cosmopolitan fashion.

Rethinking *Toward Perpetual Peace* and Other Writings on Politics, Peace, and History

Critical Essays

Kant's Theory of the State

JEREMY WALDRON

Immanuel Kant's theory of what we owe to the state presents an important alternative to traditional consent-based, utilitarian, and fairness-based accounts. On the consent-based approach, we are obligated to the state because we have consented to its authority; its authority is supposed to be based on a choice we made between two morally permissible alternatives (give one's consent to, or withhold one's consent from state authority). On Kant's theory, however, withholding one's consent is impermissible. According to the utilitarian approach, the state's claim on us is based on the benefits it provides for others; and on the fairness approach, its claim on us is based on the moral unacceptability of our accepting these benefits without contributing our fair share to their provision. On Kant's theory, however, the state's claim on us has to do not with any benefits that we receive, but with a change in the moral quality — indeed, the moral legitimacy — of certain actions of ours when they are performed under the auspices of a framework of positive law. His, therefore, is a challenging and unconventional theory of what we owe to the state, and it requires careful explication. The first step in such an explication is to figure out exactly what the state is, according to Kant, and to see whether his conception of the state differs from the conception that is used in political philosophy and social theory generally.

I

"The state" may be defined in several ways. Sometimes we use the term to apply to a whole community — a territory and everybody in it. For example, we refer to France as a state, meaning the French people considered as inhabiting the territory we commonly refer to as France. Normally, however, this usage is not just geographical. We use the term to refer to a body politic or a political community, that is, to a community *considered as governed in a certain way*. We say France is *a state*, rather than just a place or a population, because the French are governed by a certain kind of organization. Now that organization may also be referred to as a state; that is, we may use the word not only to refer to a community governed in a certain way, but also to an organization considered as governing such a community. I shall call the first sense the communal understanding and the second sense the institutional understanding of "the state." The second (institutional) sense tends to dominate, because in order to understand the first sense — community governed in a certain way — we need to understand the type of organization that is used to govern it. But the first sense never entirely drops from view, especially in those theories which treat the state-organization as a trustee or delegate of the political community or as an entity which (either directly or in the final analysis) is under the people's control.

Sociologically, we may define the state, in the institutional sense, as a certain kind of organization: it is a large entity established upon a permanent footing, with its own personnel and resources, dominant in a given territory, and dedicated to the fulfillment of certain tasks, such as keeping the peace among the people who live there. This organization comprises institutions like legislatures and tribunals, as well as organized police and armed forces, and specialized agencies devoted to the various tasks it takes on. Now, considered one by one, such institutions may be found in many settings: a feudal baron may maintain armed forces; a monastery may organize charitable relief; local notables may set up something like courts of law; a town may pay for the services of a night-watchman; and so on. But the idea of the state is not just the idea of the coexistence of such institutions: it is the idea of their being organized in a way that makes them part of a centralized apparatus, operating pervasively in the society as a single entity with a unified chain of command.

In sociology, determining the tasks or functions of the state has proven the most controversial. Max Weber warned against any attempt to seek a functional definition:

> The state cannot be defined in terms of its ends. There is scarcely any task that some political association has not taken in hand, and there is no task that one could say has always been exclusive and peculiar to those associations which are designated as political ones: today the state, or historically, those associations which have been the predecessors of the modern state. Ultimately, one can define the modern state sociologically only in terms of the specific *means* peculiar to it.[1]

And Weber went on to give his famous definition of the state as an organization "that (successfully) claims the monopoly of the legitimate use of physical force within a given territory."[2] Sociologists have not given up altogether on the attempt to define the state at least partly in terms of its function, though they have retreated to some quite abstract characterizations of function: the state is an organization devoted to the business of ruling a certain society, or it is dedicated to maintaining social order.[3]

The most striking thing about Weber's definition is its emphasis on the material aspect. The state organization controls people, resources, and power; its most important resource is its monopoly of legitimate force; and its most important functions are those that require a concentration of the means of violence. However, Hans Kelsen has suggested that we may also define the state in legalistic terms. Recognizing that "all of the external displays in which one traditionally perceives the power of the state — the prisons and fortresses, the gallows and machine guns — are in and of themselves lifeless objects,"[4] he defines the state as a system of norms — that is, as a set of rules and procedures:

> The state . . . is a legal system. Not every legal system, however, is characterized as a state; this characterization is used only where the legal system establishes certain organs — whose respective functions reflect a division of labour — for creating and applying the norms forming the legal system. When the legal system has achieved a certain degree of centralization, it is characterized as a state.[5]

The centralization referred to here involves norm-enacting and norm-applying institutions, which have certain ascendancy in relation to all the norms that are enforced in a given territory. This ascendancy, Kelsen believes, can be understood in legal as well as in material terms: the agencies of the state are those to whom the tasks of rule-making and rule-application are legally entrusted and the effective functioning of those agencies is itself constituted by the existence and application of certain rules.

To describe the state in these terms is not to say anything about its value. Kelsen is a legal positivist, and he insists that nothing can be inferred about justice or the social good from the legal fact of the state's existence. The same is true of the sociological descriptions. The state is certainly one of the more remarkable organizations that we see in the modern world, and it is natural that sociologists should try to offer a general characterization of this phenomenon, telling us how to recognize a state when we see one and telling us also what states characteristically do and why they tend to become a focus for social conflict. But it is a further step to associate any moral value with the state, so described, or to attribute to it any sort of normative significance.[6] No doubt, some of the general functions we mentioned — peace and order, etc. — are regarded as values by most people. But to treat them as values, we have to pin them down a little bit more than this: we have to stipulate that the peace is not that of a desert, that the order the state maintains is not an order devoted primarily to repression, and so on. And if we go very far in that direction, we fall foul of the earlier warning against identifying the state with too narrow a range, or too specific a conception, of its possible ends.

We should bear in mind also that if there is a value dimension associated with the state, it might well be a negative or cautionary dimension. *State,* like *army* or *coercion,* might be a concept whose definition alerts us to moral danger. This dimension is often neglected in legal and political philosophy and Kant's theory is no exception. Still, it is not out of the question that the entity described by the sociologists and positive lawyers should also be a force for good in the world. Accordingly, we may say that as well as sociological and legalistic conceptions, there can also be a *moral* conception of the state — with this caveat, that a moral conception is not so much a different kind of conception as an extra layer in our conception of the state. The moral conception offers an explanation of the moral significance of some of the features that the other conceptions emphasize already.

What would a moral account be like? What good might a state do? Under what description precisely (or under the auspices of which particular aspects of the lawyers' and the sociologists' characterizations) might an entity of this kind prove itself valuable? Sometimes the account is quite limited. The moral theorist of the state identifies worthy goals that the state might pursue — like sanitation or patronage of the arts — even though those goals might also be pursued under the auspices of other kinds of organization. And his theory is just that the state is a good thing inasmuch as it promotes goals like these. I think that such instrumental evaluation makes very little contribution to state theory. The state's ability to deploy a monopoly of force may be useful for fund-raising or for encouraging people to play their part in various beneficent schemes, but a monopolization of force is not exactly indispensable for these ends.

A more systematic moral theory would focus on the distinctive features of this kind of entity and show that they enable the state to make a moral contribution which is different in kind from the contribution that might be made by individuals acting alone or by other sorts of organizations. Such a contribution may still be thought of in terms of the state's efficacy in promoting certain goals. But we need not confine ourselves to an instrumental approach. The state may be important from a moral point of view because its presence and operations make a significant difference to ordinary moral reasoning or to our sense of what it is reasonable or right to do. Moreover a theory of this kind need not be naive. It may acknowledge the potential for abuse and subscribe to the cautions I talked about a moment ago. Nevertheless, by showing that the state makes a moral difference that no other kind of institution can make, the theory may be able to show that these risks are worth taking or — more interesting still — that they are risks we are morally *required* to incur because we are not free to turn our backs on the moral possibilities that the existence of the state opens up.

Immanuel Kant's theory of the state is roughly of this kind. As one would expect, Kant is interested in the state as an institution that makes a systematic difference to what it is morally permissible for ordinary moral agents to do. But his theory does not turn its back on the sociological and legalistic conceptions we have been considering. On the contrary, the moral difference that Kant thinks the state can make depends on its being more or less exactly the sort of organization that the sociologists and positive lawyers have described. It depends on the existence of a systematic body of enacted law, it depends on the actuality of an institution monopolizing the use of force in a territory, and it depends on the latter (coercive) resource being put at the disposal of the former (legalistic) enterprise. Only an entity with these characteristics can make the moral difference that Kant thinks the state is capable of making. And since — as we shall see — it is a moral difference, which, in Kant's view, *ought* to be made, it follows that people have a duty to see to it that such an organization comes into existence.

II

Let us turn then to the characterization of the state as it appears in Kant's political philosophy. That will be the task of this section. In section III, we will turn to the central question of the moral significance of the state as it is characterized in Kantian theory. Section IV will use the interpretation we have developed to cast light on the troubled question of resistance and civil disobedience.

The main characteristics of Kant's state are very familiar. The most prominent office in the state apparatus seems to be the chief executive, who is variously described as ruler of the state, agent of the state, directorate, government, sometimes even "supreme commander" (MM 6:316). This official "is entitled above all to the ability to *coerce* in accordance with the law" (MM 6:317). He is in charge of mobilizing fiscal resources; he commands the very considerable police apparatus that Kant envisages as well as the inspectorate that is supposed to supervise the economy and the public well-being of the society (MM 6:325); he makes appointments to an array of salaried administrative positions; and he directs the ministers, who in turn direct the administration of justice and the securing of an environment conducive to justice through their various offices (MM 6:328).[7]

The constitutional position of the chief executive, however, needs to be defined also by reference to the legislature and the judiciary. As one would expect in a late eighteenth-century theorist, the relationships between these various branches of the state are described formally in terms of constitutionalism, the rule of law, and the separation of powers. The legislature is sovereign (MM 6:313), and its function is to enact general laws, which form the basis on which the society is governed. Each institution has its proper task in relation to the rule of law, and the three of them are supposed to complement each other without usurping the others' functions (MM 6:313–16). The courts are to apply and interpret the general laws laid down by the legislature, and the executive is charged with ensuring that the laws as laid down by the legislature are carried into effect. In its relation to the judicial authority, the chief executive appoints the magistrates and he is responsible for the administration of the court system, but he does not perform the actual function of adjudication (MM 6:317). But it is interesting that Kant sees the executive as primarily an organ of the legislature, rather than of the courts. The function of the executive is to see that the laws in general are obeyed (MM 6:313), rather than to remain inactive until the laws are made determinate by the work of the judges. Whatever the judges do, the executive is bound to behave in accordance with law, and the legislature may remove and replace the executive where it considers that it has abused its authority (MM 6:317). The laws remain ascendant and in that sense the legislature really is the sovereign authority (MM 6:313). The chief executive has no authority of his own to make or vary the laws, though he does have the right to issue edicts or directives where particular decisions need to be made about the administration of the laws, or where the sentences of the courts need to be carried out in some particular way or according to some order of priorities.

Kant's discussion of all this in *The Metaphysics of Morals* is more than a little frustrating. He invokes some Latin terminology from contemporary jurisprudence — "*potestas legislatoria, rectoria, et iudicaria,*" etc. (MM 6:313) — but then, like many a philosopher after him, he is very loose in his usage of these technical terms.[8] Matters are not helped either by his characterization of what may or may not be an additional figure, called the head of state. Sometimes the head of state is identified with the ruler or chief executive, sometimes with the legislature (in a true monarchy), and sometimes (in a constitutional monarchy) with the state as a whole, that is, with all three institutions acting together. But the overall picture that emerges is clear enough. Kant is interested in a constitutional and articulated government, but above all in a *unified* system of government. And the importance of having an effective executive agency and of concentrating a power of command over the executive authority in the person of the ruler is not to provide for an institution that can stand up to or check the legislature, but to make the rule of law effective, that is, to lend force to "the constitution where the law itself rules and is tied to no particular person" (MM 6:341).

I emphasize this because it is important not to misread Kant's conception of the separation of powers. Kant was every bit as aware as his contemporary James Madison of the fetish that was made by Montesquieu and his followers of the separation of powers in the English constitution (TP 8:303). And he certainly subscribed to the conventional view that despotism would result if any one of these authorities — legislative, judicial, or executive — were to encroach on the work of any of the others (MM 6:316–17): "Republicanism," he wrote "is the principle by which the executive power . . . of a state is separated from the legislative power" (PP 8:352). Even so, the different authorities are not conceived in Kant's theory as checks and balances, and he is not interested in any version of the separation of powers that would paralyze the government in an equilibrium of mutual opposition or allow each authority to interfere with, or exercise what Madison called "partial agency" in, the others' operations.[9] The branches of the Kantian state are conceived instead as integrated and complementary parts of a functioning whole, like the propositions of a syllogism, to use one of Kant's analogies (MM 6:313).[10] It is their working together that matters. "The well-being of a state," he says, "consists in their being united," and he goes on immediately to emphasize that by well-being in this context he means a condition of the state "which reason dictates, *through a categorical imperative,* that we strive to attain" (MM 6:318). One might as well not have a legislature if there is no provision for an organ to bring overwhelming force to bear to secure the application of its laws. And one might as well not have a powerful executive if there is no legislature passing general laws to systematize the conditions under which coercive authority is properly exercised.

The features of the state that I have emphasized so far are also those that are highlighted in Kant's account of what it is to be subject to a state.

Individuals' relations to one another do not conform to principles of right (*Recht*), he says, unless they are in what he calls "the civil condition (*status civilis*)" with respect to one another. And they are not in that condition unless they have as people subjected themselves to a centralized system of "public external coercion," in which official determinations are backed up by "sufficient power" (MM 6:312).

There is nothing inevitable about this emphasis. One could imagine a theorist making more of the populist or democratic element in the modern state than Kant does, and taking that as a focus for the institution's moral significance. One might say, for example, that there is something special about being one of the people who has set up a state; or that a state to which one has consented has a particular moral authority; or that a state in which legislative decisions are made democratically has more authority than a state in which decisions are made autocratically. Kant is certainly aware of these lines of thought. In some respects his political philosophy pays tribute to that of Rousseau,[11] in its emphasis on popular sovereignty, for example, and in his equation of the authority of the sovereign legislature with that of the general will. Thus he does sometimes present the state in a contractarian light: he talks of "an original contract, on which alone a civil, and thus universally juridical constitution among human beings can be founded" (TP 8:297), and he suggests that it is not possible for anyone to be wronged by legislation inasmuch as it proceeds from "the united will of the people" (MM 6:313). Mostly, however, Kant does not regard these ideas as important, in any literal sense, for understanding the history or operation of actually existing states. The existence of an original contract, he says, cannot be proved —

> It is *futile* to try to track down the *historical document* of this mechanism [viz., of government], which is to say that one cannot arrive at the point in time at which civil society began (for savages do not draw up any document of their subjugation to the law, and it is to be presumed from the mere nature of undeveloped human beings that they began it with violence). (MM 6:339)

— and a preoccupation with it is unhealthy, inasmuch as it suggests that our obligation to the state is conditional on consent, as though our actual consent to the state were optional, something we had the right to withhold (TP 8:297) or as though we were giving up something valuable such as our freedom when we entered into the civil condition (MM 6:316). As I have already mentioned, Kant believed that the establishment of a state was a moral necessity, and if we were to oppose the establishment of a civil constitution, no wrong would be done to us if we were impelled by force to join it (MM 6:312). It is not essential to a state, then, that it be established or maintained voluntarily. The concept of its voluntary establishment is better understood as an "*idea* of reason" (TP 8:297), which according to Kant is useful mostly as a basis for assessing the output of the legislature. A state is an organization which is oriented toward law making in the name of a whole people, and this, says Kant, "is the touchstone for the lawfulness of any public law":

> If a public law is so composed that an entire people *could not possibly* give its assent to it (as, for example, in the case of a certain class of *subjects* having the hereditary privilege of a *ruling rank*), then it is unjust. If it is *only possible,* however, that a people could agree to it, then it is a duty to regard the law as just, even if the people were now in such a state or attitude of mind that, if it were asked, it would probably withhold its agreement. (TP 8:297)

Also, the fact that the state acts in the name of the whole people (as though it were set up by contract), and not in the ruler's name per se — this fact tells us something about the character of the authority that the state claims for itself. Its authority comes from its public presence, and not necessarily from the superior standing of any individual or subset of the individuals in the society. But it need not refer to any literal historical facts about the state's foundation.

That the ideal state is a republic is a proposition that Kant *was* prepared to argue for (PP 8:349–50). Unlike the reduction of the social contract to a mere idea of reason, Kant's republicanism presents itself as a practical ideal to be implemented — an ideal which state authorities are required to pursue, through gradual and continual reform (MM 6:340). His theories of representation (MM 6:341), majoritarianism (TP 8:296), and active and passive citizenship (MM 6:314–15 and TP 8:296) are part of his discussion of this ideal. Yet Kant also says that how far a commonwealth has gone down this road makes very little difference to the authority of the state that governs it. Legitimacy and aspiration are separated in this regard. The state is a morally significant entity by virtue of the tasks it takes on, the spirit in which it addresses them, and the resources it brings to those tasks. If it acts as though it embodies the united will of the whole people, operating through the medium of general laws, and deploying effective and coordinated force to secure an environment governed by those laws, then it is legitimate and the people must submit to it.

III

What moral difference, exactly, is the state supposed to make? At the beginning of his political philosophy, Kant emphasizes external freedom as the most important subject for the doctrine of right (MM 6:229ff.), and it is tempting to infer from this that the most important moral difference a state can make is to guarantee, underwrite, and protect our freedom to act in the external world. I believe this is too superficial a view; it makes the state merely an instrument, whereas everything Kant says about it points to its having inherent moral significance. External freedom may be the field in which our theory of the state is laid out, but the contribution that the state is supposed to make in that field has to do with the moral quality of our actions in respect to one another.

On Kant's account the most important difference the state makes is to the conduct of our practical reasoning. Absent a state, we have to act upon our own reasoning in every area of life. But when a state comes into existence, there are certain areas of practical decision-making in which we may not act on our own reasoning. We must act on the conclusions of the state's reasoning and do what the law says — not what we have figured out for ourselves. What are these areas, and why is it morally necessary for individuals to subordinate their practical reasoning in these areas to practical reasoning conducted in the name of a whole people with the potential backing of a monopoly of force?

Unlike Hegel,[12] Kant does not assign the state a cultural role or a mission of ethical education. His is a neutral state: it has no paternalistic responsibility and its coercive power is not to be used for promoting the welfare, virtue, or happiness of its subjects (TP 8:290).[13] Its primary mission is to maintain order by laying down and enforcing general rules of conduct to govern our interactions with one another and our use of external resources. In regard to the tasks that the state does not take on, each of us is left to his own resources: each person is to figure out how to cultivate his own powers and talents (MM 6:443–46) and "each may pursue happiness in the way that that he sees fit" (TP 8:290). In these areas our moral responsibilities are to ourselves alone, though Kant is certainly not oblivious to the fact that most of these issues also have a social dimension.[14] The only interests that the state may take in our welfare are interests related to security — "laws directed to the prosperity of citizens, increased population, etc. . . . as a means for securing a juridical condition, primarily against external enemies of the people" (TP 8:298) — and interests related to equality, that is, to the enforcement of the basic principle of right that no one may seek their happiness in a way which precludes the equal pursuit of happiness by others (TP 8:290). This sounds like a familiar version of classic liberal theory.

In fact, as soon as one goes into the detail, one starts to find a different kind of theory emerging. We know that the history of liberal thought is a history of rival and incompatible schemes for specifying principles of property, principles of justice, principles of right, and principles of public economy, to satisfy these requirements of equality, security, and freedom. And the interesting thing about the way Kant develops his theory of property is that he takes this sort of disagreement as his starting point. Among the garrulous and opinionated individuals who constitute a modern liberal state, there are many different views on all of this, and all of them, as Kant put it, "encounter in themselves the unsociable trait that predisposes them to want to direct everything only to their own ends" (IUH 8:21). And this is not just a wistful dream of political authority — "If I ruled the world . . ." It is also a matter of how we view the restraints on our own activity that we must necessarily accept for the sake of others and for the sake of the community. An individual who has thought carefully and conscientiously about justice and equality may figure that he knows as much as anyone about what is an appropriate set of restraints for him to submit to, or he may figure that he has worked out as good a theory as anyone can work out concerning property acquisition, and he may want to conduct his economic life on that basis. Anything else might seem to him an affront to his own responsible moral autonomy. To understand Kant's theory of the state, we need to understand what kind of mistake this person would be making in substituting his own conscientious thought about right for the laws that the state has laid down.

Does Kant's case depend on there being a difference in kind in the sort of reasoning that an individual might undertake and the sort of reasoning that might be undertaken in a legislature? Some have speculated that Kant's philosophy of *Recht* embodies a version of what John Rawls calls "political liberalism"[15] and that there is a radical discontinuity between his moral philosophy, which is oriented toward rich notions of dignity and individual autonomy, and his political philosophy, which explores issues about external freedom that do not involve any such comprehensive conception of ultimate worth.[16] But even if this were true, it would not show that the limited range of reasons available in the domain of right could not be dealt with by individual thinkers.

There *is* certainly a difference in subject matter, on Kant's account, between morality and right, and between the issues that are important in personal moral thinking and the issues that are important in figuring out justice and property. Morality is concerned with the quality of an agent's will (and moral philosophy investigates the conditions of such concern). Legal philosophy addresses our interest in right, and right by contrast with morality is concerned with the external character of human actions in their relation to one another. Right attends to the physical compatibility of actions in a fairly literal sense. One action is compatible with another if it does not occupy space or use material in a way that prevents the other action from taking place; and right uses that notion of compatibility as a basis for asking questions about the universalization of freedom. In the realm of right, we do not have any intrinsic interest in the character of individual motivation: we look simply to the relation between the external aspects of each individual's choices and the external aspects of similar choices by others. Thus it is assumed, in the realm of right, that action may legitimately be constrained, and rightful action legitimately motivated, by the threat of sanctions; it is assumed that the lawfulness of actions — their conformity to principle — is something that can be imposed externally by force.[17]

These are important differences, but they do not detract from the point that thinking about right is *like* individual moral thinking in a number of ways. In both realms there is an interest in universalizability and conformity to principle: in both there is an attempt to subject individual human choice to the discipline of compatibility with the similar choices of others. Indeed, something like the leading principle of right — "Any action is right if it can coexist with everyone's freedom in accordance with a universal law" (MM 6:230–31) — is already embedded in moral thinking, in the various formulations of the Categorical Imperative (G 4:421ff.). This is not just a matter of right taking its lead from morality; if anything it is the other way round. We begin with the idea of the physical compatibility of everyone's actions, and we find that morality adds to that the prospect that the very idea of such compatibility might act as an internal incentive. Put crudely, morality is *Recht*-plus-something rather than *Recht* being morality-plus-something. So we should not regard right as secondary and derivative, at least in the order of exposition. This is not to deny that Kant took a greater interest in moral philosophy and did greater work in that subject than he did in legal and political philosophy. All I am saying is that if thinking about right were something that individuals could not reliably engage in, then it would seem to follow that they could not reliably engage in moral reasoning either.

If a difference in subject matter does not explain why we must accept the authority of the state in the realm of right, should we seek an explanation in our relative incompetence as reasoners in that realm? We might invoke here the theory of authority in Joseph Raz. In Raz's account, the person or institution in authority responds to the same domain of reasons that the subject would have to respond to if the subject were figuring things out for himself, but the subject defers to the authority's reasoning because he figures he "is likely better to comply with reasons which apply to him . . . if he accepts the directives of the alleged authority as authoritatively binding, and tries to follow them, rather than if he tries to follow the reasons which apply to him directly." [18]

Now, this will not work for Kant's theory of the state if it is supposed to turn on an argument about competence. For Kant actually denies that we are any less competent as practical reasoners than our legislators. The legislator is just another human being — or bunch of human beings — trying to figure things out and their reasoning is subject to all the vicissitudes that afflict *anyone's* thinking about justice and property.[19] "The supreme authority must be just *in itself* but also a *human being* . . . [and] nothing entirely straight can be fashioned from the crooked wood of which humankind is made" (IUH 8:23). Moreover, at the same time as he lays down our duty to defer to the legislator's judgment, Kant insists that we are entitled to form and communicate opinions of our own on the matters that the legislator is addressing. We may do so, first, as individuals making provisional claims about our own rights, which we bring to civil society for ratification (MM 6:256–57); secondly, as active citizens participating in legislation if the constitution of the state is in fact republican (TP 8:294–97); and thirdly, as members of the general public exercising what Kant calls *freedom of the pen* (TP 8:304). Kant is in fact quite emphatic that we have a responsibility to participate in public life:

> But now I hear called out on all sides: *do not argue!* The officer says: do not argue, just drill! The tax collector says: do not argue, just pay! The clergyman says: do not argue, just believe! . . . I answer: the *public* use of one's reason must be free at all times, and this alone can bring about enlightenment among humans. (WE 8:37)

No doubt there are aspects of state organization in which argument is counterproductive:

> For many affairs that serve the interests of the commonwealth a certain mechanism is required . . . It would thus be very harmful if an officer who receives orders from his superiors were to publicly question the expediency or usefulness of his orders . . . A citizen cannot refuse to pay the taxes which are required of him; even a presumptuous public rebuke

of such levies, if such taxes are to be paid by him, can be punished as causing a public scandal (which could set off a more general resistance). (WE 8: 37)

Still both the soldier and the taxpayer are entitled to their opinion on the propriety or justice of the measure in question, which they may express to the general public at an appropriate time. And Kant thinks that nothing but the encouragement of people's propensity to think through public issues for themselves and "present publicly their thoughts to the world concerning a better version of his legislation" (WE 8:41) will enable man to escape what Kant calls "*his self-incurred immaturity*" (WE 8:35). Like Bentham's good citizens,[20] though they must obey punctually, they are competent to censure freely, and so the explanation of their duty of obedience must lie somewhere else than in the competence that they bring to thinking these matters through.

In Raz's account, comparative competence is just one possible way of satisfying the normal justification thesis for authority. Another has to do with coordination: "if there is any range of activities in which those who possess great power clearly can do better than most people it is in coordinating the activities of many people."[21] I believe this is also the key to the Kantian theory of the state. The realm of right is a realm in which what is important is the coordination of action: Kant argues strongly that, in this realm, it is appropriate to act only on the basis of general laws (or law-like conclusions of practical reasoning) which are actually going to be enforced, in a coordinated way on a society-wide scale, by existing state institutions.

The argument is complicated, so let me illustrate with an example. Suppose A and B are struggling for control of a portion of land. Each of them is a conscientious moral thinker, and each strives to reason responsibly about their rights. They both acknowledge — let's say they acknowledge correctly — that an equal division would be unjust, but in their individual thinking they do not come up with the same conclusion: A is convinced that he is entitled to 60 percent of the territory and B is convinced that he (B) is entitled to 60 percent of the territory. What is to be done? They can't just go their separate ways, each to act on his own practical reasoning as best he can, for the view of each conflicts directly with that of the other. I suppose they could bargain or they could fight. But there is no guarantee that the outcome of either process would correspond to any sensible view about what right requires in this case. There is certainly no sense suggesting that they should act "in a way that allows the objectively best or the correct view to prevail" — they have tried that and come up with disparate conclusions. The best they can hope for is that somehow a view of the matter will be imposed which has some internal coherence, so that at least if force is used to vindicate property claims in this territory, it will not be used arbitrarily, but in a way that represents some sort of careful thinking through of the issues. This is what a state can offer: it can offer a well-thought-through body of law which will be enforced univocally, in a way that does not represent simply a bargaining compromise or a vector of individual forces. The point is fairly trivial in a two-person case: either of the parties, A or B, could be the state for the purposes of this example, provided only that their view was able to prevail comprehensively. But it is not at all trivial — and the need for an independent source of effective, coherent, and univocal enforcement is much clearer — when we consider that it is not just A and B, but (say) a quarter of a billion highly opinionated Kantians who are offering (and preparing to act upon) their rival individual assessments about the proper distribution of resources in a large and fruitful territory.

The point can be generalized.[22] When I appropriate a piece of land for my own use, I am effectively changing the duties of everyone else: I am saying that they are no longer free to use that land, and my appropriation purports to settle any conflict they may have with me about whose use of the land should have priority. That is something, Kant says, I cannot do on my own:

> Now, a unilateral will cannot serve as a coercive law for everyone with regard to possession that is external and therefore contingent possession, since that would infringe upon freedom in accordance with universal laws. So it is only a will putting everyone under obligation, hence only a collective general (common) and powerful will, that can provide everyone this assurance. — But the condition of being under a general, external (that is, public) legislation accompanied with power is the civil condition. So only in a civil condition can something external be yours or mine. (MM 6:256)

Moreover, even if my action does not itself have these "omnilateral" consequences — even if I am not seeking a right which, in lawyers' terminology, holds against all the world — still on Kant's account *any* use of coercion in the performance of my own actions or in restraint of others raises universal issues. It is not inappropriate for force to be used to secure justice and right. But its use is justified in Kant's theory only as "a *hindering of a hindrance to freedom*" (MM 6:231), that is, only under a principle "connecting universal reciprocal coercion with the freedom of everyone" (MM 6:232). In other words, forceful action or restraint is illegitimate except when force is used systematically to vindicate rights and freedom for a whole people. And Kant's position is that only an agency vested with an actual monopoly of force has any hope of being able to act in a coordinated fashion on that sort of scale. If different people use force to secure ends which contradict one another, then this systematicity is lost. And, in this regard, it doesn't matter how conscientiously each person has thought through the universalization of his own use of force. The association that matters here is the association of power with univocality. If I am aware that there are several conceptions of justice and rights loose in the community, each upheld by its own self-righteous militia, then any sense of universalizability, reciprocity, or respect for others that I might exhibit remains merely academic. Because of cross-cutting patterns of coercion and enforcement, no *one* sense of right will ever hook up reliably with the idea of a mutually secured basis on which people might coexist in the world. At best, force is now being used simply to vindicate the moral vehemence with which each of a number of different opinions about justice is held.

If, however, there is a state in existence which lays down a single coherent set of general laws and has the capacity to enforce them on a systematic basis, then in my own practical thinking about the rights and freedoms which are appropriately upheld by force I should defer to the state and the law, and the state is justified in coercing me if I don't. For state law offers the prospect of the coordinated and systematic use of force, which can answer to the requirements of Kant's basic principles of right. My own individual practical thinking, no matter how scrupulous and no matter how universalizable, can offer only haphazard and unsystematic enforcement. [23] That is why, as Kant says, "in every commonwealth there must be obedience under the mechanism of the state constitution in accordance with coercive laws (which apply to the whole)" (TP 8:305). And that is also why in the absence of a coherent set of general norms, created and administered by a single legislature and a centralized system of courts, and backed up with the power of an armed organization that monopolizes all the force that might be thrown behind anyone's judgments about justice, right, or the common good — in the absence of all that, we are morally required to do what we can to bring these institutions into being.

IV

Kant's political philosophy is notorious for the harshness of the views he expressed about resistance and civil disobedience. I have already mentioned his opposition to any sort of legitimist inquiry: "The origin of the supreme authority is, as a matter of practical concern, *not open to examination* by the people that is subject to it" (MM 6:318). And his condemnation of resistance is really quite severe:

> All resistance against the supreme legislating authority, all incitement in order to express through action the dissatisfaction of subjects, all revolt that leads into rebellion, is the highest and most punishable offense in the commonwealth because it destroys the latter's very foundations. (TP 8:299)

Citizens may *complain* about injustice by writing letters and pamphlets (TP 8:304), but their complaints must be completely dissociated from any intention to disobey.

There are a number of things that can be said to mitigate this position, and a number of things that can be said, too, to justify and explain Kant's adoption of this authoritarian stance. But no account is complete without noticing the almost complete absence from Kant's political philosophy of any sense that the state which he calls for is an institution liable to terrible abuse. We might expect Kant to say something about the predicament faced by individual moral reasoners when abuses occur. But he says almost nothing. There is a parenthetical remark, at the end of "The Doctrine of Right" where he suggests that our duty is to obey the state only "in whatever does not conflict with inner morality" (MM 6:371); this can be read also in light of a comment in the *Second Critique* about a prince demanding that a subject give false testimony in court (PR 5:30). But the latter comment is hardly encouraging in its suggestion that the subject should accept execution rather than accede to the state's request. And I think it would be wrong to read into these spare and unexplained remarks any general suggestion of a right of conscientious refusal.[24]

The reasons supporting Kant's position are pretty clear in light of our discussion in the previous section. A person who proposes to resist or disobey some piece of legislation is offering an affront to the very idea of right, according to Kant. For even assuming that his dissent is conscientious and based on impeccable moral argument, still it is tantamount to turning his back on the idea of our *sharing* a view about right or justice and implementing it systematically in the name of the community. The one who proposes to resist or disobey is announcing in effect that it is better to revert to a situation in which each acts on his own judgment about justice. Now, we know that the fundamental argument for setting up a state in Kant's political theory is the following:

one must emerge from the state of nature in which each follows only his own thoughts and unite oneself with all others (with whom one cannot avoid interacting) in subjecting oneself to public external coercion through laws, and hence enter into a condition in which what is to be recognized as his own is *legally* established . . . (MM 6:312)

No matter what moral justification the individual sees in his own view about justice, his decision to resist the state amounts to putting this process into reverse, reverting to a situation in which each party throws its own force unilaterally and — in effect — unsystematically behind its own moral convictions. Kant cannot countenance that, not just because the result would be chaotic or unpleasant, but also because the moral condition of the use of force is its real connection to a reciprocal and systematic distribution of freedom.

In some places, Kant expresses the force of this argument in a limited and rather legalistic way, as though it concerns only the possibility of *a constitutional right of resistance.*[25] Such a right, he says, would be a contradiction in terms, and he argues in Hobbesian terms that its existence would mean "there would therefore have to be a head above the head of state, who would decide between him and the people, which is a contradiction" (TP 8:300). This line of argument might appear to leave open the question of a nonlegal right to resist quite apart from the provisions of the constitution. But I do not think we should interpret Kant this way. For elsewhere he presents the constitutional question as though it were mainly a thought-experiment to aid us in addressing the *general* question of resistance: a people, contemplating rebellion, should consider the matter from a point of view hypothesized "before establishing a civil contract, [and ask] whether it ought dare to make public the maxim of the intention to revolt on certain occasions" (PP 8:382). Just because such a right "would make all lawful constitutions uncertain" (TP 8:301), it cannot be adopted as a maxim of individual or factional decision.

However, the rigor of Kant's position can be mitigated another way. It is possible to read his strictures on resistance as limited to the question of resistance *to a state,* that is, to an entity established along the lines we have been discussing. Kant need not be read as requiring submission to any organization that *calls* itself a state or any thug who happens to wear a crown. It must actually amount to a legal system and administer what actually counts as law. In a recent paper Sarah Holtman poses the question of whether Kant would have condemned the assassination plots against Hitler in 1944, [26] and we might say that this case could be resolved for Kant by a familiar argument to the effect that the regime administered by the Nazis had few or none of the features that make the protection of states from resistance important. We are familiar with this view of the matter from Hannah Arendt's discussion of the "so-called totalitarian state,"[27] and from the jurisprudence of Lon Fuller,[28] who argued that the Nazi regime exhibited none of the formalistic features like generality, stability, prospectivity, and coherence of rules — that make a system of command worth respecting as a system of law. Recent debates in the philosophy of law have focused on the question of whether Fuller's formal features are sufficient to ensure that a regime is substantively just.[29] But that need not concern us here: whether or not some substantively unjust regimes require our submission because of their formal legality, it is pretty clear that regimes that lack formal legality cannot command our allegiance on Kant's account. Kant may occasionally have said things that appear to indicate a harder line than this: he says that the moral requirement of obedience is "unconditional" and that it applies even in cases where the ruler has breached social contract (TP 8:299–300). But at that stage, he outruns the support of any argument that possibly makes his position interesting to us.

NOTES

1. Max Weber, "Politics as a Vocation," in *From Max Weber: Essays in Sociology,* ed. H. H. Gerth and C. Wright Mills (London: Routledge & Kegan Paul, 1970), 77–78.

2. Ibid., 78.

3. See Gianfrance Poggi, *The Development of the Modern State: A Sociological Introduction* (Stanford: Stanford University Press, 1978), 1–2; and John A. Hall and G. John Ikenberry, *The State* (Minneapolis: University of Minnesota Press, 1989), 2.

4. Hans Kelsen, *Introduction to the Problems of Legal Theory,* trans. Bonnie Litschewski Paulson and Stanley L. Paulson (Oxford: Clarendon Press, 1992), 104.

5. Ibid., 99.

6. Even the term "legitimate," in Max Weber's definition of the state — "monopoly of the legitimate use of physical force" — has a nonmoral meaning: it means uses of force that people by and large regard as proper or appropriate. See Weber, *Economy and Society,* ed. Guen-

ther Roth and Claus Wittich (Berkeley: University of California Press, 1978), 31.

7. Kant even anticipates, though very briefly, Weber's account of the transition from hereditary to meritocratic and salaried officialdom (MM 6:329). Cf. Weber, *Economy and Society.*

8. In an editorial note, Mary Gregor observes the confusion in Kant's terminology. Immanuel Kant, *The Metaphysics of Morals,* trans. and ed. Mary Gregor (Cambridge: Cambridge University Press, 1991), 288–89.

9. Ibid., 304.

10. See M. J. C. Vile, *Constitutionalism and the Separation of Powers* (Indianapolis: Liberty Fund, 1998), 269–70.

11. Jean-Jacques Rousseau, *The Social Contract and Other Late Political Writings,* ed. Victor Gourevitch (Cambridge: Cambridge University Press, 1997).

12. G. W. F. Hegel, *Elements of the Philosophy of Right,* ed. Allen W. Wood (Cambridge: Cambridge University Press, 1991), 275ff.

13. For a discussion, see William Galston, "What Is Living and What Is Dead in Kant's Practical Philosophy?" in *Kant and Political Philosophy: the Contemporary Legacy,* ed. Ronald Beiner and William James Booth (New Haven: Yale University Press, 1993).

14. For an account of the social context in which human self-cultivation is possible, see the remarks about civil society and human destiny in the first five theses defended in "Idea for a Universal History from a Cosmopolitan Perspective" (8:18–22).

15. John Rawls, *Political Liberalism* (New York: Columbia University Press, 1993).

16. For an argument to this effect, see Thomas Pogge, "Is Kant's Rechtslehre a 'Comprehensive Liberalism'?" in *Kant's Metaphysics of Morals: Interpretative Essays,* ed. Mark Timmons (Oxford: Oxford University Press, 1992). Rawls, however, did not accept this characterization of Kant's political philosophy: see Rawls, *Political Liberalism,* 199ff. I have doubts about it too. What would be the motivation in Kant's philosophy for something like Rawls's political liberalism? Certainly

there is nothing corresponding to Rawls's recognition of a diversity of
reasonable comprehensive conceptions. Though Kant says each individual has his own conception of happiness (TP 8:290), he does not
concede that there could be more than one reasonable way of thinking
about the relation between one's own conception of happiness, on the
one hand, and the ideas of agency, autonomy, and principle that dominate his moral philosophy, on the other. So he has no need to withhold
the richness of his conception of moral autonomy from the working out
of his theory of *Recht.*

17. See Allen Wood's contribution in this volume, and see also Paul Guyer,
"Kant's Deductions of the Principles of Right" in *Kant's Metaphysics
of Morals: Interpretive Essays,* ed. Mark Timmons (Oxford: Oxford
University Press, 2002).

18. Joseph Raz, *The Morality of Freedom* (Oxford: Clarendon Press, 1986),
53.

19. Cf. the intriguing observations in *Toward Perpetual Peace* about the
rights of philosophers to be consulted by the state (PP 8:369).

20. Jeremy Bentham, *A Fragment of Government* (Cambridge: Cambridge
University Press, 1988), 10.

21. Raz, *Morality of Freedom,* 75.

22. See Jeremy Waldron, "Kant's Legal Positivism," *Harvard Law Review*
109 (1996): 1556ff.

23. So the mode of individual political judgment — explored for example in
Hannah Arendt's *Lectures on Kant's Philosophy* (ed. Ronald Beiner
[Chicago: University of Chicago Press, 1982]) — is not what is important here. Even if individuals can think through issues of right
from everyone's point of view, still my thinking in this mode may not
coincide in its conclusions with your thinking in this mode. Actual
coordination is not secured by universalization in the moral or political thinking of individuals. See Waldron, "Kant's Legal Positivism,"
1552–53.

24. Cf. Leslie A. Mulholland, *Kant's System of Rights* (New York: Columbia University Press, 1990), 337–40.

25. His discussion of the British constitution bears this out. He says that it is

"completely silent about the authority belonging to the people, should the monarch transgress against the contract of 1688" (TP 8:303).

26. Sarah Holtman, "Revolution, Contradiction and Kantian Citizenship," in *Kant's Metaphysics of Morals: Interpretive Essays,* ed. Mark Timmons, 209–31 (New York: Oxford University Press, 2002), 227.

27. Hannah Arendt, *The Origins of Totalitarianism,* new ed. (New York: Harcourt, Brace, Jovanovich 1973; orig. pub. 1951), 392ff.

28. Lon L. Fuller, "Positivism and Fidelity to Law: A Reply to Hart," *Harvard Law Review* 71 (1959): 630, and Lon. L. Fuller, *The Morality of Law,* rev. ed. (New Haven: Yale University Press, 1969).

29. See H. L. A. Hart, *The Concept of Law,* rev. ed., ed. Penelope A. Bulloch and Joseph Raz (Oxford: Clarendon Press, 1994), 207, for the suggestion that they are not.

Kant and Liberal Internationalism

MICHAEL W. DOYLE

What difference do liberal principles and institutions make to the conduct of the foreign affairs of liberal states? A thicket of conflicting judgments suggests that the legacies of liberalism have not been clearly appreciated. On the one hand, for many citizens of liberal states, liberal principles and institutions have so fully absorbed domestic politics that their influence on foreign affairs tends to be either perceived as exaggerated or overlooked altogether. Liberalism becomes either unselfconsciously patriotic or inherently "peace-loving." On the other hand, for many scholars and diplomats, relations among independent states appear to differ so significantly from domestic politics that the influences of liberal principles and domestic liberal institutions are either denied or denigrated. They judge that international relations are governed by perceptions of national security and the balance of power. Liberal principles and institutions, when they do intrude, confuse and disrupt the pursuit of balance-of-power politics.

Although liberalism is misinterpreted from both these points of view, a crucial aspect of the liberal legacy is captured by each. Liberalism is a distinct ideology and set of institutions that have shaped the perceptions of and capacities for foreign relations of political societies that range from social welfare or social democratic to laissez-faire. Liberalism defines much of the content of the liberal patriot's nationalism. It does appear to disrupt the pursuit of balance-of-power politics. Thus its foreign relations cannot be adequately explained (or prescribed) by a sole reliance on the balance of power. But liberalism is not inherently "peace-loving," nor is it consistently restrained or peaceful in intent. Furthermore, liberal practice may reduce the probability that states will successfully exercise the consistent restraint and peaceful intentions that world peace may well require in the nuclear age. Yet the peaceful intent and restraint that liberalism does manifest in limited aspects of its foreign affairs announces the possibility of a world peace this side of the grave or of world conquest. Liberals have created something considerably more stable than a troubled peace constantly threatening an outbreak of war. They have strengthened the prospects for a world peace established by the steady expansion of a separate peace among liberal societies.

This essay highlights the differences between liberal practice toward other liberal societies and liberal practice toward nonliberal societies. It argues that liberalism has achieved extraordinary success in the first and, yet, has contributed to exceptional confusion in the second. Appreciating these liberal legacies calls, first, for another look at one of the greatest of liberal philosophers, Immanuel Kant, for he is a source of insight, policy, and hope.

Toward Perpetual Peace

Kant's *Toward Perpetual Peace,* a mature work, written in 1795 after he had established his system of philosophy, predicted the ever-widening pacification of a liberal pacific union; it also explains that pacification and, at the same time, suggests why liberal states would not, regretfully, be pacific in their relations with nonliberal states. Kant argues that perpetual peace will be guaranteed by the widening acceptance of three Definitive Articles of peace. When all nations have accepted the Definitive Articles in a metaphorical "treaty," perpetual peace will have been established.

The importance of Immanuel Kant as a theorist of international ethics has been well appreciated.[1] Moreover, the ultimate aim of Kant's theory is to establish the grounds on which a "moral politician" — "who interprets the principles of political prudence in such a way that they can coexist with morality" — can adopt a strategy of peace as a practical duty. To show that the duty is practical, Kant wants to demonstrate that it is not impossible. He does this by showing that it can be imagined to follow logically from human beings pursuing their rational self-interest in the circumstances of the world as we know it (PP 8:372).

Kant's analytic theory of international politics is thus crucial to his project of eventual universal peace. *Toward Perpetual Peace* helps us understand the interactive nature of international relations. Methodologically, Kant tries to teach us that we cannot study either the systemic relations of states or the varieties of state behavior in isolation from each other. Like George and Martha in Edward Albee's *Who's Afraid of Virginia Woolf?*, the behavior of state A and state B cannot be understood in isolation from its pair.[2] Kant's states continue to live in international anarchy — in the sense that there is no world government — but this anarchy is tamed and made subject to law, rather than to fear and threat of war. Kant's theory is, moreover, a theory of state interest and of what does and what does not constitute a threat. Just as the superior capability of another state would be inherently threatening to Hobbes's structural realists, so autocratic regimes would be assumed to be inherently threatening to Kantians. Rather than an alternative to rational national interest theory, Kant offers a specification of what does (and should) constitute the public interest that a state should (and usually does) rationally pursue. Substantively, Kant anticipates for us the ever-widening pacification of a liberal pacific union, he explains that pacification, and at the same time suggests why liberal states are not pacific in their relations with nonliberal states.

Kant, like Hobbes, begins with the "state of nature" which is a "state of war." "States," he bluntly says, "considered in their external relations with one another (like lawless savages), are by nature in a nonjuridical condition . . . this condition is a *condition* of war" (MM 6:344). International law constitutes no guarantee of justice in these circumstances. States therefore have the right to make war in this condition when they are injured (and legal proceedings do not provide satisfaction). But they may also make war when (1) they "believe" they are injured (and legal proceedings fail to satisfy the grievance) or (2) when the state experiences a "threat" as another state makes preparations for war or (3) when another state achieves an alarming increase in power (MM 6:346). From this last consideration follows the right to maintain a balance of power.

The rights of peace include neutrality, rights to guarantees, and defensive alliances. During war all means of conflict (*jus in bello*) are allowed except those that render one's own citizens "unfit to be citizens" of a possible eventual peace based on international law. Thus spies, assassins, poisoners, sharpshooters, propaganda: all are banned (MM 6:347). So, too are war aims (*jus ad bellum*) that involve punishment, permanent conquest, subjugation, or extermination. Just wars are defensive in nature. Conquest for the sake of reforming an unjust enemy state is permitted, forcing it to "accept a new constitution, one which according to its nature is unfavorable to the inclination to wage war" (MM 6:349). But no peace should constitute a violation of the fundamental rights of the citizens of a conquered state (MM 6:347–48).

The state of war requires decisions on the basis of right, but it does not allow for security or welfare. The will to subjugate is always present and the production of armaments for defense ("which often makes peace more oppressive and destructive for internal welfare than the war itself," TP 8:312) can never be relaxed. Only a true condition of international right can establish peace. The "European balance of power" is nothing more than an illusion, like Swift's famous house constructed in such perfect harmony (balance) that as soon as a sparrow landed on it, it collapsed. Peace has to be founded on a different basis. Thus, for example, the United States and the USSR were peaceful in their Cold War relations, experiencing very few direct casualties. And Venezuela and Argentina have never fought a war against each other; nor have Iceland and Indonesia. But nuclear deterrence goes a long way to account for the Cold War "peace," and distance and lack of capacity go a long way to account for the latter peaces. None of these sets of relations escaped from the state of war. The Kantian peace on the other hand, is a state of peace, experienced while relations are close and interdependent and irrespective of arms levels or technologies.

PRELIMINARY ARTICLES

Kant begins with a set of six Preliminary Articles designed to build confidence among states still in the state of war (cf. PP 8:343–47):

1. No peace treaty will be considered valid if it harbors a secret intent to resume war at some more favorable opportunity. True peace agreements should be distinguished from truces if states are going to learn to trust each other.
2. No independent state should be subject to conquest, purchase, or inheritance. This provision is designed to establish the norm of "territorial integrity."
3. Standing armies will be gradually abolished.
4. No national debt will be incurred with the purpose of enhancing international power. This provision is designed to limit the incentives to engage in war by requiring that wars be fought from current revenues.
5. No state will forcibly interfere in the constitution or government of another. Supplementing the second provision, this guarantees "political independence" — the second of the two principles underlying modern sovereign equality.
6. No state will commit war crimes — use poisoners, assassins, promote subversion — because these are acts that destroy the mutual confidence a future peace will require.

Together these principles are designed to build the mutual confidence and respect that establishing a true peace will require. Well-intentioned, "enlightened despots" (Kant praises his own Frederick the Great) should seek to further these principles, and they sometimes have.[3] But these principles alone are not likely to be effective in the state of war when confusion and powerful incentives for aggression are prevalent. What is needed, Kant argues, is an institutionalization — a constitutionalization — of peace. The continuing dangers of the state of war make "that a league of states according to the idea of an original social contract is necessary, . . . to protect one another against attacks from the outside. . . . [The alliance] can be broken off at any time, and thus must be renewed from time to time"(PP 8:344).

THE DEFINITIVE ARTICLES

The first Definitive Article requires that the civil constitution of the state be republican. By "republican" Kant means a political society that has — from a formal-legal point of view — solved the problem of combining moral autonomy, individualism, and social order. A private property and market-oriented economy partially addresses that dilemma in the private sphere. The public, or political, sphere is more troubling. Kant's answer is a republic that preserves juridical freedom — the legal equality of citizens as subjects — on the basis of a representative government with a separation of powers. Juridical freedom is preserved because the morally autonomous individual is by means of representation a self-legislator making laws that apply equally to all citizens, including himself. Tyranny is avoided because the individual is subject to laws he does not also administer.[4]

Liberal republics will progressively establish peace among themselves by means of the pacific federation, or union (foedus pacificum), described in Kant's second Definitive Article. The pacific union will establish peace within a federation of free states and securely maintain the rights of each state. The world will not have achieved the "perpetual peace" that provides the ultimate guarantor of republican freedom until "late and after many futile attempts" (IUH 8:23). Then right conceptions of the appropriate constitution, great and sad experience, and good will have taught all the nations the lessons of peace. Not until then will individuals enjoy perfect republican rights or the full guarantee of a global and just peace. In the meantime, the "pacific federation" of liberal republics — "a lasting and continually expanding federation that prevents war" — brings within it more and more republics (despite republican collapses, backsliding, and disastrous wars), creating an expanding separate peace (PP 8:357).[5] And Kant emphasizes:

> It can be shown that the idea of federalism, which should gradually encompass all states and thereby lead to perpetual peace, is practicable (that is, has objective reality). For if fortune so determines that a powerful

and enlightened people can constitute itself as a republic (which according to its nature necessarily tends toward perpetual peace), then this republic provides a focus point for other states, so that they might join this federative union and thereby secure the condition of peace among states in accordance with the idea of international right and gradually extend this union further and further through several such associations. (PP 8:356)

The pacific union is neither a single peace treaty ending one war nor a world state or state of nations. Kant finds the first insufficient. The second and third are impossible or potentially tyrannical. National sovereignty precludes reliable subservience to a state of nations; a world state destroys the civic freedom on which the development of human capacities rests (IUH 8:27–28). Although Kant obliquely refers to various classical inter-state confederations and modern diplomatic congresses, he develops no systematic organizational embodiment of this treaty, presumably because he does not find institutionalization necessary.[6] He appears to have in mind a mutual nonaggression pact, perhaps a collective security agreement, and cosmopolitan right as set forth in the third Definitive Article.[7]

The third Definitive Article establishes cosmopolitan right to operate in conjunction with the pacific union. Cosmopolitan right "shall be limited to the conditions of universal hospitality." In this he calls for the recognition of the "the right of a stranger not to be treated in a hostile manner by another upon his arrival on the other's territory" (PP 8:358). This "does not extend beyond the conditions of the possibility of *attempting* interaction with the old inhabitants" (PP 8:358). Hospitality does not require extending to foreigners either the right to citizenship or the right to settlement, unless the foreign visitors would perish if they were expelled. Foreign conquest and plunder also find no justification under this right. Hospitality does appear to include the right of access and the obligation of maintaining the opportunity for citizens to exchange goods and ideas, without imposing the obligation to trade (a voluntary act in all cases under liberal constitutions). Liberal republican states, Kant suggests, would establish a peace among themselves while remaining in a state of war with nonrepublics.

Liberal Internationalism

The historical record of liberal international relations seems to support Kant's speculations. Liberal principles and institutions seem to have had three striking effects on the foreign affairs of liberal states. They have created incentives for a separate peace among liberal states, for aggression against nonliberals, and for complaisance in vital matters of security and economic cooperation.

The first of the effects of liberalism on the foreign relations of liberal states is the establishment of a peace among them.[8] During the nineteenth century, the United States and Great Britain engaged in nearly continual strife, including one war, the War of 1812. But after the Reform Act of 1832 defined actual representation as the formal source of the sovereignty of the British parliament, Britain and the United States negotiated their disputes despite, for example, British grievances against the North's blockade of the South, with which Britain had close economic ties. Despite severe Anglo-French colonial rivalry, liberal France and liberal Britain formed an entente against illiberal Germany before World War I. And in 1914–15, Italy, the liberal member of the Triple Alliance with Germany and Austria, chose not to fulfill its treaty obligations under the alliance to support its allies. Instead it joined in an alliance with Britain and France that had the result of preventing it from fighting other liberal states, and then it declared war on Germany and Austria. And despite generations of Anglo-American tension and Britain's wartime restrictions on American trade with Germany, the United States leaned toward Britain and France from 1914 to 1917, before entering the war on their side.

Nowhere was this special peace among liberal states more clearly proclaimed than in President Woodrow Wilson's War Message of 2 April 1917: "Our object now, as then, is to vindicate the principles of peace and justice in the life of the world as against selfish and autocratic power and to set up amongst the really free and self-governed people of the world such a concert of purpose and of action as will henceforth ensure the observance of those principles."[9] Even in the quiet recesses of secret diplomacy, liberalism has shaped the discourse of statesmen at crucial times of national emergency. In October 1938, as fears of war rose in Europe, President Roosevelt sent a special message to Britain. He asked the special envoy Col. Arthur Murray, in Murray's words, to "to convey . . . to the Prime Minister . . . an assurance — in the event of hostilities and the United States being neutral — of his [Roosevelt's] desire to help in every way in his power. . . . He [Roosevelt] said he wished the Prime Minister to feel he had, in so far as he, the President, was able to achieve it, 'the industrial resources of the American nation behind him in the event of war with the dictatorships.' "[10]

Beginning in the eighteenth century and slowly growing since then,

Table 1

The Liberal Community (by date "liberal")[a]

Period		Total Number
18th century	Swiss Cantons[b]	3
	French Republic 1790–1795	
	United States[b] 1776–	
1800–1850	Swiss Confederation,	8
	United States,	
	France 1830–1849	
	Belgium 1830–	
	Great Britain 1832–	
	Netherlands 1848–	
	Piedmont 1848–	
	Denmark 1849–	
1850–1900	Switzerland,	13
	United States,	
	Belgium, Great Britain,	
	Netherlands,	
	Piedmont –1861, Italy 1861–	
	Denmark –1866	
	Sweden 1864–	
	Greece 1864–	
	Canada[c] 1867–	
	France 1871–	
	Argentina 1880–	
	Chile 1891–	
1900–1945	Switzerland,	29
	United States,	
	Great Britain,	
	Sweden, Canada,	
	Greece –1911, 1928–1936	
	Italy –1922	
	Belgium –1940	
	Netherlands –1940	
	Argentina –1943	
	France –1940	
	Chile –1924, 1932	
	Australia 1901	
	Norway 1905–1940	
	New Zealand 1907–	
	Colombia 1910–1949	
	Denmark 1914–1940	

Table 1
Continued

Period		Total Number
	Poland 1917–1935	
	Latvia 1922–1934	
	Germany 1918–1932	
	Austria 1918–1934	
	Estonia 1919–1934	
	Finland 1919–	
	Uruguay 1919–	
	Costa Rica 1919–	
	Czechoslovakia 1920–1939	
	Ireland 1920–	
	Mexico 1928–	
	Lebanon 1944–	
1945–1990	Switzerland, United States,	68
	Great Britain, Sweden,	
	Canada, Australia, New Zealand,	
	Finland, Ireland, Mexico,	
	Uruguay –1973; 1985–	
	Chile –1973, 1990–	
	Lebanon –1975	
	Costa Rica –1948, 1953–	
	Iceland 1944–	
	France 1945–	
	Denmark 1945–	
	Norway 1945–	
	Austria 1945–	
	Brazil 1945–1954, 1955–1964, 1985–	
	Belgium 1946–	
	Netherlands 1946–	
	Italy 1946–	
	Philippines 1946–1972, 1987–	
	India 1947–1975, 1977–	
	Sri Lanka 1948–1961, 1963–1971, 1978–1983, 1988–	
	Ecuador 1948–1963, 1979–	
	Israel 1949–	
	West Germany 1949–	
	Greece 1950–1967, 1975–	
	Peru 1950–1962, 1963–1968, 1980–	
	Turkey 1950–1960, 1966–1971, 1984–	
	Japan 1951–	

Table I
Continued

Period		Total Number
	Bolivia 1956–1969, 1982–	
	Colombia 1958–	
	Venezuela 1959–	
	Nigeria 1961–1964, 1979–1984	
	Jamaica 1962–	
	Trinidad and Tobago 1962–	
	Senegal 1963–	
	Malaysia 1963–	
	Botswana 1966–	
	Singapore 1965–	
	Portugal 1976–	
	Spain 1978–	
	Dominican Republic 1978–	
	Ecuador 1978–	
	Peru 1980–1990	
	Honduras 1981–	
	Papua New Guinea 1982–	
	El Salvador 1984–	
	Argentina 1983–	
	Uruguay 1985–	
	Mauritius 1987–	
	South Korea 1988–	
	Taiwan 1988–	
	Thailand 1988–	
	Pakistan 1988–	
	Panama 1989–	
	Paraguay 1989–	
	Madagascar 1990–	
	Mongolia 1990–	
	Namibia 1990–	
	Nepal 1990–	
	Nicaragua 1990–	
	Poland 1990–	
	Hungary 1990–	
	Czechoslovakia 1990–	
1990–[d]	Switzerland, United States,	103
	Great Britain, Sweden,	
	Canada, Australia, New Zealand,	
	Finland, Ireland, Mexico, Uruguay,	

Table 1
Continued[a]

Period	Total Number
Costa Rica, Iceland, France, Denmark, Norway, Austria, Brazil, Belgium, Netherlands, Italy, Philippines, India, Sri Lanka, Ecuador, Israel, West Germany, Greece, Turkey, Japan, Bolivia, Colombia, Venezuela, Jamaica, Trinidad and Tobago, Senegal, Malaysia , Botswana, Portugal, Spain, Dominican Republic, Ecuador, Honduras, Papua New Guinea, El Salvador, Argentina, Mauritius, South Korea, Taiwan, Thailand, Panama, Paraguay, Madagascar, Mongolia, Namibia, Nicaragua, Poland, Hungary, Czechoslovakia, Singapore −1993	

Pakistan −1998
Russia 1991−1999
Jordan 1991−2001
Nepal −2003
Bulgaria 1990−
Chile 1990−
Mongolia 1990−
Albania 1991−
Bangladesh 1991−
Benin 1991−
Cape Verde 1991−
Croatia 1991−
Estonia 1991−
Latvia 1991−
Lithuania 1991−
Ukraine 1991−
Slovenia 1991−
Zambia 1991−
Armenia 1992−
Indonesia 1992−
Macedonia 1992−
Mali 1992−
Romania 1992−
Burkina Faso 1993−

Table 1
Continued[a]

Period	Total Number
Guatemala 1993–	
Lesotho 1993–	
Yemen 1993–	
Guinea-Bissau 1994–	
Malawi 1994–	
Mozambique 1994–	
South Africa 1994–	
Georgia 1995–	
Ghana, 1995–	
Sierra Leone 1998–	
Kuwait 1999–	
Nigeria 1999–	
Tanzania 1999–	
Bosnia-Herzegovina 2000–	
Djibouti 2000–	
Niger 2000–	
East Timor 2002–	
Gambia 2002–	
Kenya 2002–	

a. I have drawn up this *approximate* list of "liberal regimes" (through 2005, thus including regimes that were liberal democratic as of 2002) according to the four "Kantian" institutions described as essential: market and private property economies; polities that are externally sovereign; citizens who possess juridical rights; and "republican" (whether republican or parliamentary monarchy), representative government. This latter includes the requirement that the legislative branch have an effective role in public policy and be formally and competitively (either inter- or intra-party) elected. Furthermore, I have taken into account whether male suffrage is wide (that is, 30 percent) or, as Kant would have had it (MM, 6:314–15), open to "achievement" by inhabitants (for example, to poll-tax payers or householders) of the national or metropolitan territory. (This list of liberal regimes is thus more inclusive than a list of democratic regimes, or polyarchies [G. Bingham Powell, *Contemporary Democracies* (Cambridge: Harvard University Press, 1982), 5]). Female suffrage is granted within a generation of its being demanded by an extensive female suffrage movement, and representative government is internally sovereign (for example, including and especially over military and foreign affairs) as well as stable (in existence for at least three years). Arthur Banks and William Overstreet, eds., *A Political Handbook of the World* (New York: McGraw-Hill, 1983); United Kingdom Foreign and Commonwealth Office, *A Yearbook of the Commonwealth, 1980* (London: HMSO, 1980); *The Europa Yearbook* (London: Europa Publications, 1985); William L.

a zone of peace, which Kant called the "pacific federation" or "pacific union," began to be established among liberal societies. (Approximately 127 liberal states currently [2006] make up the union.[11] With at least three years of consolidation [2003] the number of liberal states is 103. Most are in Europe and North America, but they can be found on every continent.)

Of course, the outbreak of war, in any given year, between any two given states, is a low-probability event. But the occurrence of a war between any two adjacent states, considered over a long period of time, is more probable. The near absence of war between liberal states, whether adjacent or not, for almost two hundred years thus may have significance. More significant perhaps is that when states are forced to decide on which side of an impending world war they will fight, liberal states wind up all on the same side, despite the complexity of the paths that take them there. And we should recall that medieval and early modern Europe were the warring cockpits of states, wherein France and England and the Low Countries engaged in nearly constant strife. Then, in the late eighteenth century, liberal regimes began to emerge. At first hesitant and confused, and later clear and confident as liberal regimes gained deeper domestic foundations and longer international experience, a pacific union of these liberal states became established. These characteristics do not prove that the peace among liberals is statistically significant, nor that liberalism is the peace's sole valid explanation.[12] But they do suggest that we consider the possibility that liberals have indeed established a separate peace — but only among themselves.

Langer, *The Encyclopedia of World History* (Boston: Houghton Mifflin, 1968); U.S. Department of State, *Country Reports on Human Rights Practices* (Washington, D.C.: Government Printing Office, 1981); Raymond Gastil, *Freedom in the World* (New York: Freedom House, 1985); R. Bruce McColm and Freedom House Survey Team, eds., *Freedom in the World, 1990–1991* (New York: Freedom House, 1991); and James Finn et al., *Freedom in the World, 1994–1995* (New York: Freedom House, 1995).

b. There are domestic variations within these liberal regimes. For example, Switzerland was liberal only in certain cantons; the United States was liberal only north of the Mason-Dixon Line until 1865, when it became liberal throughout. These lists also exclude ancient "republics," since none appear to fit Kant's criteria (Stephen Holmes, "Aristippus in and out of Athens," *American Political Science Review* 89 [1979]: 113–28).

c. Canada, as a commonwealth within the British Empire, did not have formal control of its foreign policy during this period.

d. Selected list, excludes liberal regimes with populations less than one million. These include all states categorized as "free" by Freedom House and those "partly free" (four political and five civil liberties or more free).

This is a feature, moreover, that appears to be special to liberal societies. Neither specific regional attributes nor historic alliances or friendships describe the wide reach of the liberal peace. The peace extends as far as, and no further than, the relations among liberal states, not including nonliberal states in an otherwise liberal region (such as the North Atlantic in the 1930s) nor excluding liberal states in a less liberal region (such as Central America or Africa).

Relations among any group of states with similar social structures or with compatible values or pluralistic social structures are not similarly peaceful.[13] Feudal warfare was frequent and very much a sport of the monarchs and nobility. There have not been enough truly totalitarian, fascist powers (nor have they lasted long enough) to test fairly their pacific compatibility, but fascist powers in the wider sense of nationalist, military dictatorships fought each other in the 1930s in Eastern Europe. Communist powers have engaged in wars more recently in East Asia, when China invaded Vietnam and Vietnam invaded Cambodia. We have not had enough democratic socialist societies to consider the relevance of socialist pacification. The more abstract category of pluralism does not suffice. Certainly Germany was pluralist when it engaged in war with liberal states in 1914; Japan as well in 1941. But they were not liberal. Peace among liberals thus appears to be a special characteristic.

Here the predictions of liberal pacifists are borne out: liberal states do exercise peaceful restraint and a separate peace exists among them. This separate peace provides a solid foundation for the United States' crucial alliances with the liberal powers (NATO, the United States–Japanese alliance, the alliance with Australia and New Zealand). This foundation appears to be impervious to the quarrels with allies that have bedeviled many U.S. administrations. It also offers the promise of a continuing peace among liberal states. And, as the number of liberal states increases, it announces the possibility of global peace this side of the grave or world conquest.

Liberalism carries with it a second effect — what Hume called "imprudent vehemence," or aggression against nonliberals.[14] Peaceful restraint seems to work only in the liberals' relations with other liberals. Liberal states have fought numerous wars with nonliberal states.

Many of these wars have been defensive, and thus prudent by necessity. Liberal states have been attacked and threatened by nonliberal states that do not exercise any special restraint in their dealings with liberal states. Authoritarian rulers both stimulate and respond to an international political environment in which conflicts of prestige, of interest, and of pure fear of what other states might do all lead states toward war. War and conquest have thus characterized the careers of many authoritarian rulers and ruling parties — from Louis XIV and Napoleon to Mussolini's fascists, Hitler's Nazis, and Stalin's communists.

But imprudent aggression by the liberal state has also characterized many of these wars. Both liberal France and Britain fought expansionist colonial wars throughout the nineteenth century. The United States fought a similar war with Mexico in 1846–48, waged a war of annihilation against the American Indians, and intervened militarily against sovereign states many times before and after World War II. Liberal states invade weak nonliberal states and display exceptional degrees of distrust in their dealings with powerful nonliberal states.[15]

Nonetheless, establishing the statistical significance of Hume's assertion appears remarkably difficult. The best statistical evidence indicates that "libertarian" or "democratic" states (slightly different measures) are not less war-prone than nonlibertarian or nondemocratic states. Indeed, in these measures they appear to be more war-prone.[16] War-proneness is not, however, a measure of imprudent aggression since many wars are defensive. But that does not mean that we can simply blame warfare on the authoritarians or totalitarians, as many of our more enthusiastic politicians would have us do.[17] Liberal states ("libertarian") acted as initiators in 24 out of the 56 interstate wars in which they participated between 1816 and 1980 while nonliberals were on the initiating side in 91 out of the 187 times in which they participated in interstate wars.[18] Liberal metropoles were the overwhelming participators in "extrasystemic wars," colonial wars, which we can assume to have been by and large initiated by the metropole (see below). Furthermore, the United States intervened in the Third World more than twice as often in the period 1946–76 as the Soviet Union did in 1946–79.[19] Relatedly, the United States devoted one-quarter and the Soviet Union, one-tenth, of their respective defense budgets to forces designed for Third World interventions (where responding to perceived threats would presumably have a less than purely defensive character).[20]

Although liberal initiation of wars suggests some basis for Hume's assertion, it does not resolve the claim he made. Initiation or response may reflect either aggressive or defensive policy, in that an aggressive policy may provoke a rival to initiate a war and a defensive policy may require preemption. Hume appears to be suggesting that liberal policy has a tendency to be unnecessarily aggressive. To assess his assertion, we need to take into account the specific circumstances — the threats with which the state is faced, its resources, and its goals — and doing this requires an historical understanding of time and place. If liberals were always aggressive

Table 2

International Wars Listed Chronologically

Franco-Spanish, 1823	Russo-Polish, 1919–20
Russo-Turkish, 1828–29	Hungarian-Allies, 1919
Mexican-American, 1846–48	Greco-Turkish, 1919–22
Austro-Sardinian, 1848	Franco-Turkish, 1919–21
First Schleswig-Holstein, 1848	Lithuanian-Polish, 1920
Roman Republic, 1849	Sino-Soviet, 1929
La Plata, 1851–52	Manchurian, 1931–33
Crimean, 1853–56	Chaco, 1932–35
Anglo-Persian, 1856–57	Saudi-Yemeni, 1934
Italian Unification, 1859	Italo-Ethiopian, 1935–36
Spanish-Moroccan, 1859–60	Sino-Japanese, 1937–41
Italo-Roman, 1860	Changkufeng, 1938
Italo-Sicilian, 1860–61	Nomonhan, 1939
Franco-Mexican, 1862–67	World War II, 1939–45
Ecuadorian-Columbian, 1863	Russo-Finnish, 1939–40
Second Schleswig-Holstein, 1864	Franco-Thai, 1940–41
Lopez, 1864–70	First Kashmir, 1948–49
Spanish-Chilean, 1865–66	Palestine, 1948
Seven Weeks, 1866	Korean, 1950–53
Franco-Prussian, 1870–71	Russo-Hungarian, 1956
First Central American, 1876	Sinai, 1956
Russo-Turkish, 1877–78	Assam, 1962
Pacific, 1879–83	Vietnamese, 1965–75
Anglo-Egyptian, 1882	Second Kashmir, 1965
Sino-French, 1884–85	Six Days, 1967
Second Central American, 1885	Israeli-Egyptian, 1969–70
Franco-Thai, 1893	Football, 1969
Sino-Japanese, 1894–95	Bangladesh, 1971
Greco-Turkish, 1897	Yom Kippur, 1973
Spanish-American, 1898	Turco-Cypriot, 1974
Boxer Rebellion, 1900	Vietnamese-Cambodian, 1975–79
Sino-Russian, 1900	Ethiopian-Somalian, 1977–78
Russo-Japanese, 1904–5	Ugandan-Tanzanian, 1978–79
Third Central American, 1906	Sino-Vietnamese, 1979
Fourth Central American, 1907	Iran-Iraq, 1980–88
Spanish-Moroccan, 1909–10	Falklands, 1982
Italo-Turkish, 1911–12	Israel-Syria (Lebanon), 1982
First Balkan, 1912–13	Sino-Vietnamese, 1987
Second Balkan, 1913	Gulf War, 1990–91
World War I, 1914–18	

Table note on facing page

or always nonaggressive in relations with nonliberals, we could reasonably argue that they are also unnecessarily aggressive, or were not. Thus we were able to support the existence of something special in liberal foreign relations with other liberals. But relations with nonliberals appear more complicated. Unless we can normalize not just the number but the situations of liberal relations with nonliberals and nonliberal relations with nonliberals, the best we can do, if we can do that, is illustrate imprudent vehemence.

We should recall as well that authoritarian states also have a record of imprudent aggression. It was not semi-liberal Britain that collapsed in 1815, but Napoleonic France. It was the Kaiser's Germany that dissolved in 1918, not republican France and liberal Britain and democratic America. It was Imperial Japan and Nazi Germany that disappeared in 1945, not the United States or the United Kingdom.[21] It is the contrast to ideal rational strategy and even more the comparison with liberal accommodation with fellow liberals that highlight the aggressive imprudence of liberal relations with nonliberals.

Most wars, moreover, seem to arise out of calculations and miscalculations of interest, misunderstandings, and mutual suspicions, such as those that characterized the origins of World War I. But we can find expressions of aggressive intent and apparently unnecessary vehemence by the liberal state characterizing a large number of wars.[22]

Note: This partial list is based on Meredith Sarkee, "The Correlates of War Data: An Update to 1997," *Conflict Management and Peace* 18 (2000): 123–44. The definition of war used here excludes covert interventions, a few of which have been directed by liberal regimes against other liberal regimes. One example is the effort by the United States to destabilize the Chilean election and Allende's government. Nonetheless, it is significant that such interventions are not pursued publicly as acknowledged policy. The covert destabilization campaign against Chile is recounted by the U.S. Congress, Senate Select Committee to Study Governmental Operations with Respect to Intelligence Activities, *Covert Action in Chile, 1963–73,* 94th Cong., 1st sess. (Washington, D.C.: Government Printing Office, 1975).

The argument (and this list) also excludes civil wars. Civil wars differ from international wars not in the ferocity of combat but in the issues that engender them. Two nations that could abide one another as independent neighbors separated by a border might well be the fiercest of enemies if forced to live together in one state, jointly deciding how to raise and spend taxes, choose leaders, and legislate fundamental questions of value. Notwithstanding these differences, no civil wars that I recall upset the argument of liberal pacification.

In relations with powerful nonliberal states, liberal states have missed opportunities to pursue the negotiation of arms reduction and arms control when it has been in the mutual strategic interest, and they have failed to construct wider schemes of accommodation that are needed to supplement arms control. Prior to the outbreak of World War I, this is the charge that Lord Sanderson leveled against Sir Eyre Crowe in Sanderson's response to Crowe's classic memorandum on the state of British relations with Germany.[23] Sanderson pointed out that Crowe interpreted German demands to participate in the settlement of international disputes and to have a "place in the sun" (colonies), of a size not too dissimilar to that enjoyed by the other great powers, as evidence of a fundamental aggressiveness driving toward world domination. Crowe may well have perceived an essential feature of Wilhelmine Germany, and Sanderson's attempt to place Germany in the context of other rising powers (bumptious but not aggressively pursuing world domination) may have been naive. But the interesting thing to note is less the conclusions reached than Crowe's chain of argument and evidence. He rejects continued accommodation (appeasement) with Germany not because he shows that Germany was more bumptious than France and not because he shows that Germany had greater potential as a world hegemon than the United States, which he does not even consider in this connection. Instead he is (legitimately) perplexed by the real uncertainty of German foreign policy and by its "erratic, domineering, and often frankly aggressive spirit," which accords with the well-known personal characteristics of "the present Ruler of Germany."

Similar evidence of deeply held suspicion appears to characterize U.S. diplomacy toward the Soviet Union. In a fascinating memorandum to President Wilson written in 1919, Herbert Hoover (then one of Wilson's advisers), recommended that the president speak out against the danger of "world domination" that the "Bolsheviki" — a "tyranny that is the negation of democracy" — posed to free peoples. Rejecting military intervention as excessively costly and likely to "make us a party in reestablishing the reactionary classes in their economic domination over the lower classes," he proposed a "relief program" designed to undercut some of the popular appeal the Bolsheviks were garnering both in the Soviet Union and abroad. Although acknowledging that the evidence was not yet clear, he concluded: "If the militant features of Bolshevism were drawn in colors with their true parallel with Prussianism as an attempt at world domination that we do not stand for, it would check the fears that today haunt all men's minds." (The actual U.S. intervention in the Soviet Union was limited to supporting anti-

Bolshevik Czechoslovak soldiers in Siberia and to protecting military supplies in Murmansk from German seizure.)[24]

In the postwar period, and particularly following the outbreak of the
Korean War, U.S. diplomacy equated the "International Communist Movement" (all communist states and parties) with "communist imperialism"
and with a domestic tyranny in the USSR that required a Cold War contest
and international subversion as means of legitimizing its own police state.
John Foster Dulles most clearly expressed this conviction, together with his
own commitment to a strategy of "liberation," when he declared: "We shall
never have a secure peace or a happy world so long as Soviet communism
dominates one third of all the peoples that there are, and is in the process of
trying at least to extend its rule to many others."[25]

Opportunities for splitting the Communist bloc along cleavages of strategic national interest were delayed. Burdened with the war in Vietnam, the
United States took ten years to appreciate and exploit the strategic opportunity of the Sino-Soviet split. Even the signal strategic, "offensive" success of the early Cold War, the defection of Yugoslavia from the Soviet
bloc, did not receive the wholehearted welcome that a strategic assessment
of its importance would have warranted.[26] Both relationships, with Yugoslavia and China, became subject to alternating, largely ideologically derived, moods: visions of exception (they were "less ruthless," more organic
to the indigenous, traditional culture) sparred with bouts of liberal soul-
searching ("we cannot associate ourselves with a totalitarian state").

Imprudent vehemence is also associated with liberal foreign policy toward weak, nonliberal states; no greater spirit of accommodation or tolerance informs liberal policy toward the many weak, nonliberal states in the
Third World. This problem affects both conservative liberals and welfare liberals, but the two can be distinguished by differing styles of interventions.[27]

Protecting "native rights" from "native" oppressors, and protecting
universal rights of property and settlement from local transgressions, introduced especially liberal motives for imperial aggression. Ending the slave
trade destabilized nineteenth-century West African oligarchies, yet encouraged "legitimate trade" protecting the property of European merchants;
declaring the illegitimacy of "suttee" or of domestic slavery also attacked
local cultural traditions that had sustained the stability of indigenous political authority. Europeans settling in sparsely populated areas destroyed
the livelihood of tribes that relied on hunting. The tribes defensively retali-
ated in force; the settlers called for imperial protection.[28] The protection
of cosmopolitan liberal rights thus bred a demand for imperial rule that

violated the liberty of Native Americans, Africans, and Asians. In practice, once the exigencies of ruling an empire came into play, liberal imperialism resulted in the oppression of "native" liberals seeking self-determination in order to maintain imperial security, to avoid local chaos and international interference by another imperial power attempting to take advantage of local disaffection.

Thus nineteenth-century liberals, such as British Prime Minister William Gladstone, pondered whether Egypt's proto-nationalist Arabi rebellion (1881–82) was truly liberal nationalist (they discovered it was not) before intervening to protect strategic lifelines to India, commerce, and investment.[29] These dilemmas of liberal imperialism are also reflected in U.S. imperialism in the Caribbean where, for example, following the Spanish-American War of 1898, Article 3 of the Platt Amendment gave the United States the "right to intervene for the preservation of Cuban independence, the maintenance of a government adequate for the protection of life, property, and individual liberty."[30]

The invasion of Iraq in 2003 illustrated another intervention, widely regarded as imprudent by 2005. United States hostility stemmed from factors that any great power and any state committed to the international rule of law would have found provoking. These included Saddam Hussein's record of aggression against his neighbors (particularly Kuwait), the implicit threat he posed to security of oil supplies in the Persian Gulf, and his unwillingness to assure the international community that he had eliminated programs to acquire weapons of mass destruction (WMD) as he had been required to do as part of the settlement of the first Gulf War in 1991 (Security Council Resolution 687). Especially liberal factors were also at work. Saddam's genocidal campaigns against the Kurds and his record of flagrant abuses of the Iraqi population shaped his international reputation. But the particular circumstances of the run-up to the 2003 invasion appeared more significant than either of the longer trends in hostility. The Bush administration, aware that the American public held it responsible for preventing another 9/11 attack and benefiting from a public that politically rewarded a "war on terror presidency," read—and presented to the public—every piece of preinvasion intelligence according to the most threatening interpretation.[31] It attempted to justify the war by denouncing alleged Iraqi programs to build WMD and foster ties to al-Qaeda (for which no support could be found afterwards), and it promised to induce a transformative spread of democracy in the region, beginning with Iraq.[32] Reacting to the insurgency that greeted the invasion, the poor planning that characterized the occupation, and mounting U.S. and Iraqi casualties, a majority of the

U.S. public by 2005 had turned against the war, as had the publics of other democracies earlier. The long-term results of the invasion and effort to democratize Iraq were far from clear (in 2005). Iraq had experienced a referendum on a constitution and national elections, but splits among its three major communities (Shia, Sunni, and Kurd) threatened a civil war. Even aggressive liberals who might have welcomed a democratic transformation of the region questioned the method, with the questionable legality of the invasion and the long-run costs expected by some to mount to two trillion dollars.[33]

The record of liberalism in the nonliberal world is not solely a catalogue of oppression and imprudence. The North American West and the settlement colonies — Australia and New Zealand — represent a successful transplant of liberal institutions, albeit in a temperate, underpopulated, and then depopulated environment and at the cost of Native American and Aboriginal rights. Similarly, the twentieth-century expansion of liberalism into less powerful nonliberal areas has also had some striking successes. The forcible liberalization of Germany and Japan following World War II and the long-covert financing of liberal parties in Italy are the more significant instances of successful transplant. Covert financing of liberalism in Chile and occasional diplomatic démarches to nudge aside military threats to noncommunist democratic parties (as in Peru in 1962, South Korea in 1963, and the Dominican Republic in 1962[34] and again in 1978) illustrate policies that, though less successful, were directed toward liberal goals. These particular postwar liberal successes also are the product of special circumstances: the existence of a potential liberal majority, temporarily suppressed, which could be readily reestablished by outside aid or unusually weak oligarchic, military, or communist opponents.[35]

At other times in the postwar period, when the United States sought to protect liberals in the Third World from the "communist threat," the consequences of liberal foreign policy on the nonliberal society often became far removed from the promotion of individual rights or of national security. In Vietnam and elsewhere, intervening against "armed minorities" and "enemies of free enterprise" meant intervening for other "armed minorities," some sustaining and sustained by oligarchies, others resting on little more than U.S. foreign aid and troops. Indigenous liberals simply had too narrow a base of domestic support. These interventions did not advance liberal rights, and to the extent that they were driven by ideological motives they were not necessary for national security.

To the conservative liberals, the alternatives are starkly cast: Third World authoritarians with allegiance to the liberal, capitalist West or "communists" subject to the totalitarian East (or leftist nationalists, who, even if elected, are but a slippery stepping stone to totalitarianism).[36] Conservative liberals are prepared to support the allied authoritarians. The communists attack property in addition to liberty, thereby provoking conservative liberals to covert or overt intervention, or "dollar-diplomacy" imperialism. The interventions against Mossadegh in Iran, Arbenz in Guatemala, Allende in Chile, and against the Sandinistas in Nicaragua appear to fall into this pattern.[37] President Reagan's simultaneous support for the military in El Salvador and guerrilla "freedom-fighters" in Nicaragua also tracks this pattern whose common thread is rhetorical commitment to freedom and operational support for conservative, free enterprise.

To the social welfare liberals, the choice is never so clear. Aware of the need for state action to democratize the distribution of social power and resources, they tend to have more sympathy for social reform. This can produce, on the part of "radical" welfare liberals, a more tolerant policy toward the attempts by reforming autocracies to redress inegalitarian distributions of property in the Third World. This more complicated welfare liberal assessment can itself be a recipe for more extensive intervention. The large number of conservative oligarchs or military bureaucracies with whom the conservative liberal is well at home are not so congenial to the social welfare liberal, yet the communists are still seen as enemies of liberty. Left liberals justify more extensive intervention first to discover, then to sustain, Third World social democracy in a political environment that is either barely participatory or highly polarized. Thus Arthur Schlesinger recalls President Kennedy musing shortly after the assassination of General Trujillo (former dictator of the Dominican Republic): "There are three possibilities in descending order of preference, a decent democratic regime, a continuation of the Trujillo regime [by his followers], or a Castro regime. We ought to aim at the first, but we can't really renounce the second until we are sure we can avoid the third." Another instance of this approach was President Carter's support for the land reforms in El Salvador, which was explained by one U.S. official in the following analogy: "There is no one more conservative than a small farmer. We're going to be breeding capitalists like rabbits."[38] President Clinton's administration seems to have succumbed to a similar dose of optimistic interventionism in its conviction that nations could be rebuilt democratically in both Somalia and Haiti, although it had never existed in the first and was led in the second by Jean Bertrand Aristide, a charismatic socialist and an eloquent critic of American imperialism.

The third effect apparent in the international relations of liberal states is

Hume's second assertion: "supine complaisance." This takes two forms: one is failure to support allies; the other is a failure to oppose enemies.

Liberal internationalism among liberal states has been shortsighted in preserving its basic preconditions under changing international circumstances, particularly in supporting the liberal character of its constituent states. The liberal community of nations has failed on occasion, as it did in regard to Germany in the 1920s, to provide the timely international economic support for liberal regimes whose market foundations were in crisis.[39] It failed in the 1930s to provide military aid or political mediation to Spain, which was challenged by an armed minority, or to Czechoslovakia, which was caught in a dilemma of preserving national security or acknowledging the claims (fostered by Hitler's Germany) of the Sudeten minority to self-determination. Farsighted and constitutive measures seem to have been provided by the liberal international order only when one liberal state stood preeminent among the rest, prepared and able to take measures, as did Britain before World War I and the United States following World War II, to sustain economically and politically the foundations of liberal society beyond its borders. Then measures such as British antislavery and free trade and the U.S. loan to Britain in 1947, the Marshall Plan, NATO, GATT, the IMF, and the liberalization of Germany and Japan helped construct buttresses for the international liberal order.[40]

Ideologically based policies can also be self-indulgent. Oligarchic or authoritarian allies in the Third World do not find consistent support in a liberal policy that stresses human rights. Contemporary conservative critics claim that the security needs of these states are neglected, that they fail to obtain military aid or more direct support when they need it (the shah's Iran, Humberto Romero's El Salvador, Somoza's Nicaragua, and apartheid South Africa). Equally disturbing from this point of view, communist regimes are shunned even when a détente with them could further United States strategic interests (Cuba, Angola). Welfare liberals particularly shun the first group, while laissez-faire liberals balk at close dealings with the second. In both cases our economic interests or strategic interests are often slighted.[41]

A second manifestation of complaisance lies in a reaction to the excesses of interventionism. A mood of frustrated withdrawal affects policy toward strategically and economically important countries. Just as interventionism seems to be the typical failing of the liberal great power, so complaisance characterizes declined or "not quite risen" liberal states.[42] Especially following the exhaustion of wars, representative legislatures may become reluctant to undertake international commitments or to fund the military establishment needed to play a geopolitical role. Purely domestic concerns seem to take priority, as they did in the United States in the 1920s. Rational incentives for "free riding" on the extended defense commitments of the leader of the liberal alliance also induce this form of complaisance. During much of the nineteenth century the United States informally relied upon the British fleet for many of its security needs. Today, the Europeans and the Japanese, according to some American strategic analysts, fail to bear their "fair" share of alliance burdens.

Liberalism, if we take into account both Kant and Hume, thus carries with it three legacies: peace among liberals, imprudent vehemence toward nonliberals, and complaisance toward the future. The first appears to be a special feature associated with liberalism and it can be demonstrated statistically. The latter two cannot be shown to be special to liberalism, though their effects can be illustrated historically in liberal foreign policy. And the survival and growth in the number of liberal states suggests imprudent vehemence and complaisance have not overwhelmed liberalism's efficacy as a form of governance.

The Logic of a Separate Peace

How can we explain the legacies of liberalism on foreign affairs? Perpetual peace, for Kant, is an epistemology, a condition for ethical action, and (most importantly) an explanation of how the "mechanical course of nature visibly reveals a purposive plan to create harmony through discord among people, even against their own will" (PP 8:360; IUH 8:20–21). Understanding history requires an epistemological foundation, for without a teleology, such as the promise of perpetual peace, the complexity of history would overwhelm human understanding (IUH 8:29–31). But perpetual peace is not merely a heuristic device with which to interpret history. It is guaranteed, Kant explains in the First Supplement in *Toward Perpetual Peace* ("On the Guarantee of Perpetual Peace"), to result from men fulfilling their ethical duty or, that failing, from a hidden plan.[43] Peace is an ethical duty because only under conditions of peace can all men treat one another as ends (IUH 8:27–28). In order for this duty to be practical, Kant needs, of course, to show that peace is in fact possible. The widespread sentiment of approbation that he saw aroused by the early success of the French revolutionaries showed him that we can indeed be moved by ethical sentiments with a cosmopolitan reach.[44] This does not mean, however, that perpetual peace is certain. Even the scientifically regular course of the planets could be changed by a wayward comet striking them out of orbit.

Human freedom requires that we allow for much greater reversals in the course of history. We must, in fact, anticipate the possibility of backsliding and destructive wars (though these will serve to educate nations to the importance of peace, IUH 8:24–26).

But, in the end, our guarantee of perpetual peace does not rest on ethical conduct, as Kant emphasizes in *Toward Perpetual Peace:*

> The question now at hand concerns the essence with regard to perpetual peace: what nature does in this regard, or to be precise, with regard to the end that their own reason makes into a duty for human beings, and hence to further their moral aim; and how nature guarantees that that which human beings *ought* to do in accordance with the laws of freedom, but which they do not do, can be secured without injuring this freedom even through nature's compelling them to do so? . . . When I say that nature *wills* that this or that ought to happen, I do not mean that she imposes a *duty* upon us to act thus (for this can only be done by practical reason acting free of compulsion), but rather that she *does* it herself, regardless of whether we will it so or not (*fata volentem ducunt, nolentem trahunt*). (PP 8:365)

The guarantee thus rests, Kant adds, on the probable behavior not of moral angels but of devils, so long as they possess understanding (PP 8:366). In explaining the sources of each of the three Definitive Articles of the perpetual peace, Kant then tells us how we (as free and intelligent devils) could be motivated by fear, force, and calculated advantage to undertake a course of actions whose outcome we can reasonably anticipate to be perpetual peace. But while it is possible to conceive of the Kantian road to peace in these terms, Kant recognizes and argues that social evolution also makes the conditions of moral behavior less onerous, hence more likely.[45] In tracing the effects of both political and moral development, he builds an account of why liberal states do maintain peace among themselves and of how it will (by implication, has) come about that the pacific union will expand. He also explains how these republics would engage in wars with nonrepublics and therefore suffer the "lamentable experiences" (IUH 8:24) of wars that an ethical policy might have avoided.

The first source derives from a political evolution, from a constitutional law. Nature (providence) has seen to it that human beings can live in all the regions where they have been driven to settle by wars. (Kant, who once taught geography, reports on the Lapps, the Samoyeds, the Pescheras.) "Unsocial sociability" draws men together to fulfill needs for security and material welfare as it drives them into conflicts over the distribution and control of social products (IUH 8:20–21; PP 8:360–68). This violent natural evolution tends toward the liberal peace because "unsocial sociability" inevitably leads toward republican governments and republican governments are a source of the liberal peace.

Republican representation and separation of powers are produced because they are the means by which the state is "organized well" to prepare for and meet foreign threats (by unity) and to tame the ambitions of selfish and aggressive individuals (by authority derived from representation, by general laws, and by nondespotic administration) (PP 8:365–67). States that are not organized in this fashion tend to fail. Monarchs thus encourage commerce and private property in order to increase national wealth. They cede rights of representation to their subjects in order to strengthen their political support or to obtain willing grants of tax revenue.[46]

Kant shows how republics, once established, lead to peaceful relations. He argues that once the aggressive interests of absolutist monarchies are tamed and once the habit of respect for individual rights is ingrained by republican government, wars would appear as the disaster to the people's welfare that he and the other liberals thought them to be. The fundamental reason is this:

> If (as must be the case in such a constitution) the agreement of the citizens is required to decide whether or not one ought to wage war, then nothing is more natural than that they would consider very carefully whether to enter into such a terrible game, since they would have to resolve to bring the hardships of war upon themselves (which would include: themselves fighting, paying the costs of the war from their own possessions, meagerly repairing the ravages that war leaves behind, and, finally, on top of all such malady, assuming a burden of debt that embitters the peace and will never be repaid (due to imminent, constantly impending wars). By contrast, in the case of a constitution where the subject is not a citizen of the state, that is, in one which is not republican, declaring war is the easiest thing in the world, because the head of state is not a fellow citizen, but rather the owner of the state, and hence forfeits nothing of his feasts, hunts, summer residences, court festivals and such things due to the war. The head of state can decide to wage war for insignificant reasons as a kind of game for amusement and can, for the sake of decency, indifferently leave its justification up to his diplomatic corps, which always stands ready for such tasks. (PP 8:351)

These domestic restraints introduce republican caution, Kant's "hesitation," in place of monarchical caprice. Citizens become "co-legislating members" of the state and must therefore give their free consent through representatives, not only to the waging of war in general, "but rather to every particular declaration of war" (MM 6:346). Republican caution seems to save republics from the failings Hume saw as characteristic of "enormous monarchies," including "strategic over-extension," court intrigue, and praetorian rebellion.[47] Representative government allows for a rotation of elites, others have argued, and this encourages a reversal of disastrous policies as electorates punish the party in power with electoral defeat. Legislatures and public opinion further restrain executives from policies that clearly violate the obvious and fundamental interests of the public, as the public perceives those interests.[48] The division of powers among legislature, judiciary, and executive introduces salutary delay, time for reflection and adjustment in the foreign policy decision-making of republican states. In relations with fellow liberals, these delays are doubly compounded and thus can provide fertile opportunities to resolve disputes short of escalation to armed conflict.

Yet republican caution does not guarantee prudence. Liberal publics can become disaffected from international commitments and choose isolationism or appeasement, as Britain and the United States did in the 1920s and 1930s. And republican caution does not end war, or ensure that wars are fought only when necessary for national security. Many democratic and representative states have been war-prone, as was classical Athens or would have been Machiavelli's free republics. If representation alone were peace-inducing, liberal states would not be warlike or given to imprudent vehemence, which is far from the case. It does ensure that wars are only fought for popular, liberal purposes. The historical liberal legacy is laden with popular wars fought to promote freedom, protect private property, or support liberal allies against nonliberal enemies. Kant's own position is ambiguous. He regards most of these wars as unjust and warns liberals of their susceptibility to them. At the same time, he argues that each nation "can and ought to" demand that its neighboring nations enter into the pacific union of liberal states — that is, become republican (PP 6:354). Thus to see how the pacific union removes the occasion of wars among liberal states and not wars between liberal and nonliberal states, we need to shift our attention from constitutional right to international right, Kant's second source.

Complementing the constitutional guarantee of caution, international right adds a second source, a guarantee of respect. The separation of nations that unsocial sociability encourages is reinforced by the development of separate languages and religions. These further guarantee a world of separate states, an essential condition needed to avoid a "soulless despotism."

Yet, at the same time, they also morally integrate liberal states, and "in the wake of increasing culture and humankind's gradually coming within reach of an agreement regarding their principles, they lead to mutual understanding and agreement to peace" (PP 8:367). As republics emerge (the first source) and as culture progresses, an understanding of the legitimate rights of all citizens and of all republics comes into play; and this, now that caution characterizes policy, sets up the moral foundations for the liberal peace. Correspondingly, international right highlights the importance of Kantian publicity. Domestically, publicity helps ensure that the officials of republics act according to the principles they profess to hold just and according to the interests of the electors they claim to represent. Internationally, free speech and the effective communication of accurate conceptions of the political life of foreign peoples are essential to establish and preserve the understanding on which the guarantee of respect depends.

We can speculate that the process might work something like this: the leaders and publics of domestically just republics, which rest on consent, presume foreign republics to be also consensual, just, and therefore deserving of accommodation. The experience of cooperation helps engender further cooperative behavior when the consequences of state policy are unclear but (potentially) mutually beneficial. At the same time, liberal states assume that nonliberal states, which do not rest on free consent, are not just. Because nonliberal governments are perceived to be in a state of aggression with their own people, their foreign relations become deeply suspect for liberal governments. Wilhelm the II of Imperial Germany may or may not have been aggressive (he was certainly idiosyncratic); liberal democracies such as England, France, and the United States, however, assumed that whatever was driving German policy, reliable democratic, constitutional government was not restraining it. They regarded Germany and its actions with severe suspicion — to which the Reich reacted with corresponding distrust. In short, fellow liberals benefit from a presumption of amity; nonliberals suffer from a presumption of enmity. Both presumptions may be accurate. Each, however, may also be self-confirming.

Democratic liberals do not need to assume either that public opinion directly rules foreign policy or that the entire governmental elite is liberal. It can instead assume a third possibility: that the elite typically manages public affairs but that potentially nonliberal members of the elite have reason to doubt that antiliberal policies would be electorally sustained and endorsed by the majority of the democratic public.

Third and last, cosmopolitan right adds material incentives to moral commitments, for over the long run commitments unsupported by material interests are unlikely to endure. The cosmopolitan right to hospitality permits the "spirit of commerce" sooner or later to take hold of every nation, thus impelling states to promote peace and to try to avert war. Liberal economic theory holds that these cosmopolitan ties derive from a cooperative international division of labor and free trade according to comparative advantage. Each economy is said to be better off than it would have been under autarky; each thus acquires an incentive to avoid policies that would lead the other to break these economic ties. Since keeping open markets rests upon the assumption that the next set of transactions will also be determined by prices rather than coercion, a sense of mutual security is vital to avoid security-motivated searches for economic autarky. Thus avoiding a challenge to another liberal state's security or even enhancing each other's security by means of alliance naturally follows economic interdependence.

A further cosmopolitan source of liberal peace is that the international market removes difficult decisions of production and distribution from the direct sphere of state policy. A foreign state thus does not appear directly responsible for these outcomes; states can stand aside from, and to some degree above, these contentious market rivalries and be ready to step in to resolve crises. The interdependence of commerce and the international contacts of state officials help create crosscutting transnational ties that serve as lobbies for mutual accommodation. According to modern liberal scholars, international financiers and transnational and transgovernmental organizations create interests in favor of accommodation. Moreover, their variety has ensured that no single conflict sours an entire relationship by setting off a spiral of reciprocated retaliation.[49] Conversely, a sense of suspicion, such as that characterizing relations between liberal and nonliberal governments, can lead to restrictions on the range of contacts between societies. And this can increase the prospect that a single conflict will determine an entire relationship.

Immanuel Kant's 1795 treatise, *Toward Perpetual Peace,* offers a coherent explanation of two important regularities in world politics: the tendencies of liberal states simultaneously to be peace-prone in their relations with each other and unusually war-prone in their relations with nonliberal states. Republican representation, liberal respect, and transnational interdependence (to rephrase Kant's three Definitive Articles of the hypothetical peace treaty he asked states to sign) thus can be seen as three necessary and, together, sufficient causes of the two regularities. *Thus no single constitutional, international, or cosmopolitan source is alone sufficient, but together (and only together) the three sources plausibly connect the characteristics of liberal polities and economies with sustained liberal peace.*

Alliances founded on mutual strategic interest among liberal and nonliberal states have been broken, economic ties between liberal and nonliberal states have proved fragile, but the political bonds of liberal rights and interests have proven a remarkably firm foundation for mutual nonaggression. A separate peace exists among liberal states.

But in their relations with nonliberal states, liberal states have not escaped from the insecurity of the world political system considered as a whole. Moreover, the very constitutional restraint, international respect for individual rights, and shared commercial interests that establish grounds for peace among liberal states establish grounds for additional conflict irrespective of actual threats to national security in relations between liberal and nonliberal societies.

And in their relations with all states, liberal states have not solved the problems of international cooperation and competition. Liberal publics can become absorbed in domestic issues, and international liberal respect does not preclude trade rivalries or guarantee farsighted collective solutions to international security and welfare.

NOTES

This essay draws on parts of chapter 8 of my *Ways of War and Peace* (New York: W. W. Norton, 1997) and on "Liberalism and World Politics," *American Political Science Review* 80, no. 4 (December 1986): 1151–69; "Kant, Liberal Legacies, and Foreign Affairs," parts 1 and 2, *Philosophy and Public Affairs* 12 (1983): 205–35 (part 1) and 323–53 (part 2). I thank the publishers for allowing me to use material from those essays here. I would also like to thank Moza Mfuni and Olena Jennings for editorial assistance.

1. A partial list of significant studies on Kant's international theory includes: A. C. Armstrong, "Kant's Philosophy of Peace and War," *Journal of Philosophy* 28 (1931): 197–204; Karl Friedrich, *Inevitable Peace* (Cambridge: Harvard University Press, 1948); W. B. Gallie, *Philosophers of Peace and War* (Cambridge: Cambridge University Press, 1978); William Galston, *Kant and the Problem of History* (Chicago: Chicago University Press, 1975); Pierre Hassner, "Immanuel Kant," in *History of Political Philosophy,* ed. Leo Strauss and Joseph Cropsey (Chicago: Rand McNally, 1972), 554–93; F. H. Hinsley, *Power and the Pursuit of Peace* (Cambridge: Cambridge University Press, 1967);

Stanley Hoffmann, "Rousseau on War and Peace," in S. Hoffmann, *The State of War* (New York: Praeger, 1965), 45–87; George A. Kelly, *Idealism, Politics, and History* (Cambridge: Cambridge University Press, 1969); Patrick Riley, *Kant's Political Philosophy* (Totowa, N.J.: Rowman and Littlefield, 1983); Kenneth Waltz, "Kant, Liberalism, and War," *American Political Science Review* 56 (1962): 331–40; Yirmiahu Yovel, *Kant and the Philosophy of History* (Princeton: Princeton University Press, 1980); Susan Shell, *The Rights of Reason* (Toronto: University of Toronto Press, 1980); Howard Williams, *Kant's Political Philosophy* (Oxford: Basil Blackwell, 1983); Roger Sullivan, *Immanuel Kant's Moral Theory* (Cambridge University Press, 1989); Sissela Bok, *A Strategy for Peace* (New York: Pantheon, 1989); Pierre Laberge, "Kant on Justice and the Law of Nations," in *The International Society,* ed Terry Nardin and David Mapel (Princeton: Princeton University Press, 1998).

2. This was the minimum condition argued by Kenneth Waltz to be essential to a systemic, structural model of world politics. The fine analogy to Albee's play is Waltz's as well; see *Theory of International Politics* (New York: McGraw Hill, 1979), where Waltz quotes, "That which is George or Martha, individually, does not explain what is compounded between them, nor how" (75).

3. Kant remarks on Frederick in PP 8:352. This point was drawn to my attention by Dr. Dominique Leydet.

4. PP 8:349–53, and see Riley, *Kant's Political Philosophy,* 5.

5. I think Kant meant that the peace would be established among liberal regimes and would expand by ordinary political and legal means as new liberal regimes appeared. By a process of gradual extension the peace would become global and then perpetual; the occasion for wars with nonliberals would disappear as nonliberal regimes disappeared. Some have suggested, following IUH, that peace will only be achieved when all states have become republican. This interpretation suggests that "peace comes piece (peace) by piece (peace)" and that IUH should be read in light of the later and more complete PP.

6. See Wolfgang Schwarz, "Kant's Philosophy of Law and International

Peace," *Philosophy and Phenomenological Research* 23 (1962): 71–80, here 77 and Riley, *Kant's Political Philosophy,* 5.

7. Kant's *foedus pacificum* is thus neither a *pactum pacis* (a single peace treaty) nor a *civitas gentium* (a world state). He appears to have anticipated something like a less formally institutionalized League of Nations or United Nations. One could argue that these two institutions in practice worked for liberal states and only for liberal states. But no specifically liberal "pacific union" was institutionalized. Instead liberal states have behaved for the past 210 years as if such a Kantian pacific union and treaty of perpetual peace had been signed.

8. Clarence Streit, *Union Now: A Proposal for a Federal Union of the Leading Democracies* (New York: Harpers, 1938), 88, 90–92, seems to have been the first to point out (in contemporary foreign relations) the empirical tendency of democracies to maintain peace among themselves, and he made this the foundation of his proposal for a (non-Kantian) federal union of the fifteen leading democracies of the 1930s. D. V. Babst, "A Force for Peace," *Industrial Research* (April 1972): 55–58, performed a quantitative study of this phenomenon of "democratic peace." And R. J. Rummel did a similar study of "libertarianism" (in the sense of laissez-faire) focusing on the postwar period in "Libertarianism and International Violence," *Journal of Conflict Resolution* 27 (1983): 27–71. I use "liberal" in a wider (Kantian) sense in my discussion of this issue in "Kant, liberal Legacies, and Foreign Affairs," part 1, *Philosophy and Public Affairs* 12 (1983): 205–35. In that essay, I survey the period from 1790 on and find no war among liberal states. Recent work supporting the thesis of democratic pacification is discussed in Zeev Maoz and Nasrin Abdolali, "Regime Types and International Conflict, 1816–1976," *Journal of Conflict Resolution* 33 (March 1989), and John Oneal, Frances Oneal, Zeev Maoz, and Bruce Russett in "The Liberal Peace: Interdependence, Democracy and International Conflict, 1950–1985," *Journal of Peace Research* (February 1996). A valuable survey of the debate over the empirical evidence for the democratic peace, assembling much of the best of the criticism and responses to that criticism, can be found in Michael Brown, Sean Lynn-

Jones, and Steven Miller, eds., *Debating the Democratic Peace* (Cambridge: MIT Press, 1996).

9. Woodrow Wilson, *The Messages and Papers of Woodrow Wilson,* ed. Albert Shaw (New York: The Review of Reviews, 1924), 378.

10. From Barbara Farnham, *Roosevelt and the Munich Crisis: A Study of Political Decision-Making* (Princeton: Princeton University Press, 1997). One can presume that his motivation as in most political events was complex. He did not categorically support every foreign policy of a democracy (nor should he). He, for example, questioned the legitimacy of the British Empire. America had failed to support the democracies financially in the 1920s. Roosevelt was also concerned to avoid a Nazi conquest of Europe and the threat a united Nazi Europe would pose to the United States. "On the Atlantic," the president also said, "our first line is the continued independent existence of a very large group of nations." (From January 1939 briefing to the Senate Military Affairs Committee, quoted in Haight, *American Aid,* 98.) But Roosevelt's aim was not to establish a balance of power in Europe between Nazi Germany and democractic Britain and France, but to defeat the former forces altogether. See also Haight, *American Aid,* 30–31.

11. I am including all states listed by Freedom House as "free" and those "partly free" with a four or less on the political scale and five or less on the civil liberties scale; http://www.freedomhouse.org/template.cfm ?page211.

12. Babst, "Force for Peace," did make a preliminary test of the significance of the distribution of alliance partners in World War I. He found that the possibility that the actual distribution of alliance partners could have occurred by chance was less than 1 percent (56). But this assumes that there was an equal possibility that any two nations could have gone to war with each other; and this is a strong assumption. Rummel, "Libertarianism and International Violence," has a further discussion of significance as it applies to his libertarian thesis.

13. There is a rich contemporary literature devoted to explaining international cooperation and integration. Karl Deutsch's *Political Community and the North Atlantic Area* (Princeton: Princeton University Press,

1957) develops the idea of a "pluralistic security community" that bears a resemblance to the "pacific union," but Deutsch limits it geographically and finds compatibility of values, mutual responsiveness, and predictability of behavior among decision-makers as its essential foundations. These are important but their particular content, liberalism, appears to be more telling. Joseph Nye in *Peace in Parts* (Boston: Little, Brown, 1971) steps away from the geographic limits Deutsch sets and focuses on levels of development; but his analysis is directed toward explaining integration — a more intensive form of cooperation than the pacific union.

14. David Hume, "Of the Balance of Power," in *Essays: Moral, Political, and Literary* (1741–42) (Oxford University Press, 1963), 346–47. With "imprudent vehemence," Hume referred to the English reluctance to negotiate an early peace with France and the total scale of the effort devoted to persecuting that war, which together were responsible for over half the length of the fighting and an enormous war debt. Hume, of course, was not describing fully liberal republics as defined here; but the characteristics he describes do seem to reflect some of the liberal republican features of the English eighteenth-century constitution (the influence of both popular opinion and a representative [even if severely limited] legislature). He contrasts these effects to the "prudent politics" that should govern the balance of power and to the special but different failings characteristic of "enormous monarchies." The monarchies are apparently worse; they risk total defeat and collapse because they are prone to strategic overextension, bureaucratic, and ministerial decay in court intrigue, and praetorian rebellion (347–48). In this connection one can compare the fates of Britain with its imprudence to Louis XIV's or Napoleon's France or, for that matter, Hitler's Germany or Mussolini's Italy or Brezhnev's Soviet Union. Overextension to the extent of destruction is clearly worse, from the strategic point of view, than a bit of imprudence.

15. For a discussion of the historical effects of liberalism on colonialism, the U.S.-Soviet Cold War, and post–World War II interventions see

"Kant, Liberal Legacies, and Foreign Affairs," part 2, *Philosophy and Public Affairs* 12 (1983): 323–53 , and the sources cited there.

16. See Steve Chan, "Mirror, Mirror on the Wall . . . : Are Freer Countries More Pacific?" *Journal of Conflict Resolution* 28 (December 1984): 617–48; and Erich Weede, "Democracy and War Involvement," *Journal of Conflict Resolution* 28 (December 1984): 649–64. Their argument supports the conclusions reached by M. Small and J. David Singer, "The War-Proneness of Democratic Regimes, 1816–1965," *Jerusalem Journal of International Relations* 1 (summer 1976): 50–69. Both counter Rummel's view (in "Libertarianism and International Violence") that libertarian states are less prone to violence than non-libertarian states, which he based on a sample of 1976–80 data not representative of the war year data of 1816–1980 of Chan or the 1960–80 data of Weede.

17. There are, however, serious studies that show that Marxist regimes have higher military spending per capita than non-Marxist regimes (James Payne, "Marxism and Militarism," *Polity* 19 [1987]: 270–89). But this should not be interpreted as a sign of the inherent aggressiveness of authoritarian or totalitarian governments or — with even greater enthusiasm — the inherent and global peacefulness of liberal regimes. Marxist regimes, in particular, represent a minority in the current international system; they are strategically encircled, and, due to their lack of domestic legitimacy, they might be said to "suffer" the twin burden of needing defenses against both external and internal enemies. Stanislav Andreski in "On the Peaceful Disposition of Military Dictatorships," *Journal of Strategic Studies* 3 (1980): 3–10, moreover, argues that (purely) military dictatorships, due to their domestic fragility, have little incentive to engage in foreign military adventures.

18. Chan, "Mirror, Mirror on the Wall," 636.

19. Walter Clemens, "The Superpowers and the Third World," in *Foreign Policy; USA/USSR,* ed. Charles Kegley and Pat McGowan (Beverly Hills: Sage, 1982), 117–18.

20. Barry Posen and Stephen VanEvera, "Overarming and Underwhelming,"

Foreign Policy 40 (1980): 99–118; and "Reagan Administration Defense Policy," in *Eagle Defiant,* ed. Kenneth Oye, Robert Lieber, and Donald Rothchild (Boston: Little, Brown, 1983), 86–89.

21. This does not necessarily mean that the nonliberals are strategically inferior or less capable of mobilizing the resources needed to win. Nonliberal Russia bore the burden of both those sets of victories. The liberal advantage in World Wars I and II was in not fighting each other and being resistant to defection to the nonliberal camp.

22. The following paragraphs build on arguments I presented in "Kant, Liberal Legacies, and Foreign Affairs," part 2, *Philosophy and Public Affairs* 12 (1983): 323–53.

23. Memoranda by Mr. Eyre Crowe, 1 January 1907, and by Lord Sanderson, 25 February 1907, in *British Documents on the Origins of the War, 1898–1914,* ed. G. P. Gooch et al. (London: HMSO, 1928), vol. 3, pp. 397–431.

24. Herbert Hoover to President Wilson, 29 March 1919, excerpted in *Major Problems in American Foreign Policy,* ed. Thomas Paterson (Lexington, Mass.: D. C. Heath, 1978), vol. 2, p. 95.

25. U.S. Senate, *Hearings Before the Committee on Foreign Relations on the Nomination of John Foster Dulles, Secretary of State Designate,* 15 January 1953, 83rd Cong., 1st sess. (Washington D.C.: G.P.O., 1953), 5–6. John L. Gaddis has noted logistical differences between laissez-faire and social welfare liberals in policy toward the Soviet Union. In U.S. policy, until the advent of the Reagan administration, the fiscal conservatism of Republicans led them to favor a narrow strategy; the fiscal liberality of Democrats led to a broader strategy. See, *Strategies of Containment* (New York: Oxford University Press, 1982).

26. Thirty-three divisions, the withdrawal of the Soviet bloc from the Mediterranean, political disarray in the communist movement: these advantages called out for a quick and friendly response. An effective U.S. ambassador in place to present Tito's position to Washington, the public character of the expulsion from the Cominform (June 1948), and a presidential administration in the full flush of creative statesmanship (and an electoral victory) also contributed to Truman's decision to res-

cue Yugoslavia from the Soviet embargo by providing trade and loans (1949). Nonetheless (according to Yugoslav sources), this crisis was also judged to be an appropriate moment to put pressure on Yugoslavia to resolve the questions of Trieste and Carinthia, to cut its support for the guerrillas in Greece, and to repay prewar (prerevolutionary) debts compensating the property owners of nationalized land and mines. Nor did Yugoslavia's strategic significance exempt it from inclusion among the countries condemned as "captive nations" (1959) or secure most-favored-nation trade status in the 1962 Trade Expansion Act. Ideological anticommunism and the porousness of the American political system to lobbies combined (according to Kennan, ambassador to Yugoslavia at that time) to add these inconvenient burdens to a crucial strategic relationship. (John C. Campbell, *Tito's Separate Road* [New York: Council on Foreign Relations/Harper and Row, 1967], 18–27; Suctozar Vukmanovic-Tempo, in Vladimir Dedijer, *The Battle Stalin Lost* [New York: Viking, 1970], 268; George F. Kennan, *Memoirs, 1950–1963* [Boston: Little, Brown, 1972], chap. 12).

27. See Robert A. Packenham, *Liberal America and the Third World* (Princeton: Princeton University Press, 1973), for an interesting analysis of the impact of liberal ideology on American foreign aid policy, esp. chap. 3, 313–23.

28. Alexis de Tocqueville, *Democracy in America* (New York: Vintage, 1945), vol. 1, p. 351. De Tocqueville describes how European settlement destroys the game; the absence of game reduces the Indians to starvation. Both then exercise their rights to self-defense. But the colonists are able to call in the power of the imperial government. Palmerston once declared that he would never employ force to promote purely private interests — whether commercial or settlement. He also declared that he would faithfully protect the lives and liberty of English subjects. In circumstances such as those de Tocqueville described, Palmerston's distinctions were irrelevant. See Kenneth Bourne, *Palmerston: The Early Years* (New York: Macmillan, 1982), 624–26. Other colonial settlements and their dependence on imperial expansion are examined in Ronald Robinson, "Non-European Foundations of

Imperialism," in *Studies in the Theory of Imperialism, ed. Roger Own and Bob Sutcliffe* (London: Longmans, 1972).

29. Gladstone had proclaimed his support for the equal rights of all nations in his Midlothian speeches. Wilfrid Scawen Blunt served as a secret agent in Egypt keeping Gladstone informed of the political character of Arabi's movement. The liberal dilemma in 1882 — were they intervening against genuine nationalism or a military adventurer (Arabi)? — was best expressed in Joseph Chamberlain's memorandum to the cabinet, 21 June 1882, excerpted in J. L. Garvin and J. Amery, *Life of Joseph Chamberlain* (London: Macmillan, 1935), vol. 1, p. 448. And see Peter Mansfield, *The British in Egypt* (New York: Holt, Rinehart and Winston, 1971), chaps. 2–3; Ronald Hyam, *Britain's Imperial Century: 1815–1914* (London: Batsford, 1976), chap. 8; and Robert Tignor, *Modernization and British Colonial Rule in Egypt* (Princeton: Princeton University Press, 1966).

30. The Platt Amendment is excerpted in *Major Problems in American Foreign Policy,* ed. Thomas Paterson (Lexington Mass.: D. C. Heath., 1978), vol. 1, p. 328.

31. One instance was the neglect of information widely available in the administration that Niger was very unlikely to have sold uranium ore to Iraq. The charge that it did nonetheless wound up as the infamous sixteen words in the president's 2003 State of the Union address justifying the march to war. See Eric Lichtblau, "2002 Memo Doubted Uranium Sale Claim," *New York Times,* 18 January 2006.

32. For an informative collection of speeches by President Bush and Secretary Powell justifying the war and Senator Byrd and others criticizing those rationales, see the section "Why Attack Iraq?"in Amy Gutmann and Dennis Thompson, eds., *Ethics and Politics: Cases and Comments,* 4th ed. (Belmont: Wadsworth, 2006), 45–60, 88–95. For a thoughtful legal analysis, pro and con, see Lord Peter Goldsmith, "Downing Street Memo to Tony Blair" (Office of the Prime Minster, 2002; first published in *The Sunday Times,* 1 May 2005), and Thomas Franck, "Agora: What Happens Now? The United Nations after Iraq," *American Journal of International Law* 97 (2003): 607. And, for policy analysis, pro

and con, see Kenneth Pollack, *The Threatening Storm* (New York: Random House, 2002), chaps. 5 and 11, and Chaim Kaufmann "Threat Inflation and the Failure of the Marketplace of Ideas: The Selling of the Iraq War," *International Security* 29, no. 1 (summer 2004): 5–48.

33. See the January 2006 paper by Joseph Stiglitz and Linda Bilmes in which one trillion is the low estimate and two the high, taking into account the long-term medical and other indirect costs associated with the war, http://www2.gsb.columbia.edu/faculty/jstiglitz/Cost _ of _ War _ in _ Iraq.pdf.

34. During the Alliance for Progress era in Latin America, the Kennedy administration supported Juan Bosch in the Dominican Republic in 1962. See also William P. Bundy, "Dictatorships and American Foreign Policy," *Foreign Affairs* 54 (1975): 51–60.

35. See Huntington, "Human Rights and American Power," in *Commentary* (September 1981), and Quester, "Consensus Lost," in *Foreign Policy* 40 (fall 1980), for argument and examples of the successful export of liberal institutions in the postwar period. A major study of the role of democratic expansion in U.S. foreign policy is Tony Smith, *America's Mission* (Princeton: Princeton University Press, 1994).

36. Jeane Kirkpatrick, "Dictatorships and Double Standards," in *Commentary* 68 (November 1979): 34–45. In 1851 the liberal French historian Guizot, made a similar argument in a letter to Gladstone urging that Gladstone appreciate that the despotic government of Naples was the best guarantor of liberal law and order then available. Reform, in Guizot's view, meant the unleashing of revolutionary violence (Philip Magnus, *Gladstone* [New York: Dutton, 1964], 100).

37. Richard Barnet, *Intervention and Revolution: The United States in the Third World* (New York: Meridian, 1968), chap. 10, and on Nicaragua, see *New York Times,* 11 March 1982, for a description of the training direction, and funding ($20 million) of anti-Sandinista guerrillas by the United States.

38. Arthur Schlesinger, *A Thousand Days* (Boston: Houghton Mifflin, 1965), 769, and quoted in Richard Barnet, *Intervention and Revolution* (New York: Meridian, 1968), 158. And for the U.S. official's comment

on the Salvadoran land reform, see Simon and Stephen, *El Salvador Land Reform 1980–1981* (Boston: Oxfam-America, 1981), 38.

39. France and Britain were insisting on prompt payment of wartime reparations, just as the United States was insisting on prompt repayment of wartime loans. The U.S. government formally refused to consider the problem in a comprehensive light. American bankers stepped in; but in light of the needs for financial accommodation, the Dawes and Young Plans were helpful but still feeble stopgaps to finance German reparations and Allied debts with lower interest packages of loans. Two contemporary classics that discuss the problem are Arnold Wolfers, *Britain and France between Two Wars* (1940) and Harold G. Moulton and Leo Pasvolsky, *War Debts and World Prosperity* (1932).

40. Charles Kindleberger, *The World in Depression* (Berkeley: University of California Press, 1973); Robert Gilpin, *U.S. Power and the Multinational Corporation* (New York: Basic Books, 1975); Stephen Krasner, "State Power and the Structure of International Trade," *World Politics* 28, no. 3 (1976): 317–47, and Fred Hirsch and Michael Doyle, "Politicization in the World Economy" in Fred Hirsch, Michael Doyle and Edward Morse, ed., *Alternatives to Monetary Disorder* (New York: Council on Foreign Relations/McGraw Hill, 1977).

41. Kirkpatrick, "Dictatorships and Double Standards," points out our neglect of the needs of the authoritarians. Theodore Lowi argues that Democratic and Republican policies toward the acquisition of bases in Spain reflected this dichotomy; "Bases in Spain," in *American Civil-Military Decisions,* ed. Harold Stein (University: University of Alabama Press, 1963), 699. In other cases where both the geopolitical and the domestic orientation of a potential neutral might be influenced by U.S. aid, liberal institutions (representative legislatures) impose delay or public constrains and conditions on diplomacy that allow the Soviet Union to steal a march. Warren Christopher has suggested that this occurred in U.S. relations with Nicaragua in 1979. Warren Christopher, "Ceasefire between the Branches," in *Foreign Affairs* 60 (1982): 989–1005, here 998.

42. Ideological formulations often accompany these policies. Fear of Bol-

shevism was used to excuse not forming an alliance with the Soviet Union in 1938 against Nazi aggression. And Nazi and fascist regimes were portrayed as defenders of private property and social order. But the connection liberals draw between domestic tyranny and foreign aggression may also operate in reverse. When the Nazi threat to the survival of liberal states did require a liberal alliance with the Soviet Union, Stalin became for a short period the liberal press's "Uncle Joe."

43. In the *Metaphysics of Morals,* Kant seems to write as if perpetual peace is only an epistemological device and perpetual peace, while an ethical duty, is empirically merely a "pious wish" (MM, 6:355, 343– 51). (Though even here Kant finds that the pacific union is not unrealizable, MM 6:350.) In the "Idea for a Universal History" Kant writes as if the brute force of physical nature drives men toward inevitable peace. Yovel, *Kant and the Philosophy of History,* 168ff., argues that *Toward Perpetual Peace* reconciles the two views of history, from a postcritical (post–*Critique of Judgment*) perspective. "Nature" is human-created nature (culture or civilization). Perpetual peace is the "a priori of the a posteriori" (a critical perspective that then enables us to discern causal, probabilistic patterns in history). Law and the "political technology" of republican constitutionalism are separate from ethical development. But both interdependently lead to perpetual peace: the first through force, fear, and self-interest; the second through progressive enlightenment; and both together through the widening of the circumstances in which engaging in right conduct poses smaller and smaller burdens.

44. CF 7:85–89. This view is defended by Yovel, *Kant and the Philosophy of History,* 153–54.

45. CF 7:91–93. See Kelly, *Idealism, Politics, and History,* 106–13 for a further explanation.

46. Hassner, "Immanuel Kant," 583–86. The Kantian pacific union has in fact expanded steadily, but whether we can anticipate its continued expansion much beyond the current numbers of liberal democracies has been called into question by Samuel Huntington in "Will More Countries Become Democratic?" *Political Science Quarterly* 99 (1984): 193–218 — an issue which he revisits in a more optimistic vein in *The*

Third Wave: Democratization in the Late Twentieth Century (Norman: University of Oklahoma Press, 1991).

47. See the discussion of Hume in footnote 13, above; Hume, "Of the Balance of Power," 347–48.

48. For a confident reading of democratic capacities both to defer to prudent leadership and to make prudent judgments in this regard, see Waltz, *Foreign Policy and Democratic Politics* (Boston: Little, Brown, 1967), 288–97. Joseph Nye concludes that the U.S. record in postwar diplomacy is more mixed, finding that nuclear war has been successfully avoided but containing Soviet power and fostering moderation in and by the Soviet Union have been less successful: "Can America Manage Its Soviet Policy?" in *The Making of America's Soviet Policy,* ed. Joseph S. Nye, Jr. (New Haven: Yale, 1984), 325–29.

49. Karl Polanyi, *The Great Transformation* (Boston: Beacon Press, 1944), chaps. 1–2; Zbigniew Brzezinski and Samuel Huntington, *Political Power: USA/USSR* (New York: Viking Press, 1963), chap. 9: Robert Keohane and Joseph Nye, *Power and Interdependence* (Boston: Little, Brown, 1977), chap. 7: Richard Neustadt, *Alliance Politics* (New York: Columbia University Press, 1970). Daniele Archibugi, "Immanuel Kant, Cosmopolitan Law, and Peace," *European Journal of International Relations* 1 (1995): 429–56.

Kant's Philosophy of History

ALLEN W. WOOD

Kant's writings on human history appear at first glance to constitute only a small part of his literary output and to have only marginal significance for his philosophy. Unlike some other great modern philosophers, such as Leibniz, Hume, and Hegel, Kant was not himself a historian, not even a very well read historian of philosophy. The essays devoted chiefly to the philosophy of history consist in a few brief occasional pieces, such as "Idea for a Universal History from a Cosmopolitan Perspective" (1784) and "Conjectural Beginning of Human History" (1786), plus some parts of other essays, such as the one about the common saying on theory and practice (1794) or the *Contest of the Faculties* (1798). But if we look more closely at some of his most important works, we begin to see that views about history, even quite distinctively Kantian views, play a major role in their arguments and even in their very conception.

Kant and the Philosophy of History

Probably Kant's most conspicuous appeal to his philosophy of history occurs in the First Supplement in *Toward Perpetual Peace,* in the form of the "guarantee" he offers for the terms of peace between nation states that he has proposed (PP 8:360–68). But a moment's consideration of the prefaces to both the first and second editions of the *Critique of Pure Reason* reveals that his very conception of that work (and with it, of the entire critical philosophy) is framed in terms of a conception of the *history* of metaphysics as a science, which is understood either (as in the second edition) in terms of the course pursued by a branch of inquiry when it is converted from a mere "random groping" into "the secure course of a science" (CPuR B vii–xviii) or else (as in the first edition), when it is seen as a stage in the enlightenment of social inquiry generally and placed in the context of the political reform of society (CPuR A viii–xiii). Reflections on the philosophy of history also play a role in the argument of the closing pages of the

Critique of Judgment, where Kant is attempting to bridge the gulf between theoretical understanding and practical reason by relating the ultimate end of nature (regarded theoretically as a teleological system) to the final end set by morality (CJ 5:429–34). Reflections on the history of religion are prominent in Kant's expression of hope for the moral progress of humanity (R 6:124–37). And Kant's anthropology concludes with reflections on the history of the human species (A 7:321–33). Indeed, Kant's basic characterization of the human species in terms of its collective possibilities for rational self-direction indicates that his conception of human nature itself is a historical one.

Human history is first of all a collection of facts about what human beings have done and undergone, in which human inquiry needs to find some kind of intelligibility. But history seems to be made up of merely contingent facts about the arbitrary actions and accidental good or bad fortune of individuals. There seems no guarantee in advance that as a whole, or even in any significant parts, it should be comprehensible at all. Our very need to find history intelligible, moreover, is inevitably bound up with a practical interest in it. We hope to find history intelligible in order to make our own actions intelligible to ourselves insofar as they constitute a part of history, perhaps also in order to direct our actions in accordance with historical trends or movements because of the intelligibility they have, especially because of the way our actions may fulfill possibilities or purposes we discover in history. Kant's philosophy of history is fundamentally guided first by the concern to discover something rationally comprehensible in the seemingly accidental occurrences that make up history, and second to relate that understanding to our practical concerns and hopes.

In Kant's writings about history it is especially conspicuous that his project of understanding human history is bound up with certain rational aims and hopes — for the growth of enlightenment, moral progress of the human species, perpetual peace between nations. These hopes are sometimes related by Kant himself to religious hopes, as when he describes the hope for perpetual peace by saying that "philosophy too can have its chiliastic beliefs" — its millenarian expectations (IUH 8:27).

It is not uncommon for expositions of Kant's philosophy of history to interpret this entire philosophy as motivated by practical considerations and consisting in large part of rational hopes analogous to his "practical postulates" of God, freedom, and immortality. Kant's theory of history is then seen as basically an expression of moral-religious hope rather than a program for empirical-factual inquiry. On this interpretation, it consists not of a theory about facts grounded on evidence but in a kind of religious faith grounded a priori on moral duties and ends. There is no doubt that Kant sometimes looked at history in light of our moral vocation and the moral-religious hopes grounded on it. This approach is particularly prominent in his reply to Moses Mendelssohn's rejection of the idea of moral progress in history, found in the third part of Kant's essay on theory and practice (TP 8:307–13).

Yet such a reading of Kant's philosophy of history as a whole, and especially of the project set forth in Kant's chief and basic work on the subject — the "Idea for a Universal History" — seems to me fundamentally mistaken, a gross distortion of Kant's views about the way human history should be studied. In fact, Kant is concerned to reconcile and integrate a purely theoretical concern with making theoretically intelligible the welter of contingent facts of which human history consists, with our inevitable and proper concern about the course of history as historical beings and moral agents. This project of reconciliation is quite subtle, and also presents us with a model for the many-sided approach to history found in the great nineteenth-century theorists of history in the German Idealist tradition, Fichte, Hegel, and Marx.

A close look at the text of "Idea for a Universal History" reveals that Kant's starting point for the philosophy of history in general is purely theoretical. He does not introduce considerations of a moral-religious nature until the Ninth (and last) Proposition of that essay. The right way to describe his approach is to say that he proceeds from considerations of theoretical reason, projecting the "idea" (or a priori rational concept) of a purely theoretical program for making comprehensible sense of the accidental facts of human history. He then attempts to bring history as a theoretical object of study, so conceived, into a kind of *convergence* with our practical concerns, so as to unite our theoretical understanding of history with our moral-religious hopes as historical beings. Thus although this essay was written six years before the *Critique of Judgment,* it already exhibits Kant's attempt in the Methodology of Teleological Judgment to bridge the gulf between theoretical and practical reason. But it can do this regarding history only if it begins by studying history from a purely theoretical standpoint, since otherwise there would be nothing with which to bring our practical hopes into convergence.

The attempt to read Kant's entire philosophy of history as exclusively, or even fundamentally, an exercise in practical faith not only conflicts with the text of "Idea for a Universal History," but considered in the context of Kant's philosophy as a whole it makes little sense. For Kant the ideas of God, freedom, and immortality are proper objects of rational faith only because their objects, if they have any, would be transcendent to any possible experience, and hence it would be theoretically undecidable in principle whether such objects exist. It is only in the case of such theoretically problematic objects that moral faith is permitted to decide the question (CPuR A828–29/B856–57). But human history is a domain within the empirical world, and the undecidability of any beliefs or hopes we might have about it is due not to the fact that no experience is relevant to them, but to the fact that the evidence is too complex or mixed to permit any firm conclusions.

In Kant's view, it would be intellectually dishonest to appeal to practical faith to decide dubious matters of empirical fact. Also, the historical ends regarding which we might have practically grounded hope — for instance, the end of perpetual peace between nations — are not (like the pure ideal of the highest good) set a priori by reason. They are formed through the application of a priori practical principles to the empirical conditions of human life. The setting of these ends thus depends in part on propositions about history that must be arrived at through the working out of Kant's philosophy of history. There is a strong temptation, which readers of Kant must resist, to treat certain general conditions of human life, or even certain historically evolved conditions of society, as if they were a priori conditions of rational nature generally, and therefore to promote to a priori status certain features of Kant's theory of our rational ends that are not a priori at all, but empirically and historically conditioned.

For example, the mere existence of a plurality of rational beings does not yet make it imperative on Kantian principles to found a civil union among them guaranteeing external freedom according to universal laws. In addition, it must be assumed that they are in some form of interaction with one another, able to violate one another's external freedom and able to be mutually protected from such violation through the application of external constraint. The specific conditions under which Kant describes the creation of such a civil society in the Doctrine of Right, moreover, further assumes that people's exercise of their freedom involves their separate use of portions of the external world, especially portions of the earth's surface. Kant's philosophy of history treats these circumstances of human life as the product of a historical evolution, specifically of the emergence of an agricultural mode of life. It is a further empirically conditioned historical development that civil societies protecting the rights of persons arise first as despotisms needing to be reformed through a historical process in order to approach the ideal of a perfect constitution maintaining justice between individuals. Moreover, it is also a historical development (that is, even distinctive of

Kant's philosophy of history) that these states come into conflict with one another and that the teleology of nature, as well as the aims of morality, come to require that people create an international federation of states maintaining international peace between them.

It would therefore be incoherent, or at least question-begging, to attempt to base the philosophy of history itself solely on beliefs held purely on practical grounds, where it turns out that the ends grounding the practical justification of these beliefs (for instance, the end of achieving a perfect civil constitution, or the end of achieving a federation of states maintaining perpetual peace between nations) must depend in part on that very philosophy of history itself. Practically grounded hopes and beliefs regarding history make sense only relative to a theoretical understanding of history and the practical possibilities it affords the human species, on the basis of which we might formulate ends for whose attainment we might have moral grounds to hope. Kant's philosophy of history, as outlined in the "Idea for a Universal History," aims at that theoretical understanding.

Natural Teleology and Human History

The "idea" referred to in the title of Kant's essay is the conception of a *theoretical* project whose aim is to ground the empirical inquiry into human history. It is an "idea" because it is a concept devised starting with a priori regulative principles of reason. More specifically, it is devised in accordance with Kant's theory of natural teleology (of which he did not give a full account until the *Critique of Judgment* six years later), and in particular in accordance with Kant's conception of the natural teleology of human beings regarded as an animal species.

Kant begins "Idea for a Universal History" by reflecting on the fact that human history is a realm of empirical contingencies, of which, however, rational inquiry has the task of making sense according to regularities of some kind. As the chief source of this contingency he cites human freedom, which releases people from the regularities of animal instinct but (so far, at any rate) subjects their actions to no conscious collective rational plan (IUH 8:17–18). On the basis of Kant's solution to the metaphysical problem of free will in the first and second *Critiques*, it is sometimes thought that he regards human actions in the phenomenal world as capable of being brought under necessary causal laws and investigated like the motions of the heavens or other physical phenomena (see CPuR A550/B578, CPrR 5:99), while freedom belongs entirely to the noumenal self. But this is a misreading of (or rather a fallacious inference from) Kant's solution to the problem of freedom. Kant does think that the metaphysical problem of freedom can be solved only by postulating a transcendentally free cause in the noumenal world, and he does think that human actions in the phenomenal world are not exempted from natural necessity. But it does not follow that the species of natural necessity governing human volition is knowable by us, and in fact Kant thinks it is not knowable. Regarding our actions, the future is therefore "not discoverable from known laws of nature (as are solar and lunar eclipses)" (CF 7:79). Kant's entire "pragmatic" approach to anthropology (the study of human nature) was predicated on his rejection in the early 1770s of Ernst Platner's "physiological" approach to the subject (see Ak 10:146). For Kant, it is an empirical sign (though not a proof) of our freedom that our volitions are not governed by instinct or physiological laws or other discoverable natural regularities.

Organized Beings

Kant regards living organisms generally as beings whose arrangement and behavior exhibits conceptualizable regularities that cannot be explained by being brought under the kinds of (mechanical) causal laws that make physical phenomena intelligible to us. Instead, they can be brought under the regulative concept of an "organized being" — a being whose internal arrangements and behavior produce its own organic form, and which can therefore be described as "*both cause and effect of itself*" (CJ 5:370). No being in nature corresponds perfectly to this concept, but there are beings in nature (living organisms) that approximate it, and the investigation of their life processes is governed by a set of regulative principles or maxims, amounting to the assumption (which is not to be taken dogmatically, but used only heuristically) that in an organized being "everything is an end and reciprocally a means as well" (CJ 5:376) — in other words, that the life processes of the organism *maximize* the teleological intelligibility we are looking for. The rationale for this assumption is that we have everything to gain by assuming maximal teleological interconnection in organized beings, since this will guide us toward discovering whatever teleology is present there, and the absence of teleology represents only an empirical limit to the intelligibility of the organism for us, so that there is no cognitive gain to us in ever being satisfied that teleology is absent.

"Since human beings do not, in the pursuit of their endeavors, follow merely their instincts as do animals, and yet also do not, as would rational citizens of the world, proceed in accordance with a previously arranged plan, it does not seem possible to present a systematic history of them (as could be given for bees or beavers, for instance)" (IUH 8:17). Yet there are observable regularities among the free actions of human beings as regards their effects.

Given that the free will of humans has such a great influence on marriages, on the births that result from these, and on dying, it would seem that there is no rule to which these events are subject and according to which one could calculate their number in advance. And yet the relevant statistics compiled annually in large countries demonstrate that these events occur just as much in accordance with constant natural laws as do inconstancies in the weather, which cannot be determined individually in advance, but which, taken together, do not fail to maintain a consistent and uninterrupted process in the growth of the plants, the flow of the rivers, and other natural arrangements (IUH 8:17).

Kant's philosophy of history depends on attributing a natural teleology or unconscious, unintended goal-directedness, to historical events. Because the facts to be made sense of involve the behavior over long periods of time of many human individuals, the natural teleology in history must involve ends that direct the *collective* actions of many human beings, in fact, of many generations of human beings. But because human beings do not coordinate their actions "as would rational citizens of the world, . . . in accordance with a previously arranged plan," this purposiveness must be unconscious, unintended; it must be a *natural* purposiveness, like that found in the organic arrangement of plants and animals. Kant's idea for a universal history is a regulative idea for the investigation of history, guided by the heuristic assumption that human history is guided by a natural teleology.

Since humanity is a species of living organisms, Kant looks for a natural teleology in history in connection with the natural teleology we discover in human beings as living organisms. One heuristic assumption we employ in the investigation of organisms has to do with the development of individual specimens to maturity. It involves the conception of a natural "predisposition" — a global tendency of the organism to develop the set of capacities best suited to carrying on its mode of life. The regulative maxim governing the investigation of predispositions is: "*All of a creature's natural predispositions are destined eventually to develop fully and in accordance with their purpose*" (IUH 8:18). That is, we count something as a natural predisposition only if, in the normal and unhindered development of the organism, it develops completely and suitably to the life processes of the species. And in investigating the growth processes of an organism, we conceptualize the global tendencies that show themselves in these processes around the full development of such predispositions. A predatory animal, for example, develops predispositions enabling it to stalk and kill its prey, while the prey animal develops predispositions enabling it to hide, flee, or repel predators, as well as predispositions enabling it to find and eat the kinds of plants on which it lives.

Kant's First Proposition in the "Idea for a Universal History" invokes this teleological maxim, and then the Second Proposition applies it, in an extended and creative way, to the human species, in light of its distinctive capacities as a species of free and rational beings. Reason is a capacity that frees those beings that have it from the limitation to only one way of life and enables them to invent, so to speak, their own nature and their role in the natural world (CB 8:111–12). It gives human beings what Rousseau called "perfectibility."[1] The predispositions of rational beings, therefore, are not fixed by instinct, as they are for other animals, but devised by human beings themselves. From this follows Kant's Third Proposition: *"Nature has willed that human beings produce everything that extends beyond the mechanical organization of their animal existence completely on their own, and that they shall not partake in any happiness or perfection other than that which they attain free of instinct and by means of their own reason"* (IUH 8:19).

The Economic Basis of History

Further, it implies that human predispositions are handed down from one generation of human beings to the next, and then they are modified or augmented by the reason of those who receive them. Consequently, what we count as the predispositions of the human species are continually developing and growing, and the heuristic maxim that nature has ordered things in such a way that all of them eventually develop fully amounts to the claim that human history exhibits a tendency, unintended by human beings themselves, toward the accumulation and boundless development of human faculties and diverse ways of life, with those ways of life predominating that enable these faculties to be exercised to the full and to develop further. In his essay "Conjectural Beginning of Human History," Kant distinguishes different phases or stages of human history, based on the historically developed way of life that is dominant in them. In the first phase, people lived as hunter-gatherers; in the next, they tamed animals and lived a pastoral life as nomadic herders (CB 8:118–19). Then came, in Kant's view, the true revolution in human history, when people developed the capacity to plant and grow crops. Agriculture necessitated a settled mode of life, both in order to reap the harvests they sowed and in order to live off the stored up products. It required that the producers limit themselves to certain parts of the earth's surface, but also that they defend those parts against others, and in particular against the incursions of those who still practiced the more primitive ways of life, such as the herdsmen who wanted to drive their flocks across the cultivated land. Farming was the most productive mode of life devised so far, creating a surplus, teaching people to plan their lives, defer the satisfaction of their needs, and freeing them to diversify their activities. This led to the creation of towns and the development of diverse practical arts, and a division of labor. Part of the productive surplus could be, and had to be, devoted to the creation of the coercive force needed to protect the rights of property, both in land and stored up goods, that made the agricultural and urban ways of life possible (CB 8:119–20). The protection of property for Kant, as for Locke, Rousseau, and many other modern political theorists, represents the fundamental rationale and function of civil society and the foundation of all those legitimate coercive institutions concerned with the protection of rights and justice.

Not to be missed is the way in which Kant's philosophy of history on these points anticipates the Marxian materialist conception of history. Marx too sees history as divided into stages that are distinguished by modes of production fundamentally distinguished by the degree of development of the productive forces of society. And he too sees political institutions as based on the property relations corresponding to the prevailing mode of production. Kant's theory lacks the Marxian conception of class conflict as the determinant of social dynamics, but Kant does view social change as involving conflict between higher and lower productive modes — such as the conflict between the pastoral and agricultural ways of life.

Unsociable Sociability

In another way, however, Kant's philosophy of history also grounds social progress just as deeply on social conflict. For in his Fourth Proposition in the *Idea for a Universal History*, Kant identifies the mechanism through which he thinks human predispositions unfold in history. This mechanism is social antagonism, a propensity in human nature to compete with other human beings, to have its own way against their will and to achieve superior rank or status in the opinion of others. Alluding to a remark by Montaigne (one of Kant's favorite authors), he calls this propensity of human nature "unsociable sociability"[2] — meaning that it is simultaneously a propensity to be dependent on others (for one's sense of superiority to them) and also a propensity to cross others, isolate oneself from them, and to behave unsociably within this fundamental relation of interdependency. Through unsociable sociability, we seek honor, power, and wealth, that is, superiority to others exercised over them (respectively) through their opinion, their fear, or their interest. These are the three objects of the social passions (A 7:271–75), that is, inclinations that are difficult for us to control through reason. In the *Critique of Practical Reason,* unsociable sociability appears as "self-conceit" (CPrR 5:72); in *Religion within the Boundaries of Mere Reason,* it appears as the radical propensity to evil in human nature.

Unsociable sociability develops along with the same faculty of reason that enables us to know that it is evil; both are products of society. Acting from our propensity to unsociable sociability is something we do freely, and for which we are to blame. But there is natural purposiveness in unsociable sociability — in other words, nature employs this propensity to further the development of the predispositions of the human species. When people seek to gain superiority over others, they make themselves both unhappy and evil. But in the process they develop capacities that are passed along to later generations and enrich both human nature and human history.

The Political State

Yet as a mechanism for developing human predispositions, unsociable sociability reaches a limit at the point where human conflict disrupts the stable life of civilization that is needed for the preservation and further development of human faculties. If life and property become insecure, then people have no opportunity to perfect themselves and no incentive to accumulate products of labor, which may be taken from them before they can be enjoyed. At a certain point, therefore, nature's end of endlessly developing the predispositions of the human species requires a stable and ordered society, a condition of peace with justice. When civilization reaches this point, natural purposiveness requires another device alongside unsociable sociability to balance its counterpurposive effects. This device, which Kant introduces in the Fifth and Sixth Propositions of "Idea for a Universal History," is the establishment of "*a civil society which administers right universally*" (IUH 8:22). This civil society, characterized by a coercive power protecting rights and property, is the political state. It is a voluntary creation of human beings themselves and is subject to ideal rational principles (of right or justice) that people are capable of recognizing and obeying; but in promoting the full development of our species predispositions, the establishment of a political state also accords with natural teleology.

The creation of a perfect civil constitution for the state presents itself to the human species as a "problem" to be solved by people themselves, because in addition to being an end of nature (needed to facilitate nature's more basic end of developing human faculties), justice among human beings also presents itself to them as a demand of reason, something they unconditionally ought to achieve. In the Seventh Proposition, Kant argues that this problem cannot be solved as long as states remain in a permanent state of war in relation to one another. For not only are wars themselves destructive of the conditions needed to develop human faculties, but the continuous need to be prepared for war distorts the state by putting power in the hands of those who would govern in the spirit of military despotism and by diverting human talents and resources to aims irrelevant or hostile to human progress.

Kant is not ignorant of the arguments, advanced in his century by Turgot and renewed in the last century by partisans of the cold war, that military technologies too can serve human progress.[3] Nor is he unsusceptible to the idea, most often associated with Hegel, that the sublimity of war helps to unite the state and raise individuals above the ignoble disposition to complacent self-seeking that characterizes private economic life in peacetime (indeed, Kant expresses this "Hegelian" idea himself, CJ 5:263).[4] But he thinks that the stage of history in which armed conflict between states, and the preparations for conflict, are conducive to human progress, is a cruder one than that which the human species has now attained in civilized parts of the world.

Kant never presented a clear and detailed model of the federation of states he hoped would achieve perpetual peace. His works suggest at least two possibilities, a "federation of nations" (*Völkerbund*) or *foedus pacificum* and a "state of nations" (*Völkerstaat*) or *civitas gentium* (PP 8:356–57). The former would be a league or pact between states aiming at maintaining peace and independence among its members, while the latter would be a state whose members are themselves states (not, therefore, a single world-state directly governing human beings — an idea Kant rejects). The suggestion in *Toward Perpetual Peace* seems to be that a federation between nations might evolve toward a state of nations, whose members would grow until it encompassed all the nations of the earth (PP 8:357). Even the weaker model of a federation of nations, however, is conceived as maintaining peace by exercising "a united power" "from the decision based on laws of the united will" (IUH 8:24).

The Theoretical Comprehension of History and Moral Striving

The result is, as Kant puts it in the Eighth Proposition, that both progress toward a perfect state constitution and the creation of a peaceful international order among states may be regarded as ends of nature in history. *"One can regard the history of the human species at large as the realization of a concealed plan of nature, meant to bring into being an internally and, to this end, externally perfect state constitution, as the only condition in which nature can fully develop all of its predispositions in humankind"* (IUH 8:27).

It is important to distinguish between two quite different (and largely independent) theses that Kant maintains here. The first thesis, which is the primary focus of "Idea for a Universal History," is a wholly theoretical one: Under the guidance of heuristic or regulative principles of reason, we should attempt to make sense of human history as a process involving an unconscious and unintended teleology of nature, whose ultimate end regarding the human species is the open-ended development of its predispositions, and whose ends, subordinate to this one, also include the creation of a perfectly just civil constitution and a peaceful international order among states. A second thesis, evident at many points in Kant's writings, extremely important to his philosophy as a whole but of only ancillary significance in the "Idea for a Universal History," is a practical or moral one: As human beings, we have a duty to work together toward devising and realizing the end of a perfect civil constitution administering justice among human beings, and to this end we are also required to seek an order guaranteeing perpetual peace among states.

The first thesis is a purely theoretical one, having no moral presuppositions. It results in part from a priori regulative principles of reason when they are applied to the facts of human history, and partly from these facts themselves, such as the fact that nature is seen to employ unsociable sociability as the device for unfolding the predispositions of the human species, and the fact that beyond a certain point this device can continue to operate toward nature's end only if it is counterbalanced by a humanly created order of peace with justice within the political state and between states. The second thesis is a purely practical (or moral) one, deriving from the fact that human beings, as rational beings, are ends in themselves, consequently beings whose external freedom ought to be protected and whose perfection and happiness ought to be set as ends by all rational beings.

The first (theoretical) thesis is in no way dependent on the second (practical or moral) thesis. For Kant it is practical reason, not natural purposiveness, that fundamentally sets our moral duties. If something is an end of morality for practical purposes, it does not follow that it should be regarded by theoretical reason as an end of nature. Nor does the fact that something should be treated for heuristic purposes as an end of nature necessarily imply that there is any moral reason to promote it. Kant does think that some of our duties (for instance, our duties to ourselves regarding self-preservation and the use of food, drink, and sex) derive from respecting the natural purposiveness of our organization as living beings. But unsociable sociability also introduces a natural purposiveness into our lives, which inclines us to seek superiority — through honor, wealth, and tyrannical dominion — over other human beings, who are our equals in the eyes of reason, and to treat them as mere means to our own selfish ends. But such conduct is paradigmatic of what violates the moral law, and the fact that such conduct serves natural purposes is no justification or excuse for it. Kant is quite explicit that natural teleology by itself does not entail any moral duty to cooperate with it: "When I say that nature *wills* that this or that ought to happen, I do not mean that she imposes a *duty* upon us to act thus (for this can only be done by practical reason acting free of compulsion), but rather that she *does* it herself, regardless of whether we will it so or not (*fata volentem ducunt, nolentem trahunt*)" (PP 8:365).[5] In other words, when we have a duty to do something that accords with nature's ends, natural teleology cooperates with us, but when moral ends oppose natural ends, nature will offer resistance to the good will.

Yet there is one connection between Kant's theoretical theses about history and his practical ones. This connection makes the former thesis part of our grounds for the latter. The fact that, according to a teleologically conceived theoretical philosophy of history, a natural purposiveness leads toward an ideal civil constitution and toward perpetual peace between nations — and even more, the factual reasons why it does so — constitutes part of the reason why we have a moral duty to place an ideal civil constitution and perpetual peace among the ends of our action. Moral reason, which recognizes human beings as ends in themselves, provides us with a ground for respecting their rights and for valuing arrangements that protect those rights. But it gives us moral grounds for pursuing an ideal civil constitution only under certain contingent, empirical conditions, specifically, under conditions where human beings themselves have established institutions for the protection of human rights through collective coercive action in the form of a civil constitution, and where there exist imperfect forms of civil constitution presenting us with historical possibilities for improving them. When we look at history as containing a natural purposiveness toward the perfection of civil constitutions, this gives us a moral reason for cooperating with that purposiveness. We have seen that for Kant himself, the very existence of civil constitutions themselves is historically contingent on the emergence of an agricultural way of life, the growth of urban centers, and the productive surplus made possible by these socioeconomic forms; he further understands the imperfect state of civil constitutions as resulting from the fact that they arose as military despotisms arising under social conditions determined by the unsociable sociability of human beings. The entire context in which it is rational to set the improvement of civil constitutions as a moral end is conditioned by empirical contingencies highlighted by Kant's philosophy of history.

It is also at most a contingent fact that at the present stage of history the further improvement of civil constitutions must depend on achieving peace between nations. (As we have seen, not everyone, either in Kant's day or our own, even thinks this is a fact at all.) It is therefore only contingent historical facts, along with a priori moral principles, that give us any reason to seek perpetual peace as part of the process of striving toward a perfect civil constitution. Only Kant's philosophy of history, regarded as a heuristically motivated project for obtaining and systematizing theoretical knowledge about history, could deliver the kinds of information necessary to warrant our setting perpetual peace between nations and a perfect civil constitution as ends of morality.

This entails that it could make no sense to view Kant's philosophy of history itself as motivated by moral faith in, or hope for, the achievement of these historical ends. For the rationale for setting these ends themselves is not wholly a priori, but it depends on theoretical conclusions of fact that, in the context of Kant's philosophy of history, could be motivated only by the results of his project of theoretical inquiry. To interpret Kant as reasoning in such a manner solely from moral aspirations to historical conclusions is not only to caricature Kantian moral faith as nothing but groundless wishful thinking, but it is also to display the moral hopes themselves as grounded on ends that are without adequate rational motivation in the first place. Such an interpretation, therefore, not only fails to correspond to the letter of Kant's texts on the philosophy of history, but it is also a conspicuously hostile interpretation, which, if correct, could only invite us to dismiss Kant's entire philosophy of history as rationally unmotivated and not to be taken seriously. Kant's philosophy of history makes sense at all only if, in the words of one recent writer on this topic, we see it as satisfying *both* a theoretical and a practical need of reason.[6] Further, we have to see the mode of satisfaction of the theoretical need as coming prior in the rational order even to the emergence of the practical need.

But here is a harder question: How far does Kant's philosophy of history give us reason for *expecting* or *predicting* the success of our moral strivings — the actual progress of civil constitutions toward perfection, the actual cooperation of states in a lawful federation maintaining perpetual peace between them? Kant must be seen as thinking that it does provide such reasons, for in *Toward Perpetual Peace* he offers conclusions from the philosophy of history as providing a "guarantee" of the terms of perpetual peace he has outlined (PP 8:360–68). Kant realizes that before the skeptical (sometimes cynical, often fearful) heads of state to whom he is addressing his treatise are going to take steps to bring about a peaceful federation, they will need reassurances that the course to which Kant is directing them has some prospect of success in human history. But it is not immediately clear that his philosophy of history can offer them these reassurances while remaining consistent with its own theoretical claims. For Kant, to identify something as an end of nature is to say that we have heuristic or regulative reasons to look at the facts on the assumption that there are natural tendencies at work to actualize it. But these heuristic reasons by themselves provide us with no theoretical guarantee, no real *evidence* at all, in fact, that what has been identified as a natural end will actually come about. The heuristic recommendation says only that we maximize intelligibility by *looking for* such evidence; it does not say that we are guaranteed to find what we are looking for.

Yet it would not make empirical sense, even for heuristic purposes, to identify something as a *natural* end if we could observe no mechanisms toward achieving it at work in nature. We say that maintaining a constant body temperature is an end of nature in animals because we notice instinctive behaviors and mechanisms that tend toward increasing their body heat when they are too cold and toward losing body heat when they are too warm. Likewise, it is a necessary condition for viewing the achievement of perpetual peace among nations as an end of nature that we should find some mechanisms at work that tend in that direction. Along these lines, Kant cites the fact that nations can be strong militarily only if they are strong economically, and that the more civilized a nation becomes, the more its economic strength depends on peaceful prosperity. Those nations that do not value peaceful relations with their neighbors, therefore, should increasingly be unable to make war successfully on them, and those nations that are in the best position to defend themselves should also be the ones most ready to join in a peaceful federation (see PP 8:368, IUH 8:27–28).

But Kant also appears to acknowledge that the heuristic reasons provided by his theoretical philosophy of history for expecting the success of his project of perpetual peace fall short of providing a genuine theoretical guarantee. It is at this point that he falls back on the moral duty we have to promote the end of perpetual peace, and to hope, on practical or rational-religious grounds, that the end will be achieved. It is this rational hope, more than any theoretical expectation, that he emphasizes as the "guarantee" of perpetual peace (PP 8:360–62). But he apparently concedes that even that hope would be irrational if there were no theoretical grounds at all for expecting it to succeed. And he therefore offers the admittedly less than conclusive combination of heuristic expectations and empirical reasons supporting them as sufficient to constitute those grounds: "In this way nature guarantees perpetual peace through the mechanism of human inclinations itself. To be sure, it does this with a certainty that is not sufficient to *foretell* the future of this peace (theoretically), but which is adequate from a practical perspective and makes it a duty to work toward this (not simply chimerical) goal" (PP 8:368).

Critical Assessment of Kant's Philosophy of History

Even when Kant's views are correctly and sympathetically interpreted, how seriously do they deserve to be taken?

Kant's philosophy of history depends on postulating, at least for heuristic purposes, a natural teleology in human history, whose goals are both collective and unconscious. This aspect of Kant's theory may make it seem extravagant, speculative, anti-empirical and even obscurantist. His philosophy of history in this respect may seem starkly at odds with his reputation for skeptical modesty and epistemic humility and caution. Proponents of so-called methodological individualism will say that it makes sense to appeal to historical tendencies or trends only when their existence can be authenticated and explained in terms of the choices and motivations of individuals, by way of providing "microfoundations" for them.

Kant is no methodological individualist, but the unconscious collective ends he posits in human history for regulative purposes are not meant to be postulated arbitrarily and not supposed to be divorced from empirically observable motivations and actions of individuals. The whole aim of the theory itself is to use these ends to identify those patterns of human motivation and action that have historical efficacy, distinguishing these from the accidental factors in human choice whose relation to history is merely accidental and insignificant. Kant's method, however, is not to begin with microfoundations and generate historical trends or natural purposes, but to assume certain natural purposes heuristically and use these as a guide to the discovery of the kinds of motives and actions that are historically potent. The natural end of endlessly developing humanity's species-predispositions leads, for instance, to the specification of unsociable sociability (the human traits of discontent and competitiveness) as the basic mechanism for this development; the historical need, at a certain stage of history, for nations to remain at peace in order to perfect their civil constitutions and continue the development of new human capacities, leads us to recognize the importance of commerce and economic prosperity in making nations powerful, and the reluctance of commercially oriented citizens to turn their lives and property over to warlike heads of state to pursue their greedy and barbaric fantasies of military conquest. Kant also attempts to render the natural teleology of history nonarbitrary by linking it to the natural teleology found in human beings as a species of organisms, as he thinks this teleology plays a role in biological investigations.

No doubt there is a measure of theoretical adventurousness in Kant's historical teleology that might unnerve a traditional empiricist. But there is a very analogous but much less often appreciated departure from empiricist caution involved in the abstract idealizations used by methodological individualists in constructing their "microfoundations" for the social trends and tendencies they are willing to countenance. In both cases, an honest assessment of what is going on must take note of the fact that empiricist reconstructions of theoretical practice underestimate the creative role of theorizing. There are usually macro-level assumptions built into the choices of abstraction and idealization used to construct microfoundations, and these are all the less subject to empirical constraint and criticism to the extent that they are not acknowledged for what they are. The Kantian choice to begin with the macro-level is more forthright in acknowledging the importance of our a priori cognitive ambitions than are the methodological individualists who deceptively pretend they are always sticking close to empirical observation.

A more serious problem for Kant's philosophy of history is that we can no longer believe, for instance, in Kant's heuristically motivated natural teleology as the right way for investigating the structure and behavior of living organisms. Since Darwin, it has been recognized that the unconscious and unintended purposive arrangements in living things have a determinate empirical explanation based on natural selection. Moreover, this explanation reveals that Kant's heuristic assumption that the teleology in organisms is maximal is empirically and explainably false. When we learn how the organs of a living thing evolved, for instance, we sometimes come to understand why they are not optimally suited for the function they perform. And it might turn out, for similar reasons, that not everything we rightly conceptualize as one of the "species predispositions" of an organism would have to be fully developed in the normal course of the organism's development. The biological basis of Kant's philosophy of history therefore seems to have been undermined by scientific developments between his time and ours.

Yet it is not so clear that the methodological considerations motivating Kant's philosophy of history are less applicable today than they were in the eighteenth century. Biology may have made advances that undermine the application to it of Kant's heuristically motivated natural teleology, but human history is still an area of inquiry to which no similar empirical theory has been applied with success. It may be that our best chance of making it intelligible is still the regulative-teleological one that Kant adopts. Kant's approach also has the other benefit it had for him, that it enables us to connect an empirical, theoretical study of history to our practical concern with history as historical agents, by identifying historical tendencies (which Kant calls unintended "ends of nature") with which our efforts as moral beings might harmonize. Historical theories since Kant's time (most famously, the historical materialism of Marx) have taken up the idea that historical changes can be understood as functions of the progressive development of collective human capacities and consequent changes in economic forms over time. Many others besides Marx have used this idea in a wide variety of contexts to deal with social and historical change (for instance, in the wide variety of so-called theories of modernization). The basic ideas of Kant's philosophy of history, though they may not always be easily recognizable in their more recent guises, are very far from having been discredited.

Easier to recognize is the way the practical or moral-religious side of Kant's philosophy of history is still with us. We are also still practically concerned with the direction of economic growth and the relation of it to the prospects for peace between nations. Twentieth-century projects for peace — the League of Nations, the United Nations, and the European Union — are all attempts to fulfill hopes that Kant was among the first to articulate.

Also still with us is Kant's cosmopolitanism, which is most fundamentally a view about the historicity of human nature. Kant holds that each of us, while being a citizen of an empirically determinate civil order or political state, is also a citizen of a single world community — our attempt to realize on earth the idea of an ethical *realm of ends* in which all rational beings are accorded a dignity that is beyond price and all the ends and maxims should harmonize in one systematic combination. This side of Kant's is still with us not in the sense that we are very much closer to actualizing the idea, but rather in the sense that it is much more difficult today than it was two centuries ago for a thinking person not to share Kant's sense that we fulfill our nature as human beings only insofar as our species makes historical progress toward it. This in fact is precisely the thought with which Kant closes his last work: *Anthropology from a Pragmatic Point of View*.

In concluding his attempt to identify the "character of the human species" as a whole, he describes it first in terms of unsociable sociability: "The character of the species, as evident based on the collected historical experience of all times and among all peoples, is the following: that they, taken collectively (as the human race as a whole), are a mass of persons that exist one next to one another and after one another and who cannot *do without* peaceful coexistence and yet cannot *avoid* constant strife amongst one another" (A 7:331). Then he asks whether such a species should be considered a good race or an evil one, and seems at first to side with those misanthropic critics who either censure humanity for its wickedness or else laugh at it for its folly — and this not only, he says, through good-natured laughter, but also through a derision of contempt. And these attitudes would be correct, Kant concludes, but for one thing: they themselves reveal "a moral predisposition in us, an innate appeal of reason, to work against that tendency [toward evil]." His final conception of human nature, therefore, consists in a *historical* vision of the human species that unites the basis for our criticism with the moral predisposition this criticism reveals, namely:

to present the human species not as evil, but rather as a race of rational beings that strive continually to make progress, against obstacles, from evil to the good. Its will would be good in general, but carrying it through is hindered by the fact that reaching the end cannot be expected simply on the basis of a free agreement of *individuals*. Rather reaching that end can only be expected from the progressive organization of the citizens of the earth within and into the species as a system that is interconnected in a cosmopolitan fashion." (A 7:333)

NOTES

1. Jean-Jacques Rousseau, *Discourse on the Origin of Inequality*, trans. Donald Cress (Indianapolis: Hackett 1992), 26.

2. "Il n'est rien si dissociable et sociable que l'homme: l'un par son vice, l'autre par sa nature." Michel Eyquem de Montaigne, "De la solitude," *Essais,* ed. André Tournon (Paris: Imprimerie nationale Éditions, 1998), vol. 1, p. 388. "There is nothing so unsociable and sociable as man; the one by his vice, the other by his nature," "Of Solitude," *Selected Essays,* trans. C. Cotton, rev. W. Hazlitt, ed. Blanchard Bates (New York: Random House, 1949), 91.

3. See Anne-Robert-Jacues Turgot, *Turgot on Progress, Sociology and Economics: A Philosophical Review of the Successive Advances of the Human Mind, On Universal History [and] Reflections on the Formation and the Distribution of Wealth,* ed., trans., and with an intro. by Ronald L. Meek (Cambridge: Cambridge University Press, 1973). For a recent defense of this idea in the Cold War context, see Diane R. Kunz, *Guns and Butter: America's Cold War Economic Diplomacy* (New York: Free Press, 1997).

4. Compare Hegel, *Elements of the Philosophy of Right,* ed. Allen W. Wood, trans. H. B. Nisbet (Cambridge: Cambridge University Press, 1991), § 324.

5. "The fates lead the willing, drive the unwilling," in Seneca, *Moral Epistles* 18.4.

6. Pauline Kleingeld, *Fortschritt und Vernunft: Zur Geschichtsphilosophie Kants* (Würzburg: Königshausen & Neumann, 1995), 215.

Bibliography

Arendt, Hannah. *Lectures on Kant's Political Philosophy,* ed. Ronald Beiner. Chicago: University of Chicago Press, 1982.

Beiner, Ronald, and William James Booth, eds. *Kant and Political Philosophy: The Contemporary Legacy.* New Haven: Yale University Press, 1993.

Beiser, Frederick C. *Enlightenment, Revolution, and Romanticism: The Genesis of Modern German Political Thought, 1790–1800.* Cambridge: Harvard University Press, 1992.

Bohman, James, and Matthias Lutz-Bachmann, eds. *Perpetual Peace: Essays on Kant's Cosmopolitan Ideal.* Cambridge: MIT Press, 1997.

Booth, William James. *Interpreting the World: Kant's Philosophy of History and Politics.* Toronto: Toronto University Press, 1986.

Cavallar, Georg. *Kant and the Theory and Practice of International Right.* Cardiff: University of Wales Press, 1999.

Covell, Charles. *Kant and the Law of Peace.* London: Macmillan, 1998.

Despland, Michel. *Kant on History and Religion.* Montreal: McGill–Queens's University Press, 1973.

Dietze, Anita, and Walter Dietze, eds. *Ewiger Friede? Dokumente einer deutschen Diskussion um 1800.* Leipzig: Kiepenheuer Verlag, 1989.

Doyle, Michael W. *Ways of War and Peace: Realism, Liberalism, and Socialism.* New York: W. W. Norton, 1997.

Flikshuh, Katrin. *Kant and Modern Political Philosophy.* Cambridge: Cambridge University Press, 2000.

Franceschet, Antonio. *Kant and Liberal Internationalism.* New York: Palgrave Macmillan, 2002.

Gallie, Walter B. *Philosophers of Peace and War: Kant, Clausewitz, Marx, Engels, and Tolstoy.* Cambridge: Cambridge University Press, 1978.

Galston, William A. *Kant and the Problem of History.* Chicago: University of Chicago Press, 1975.

Gerhardt, Volker. *Immanuel Kants Entwurf, "Zum ewigen Frieden": Eine Theorie der Politik.* Darmstadt: Wissenschaftliche Buchgesellschaft, 1995.

Guyer, Paul. *Kant on Freedom, Law, and Happiness.* Cambridge: Cambridge University Press, 2000.

Höffe, Otfried, ed. *Immanuel Kant: Zum ewigen Frieden.* Berlin: Akademie Verlag, 1995.

————. *Immanuel Kant: Metaphysische Anfangsgründe der Rechtslehre.* Berlin: Akademie Verlag, 1999.

Kersting, Wolfgang. *Wohlgeordnete Freiheit: Immanuel Kants Rechts- und Sozialphilosophie,* 2nd ed. Frankfurt am Main: Suhrkamp, 1993.

Kleingeld, Pauline. *Fortschritt und Vernunft: Zur Geschichtsphilosophie Kants.* Würzburg: Königshausen und Neumann, 1995.

Kneller, Jane, and Sidney Axinn, eds. *Autonomy and Community: Readings in Contemporary Kantian Social Philosophy.* Albany: SUNY Press, 1998.

Kuehn, Manfred. *Kant: A Biography.* Cambridge: Cambridge University Press, 2001.

Ludwig, Bernd. *Kants Rechtslehre.* Hamburg: Felix Meiner Verlag, 1988.

Mulholland, Leslie A. *Kant's System of Rights.* New York: Columbia University Press, 1990.

O'Neill, Onora. *Bounds of Justice.* Cambridge: Cambridge University Press, 2000.

Raumer, Kurt von, ed. *Ewiger Friede: Friedensrufe und Friedenspläne seit der Renaissance.* Freiburg: Karl Alber Verlag, 1953.

Riley, Patrick. *Kant's Political Philosophy.* Totowa, N.J.: Rowman and Littlefield, 1983.

Rosen, Allen D. *Kant's Theory of Justice.* Ithaca: Cornell University Press, 1993.

Saner, Hans. *Kant's Political Thought: Its Origins and Development.* Trans. E. B. Ashton. Chicago: University of Chicago Press, 1973.

Shell, Susan Meld. *The Rights of Reason: A Study of Kant's Philosophy and Politics.* Toronto: University of Toronto Press, 1980.

Schmidt, James, ed. *What Is Enlightenment? Eighteenth-Century Answers and Twentieth-Century Questions.* Berkeley: University of California Press, 1996.

Timmons, Mark, ed. *Kant's Metaphysics of Morals: Interpretative Essays.* Oxford: Oxford University Press, 2002.

Tuck, Richard. *The Rights of War and Peace: Political Thought and the International Order from Grotius to Kant.* Oxford: Oxford University Press, 2001.

Waldron, Jeremy. *The Dignity of Legislation.* Cambridge: Cambridge University Press, 1999.

Williams, Howard. *Kant's Political Philosophy.* Oxford: Basil Blackwell, 1983.

Williams, Howard, ed. *Essays on Kant's Political Philosophy.* Chicago: University of Chicago Press, 1992.

Wood, Allen W. *Kant's Ethical Thought.* Cambridge: Cambridge University Press, 1999.

Yovel, Yirmiyahu. *Kant and the Philosophy of History.* Princeton: Princeton University Press, 1980.

Rethinking the Western Tradition

On Liberty
by John Stuart Mill
Edited by David Bromwich and George Kateb

Two Treatises of Government and *A Letter Concerning Toleration*
by John Locke
Edited by Ian Shapiro

Reflections on the Revolution in France
by Edmund Burke
Edited by Frank M. Turner

Toward Perpetual Peace and Other Writings on Politics, Peace, and History
by Immanuel Kant
Edited by Pauline Kleingeld